Essential
Study Skills

SAGE was founded in 1965 by Sara Miller McCune to support the dissemination of usable knowledge by publishing innovative and high-quality research and teaching content. Today, we publish over 900 journals, including those of more than 400 learned societies, more than 800 new books per year, and a growing range of library products including archives, data, case studies, reports, and video. SAGE remains majority-owned by our founder, and after Sara's lifetime will become owned by a charitable trust that secures our continued independence.

Los Angeles | London | New Delhi | Singapore | Washington DC | Melbourne

SAGE Study Skills

Essential
Study Skills

The Complete Guide to
Success at University

Tom Burns & Sandra Sinfield

4th Edition

SAGE

Los Angeles | London | New Delhi
Singapore | Washington DC | Melbourne

Los Angeles | London | New Delhi
Singapore | Washington DC | Melbourne

SAGE Publications Ltd
1 Oliver's Yard
55 City Road
London EC1Y 1SP

SAGE Publications Inc.
2455 Teller Road
Thousand Oaks, California 91320

SAGE Publications India Pvt Ltd
B 1/I 1 Mohan Cooperative Industrial Area
Mathura Road
New Delhi 110 044

SAGE Publications Asia-Pacific Pte Ltd
3 Church Street
#10-04 Samsung Hub
Singapore 049483

Editor: Marianne Lagrange
Editorial assistant: Robert Patterson
Production editor: Tom Bedford
Copyeditor: Gemma Marren
Proofreader: Andy Baxter
Marketing manager: Catherine Slinn
Cover design: Stephanie Guyaz
Typeset by: C&M Digitals (P) Ltd, Chennai, India
Printed and bound in Great Britain by Bell and
Bain Ltd, Glasgow

MIX
Paper from
responsible sources
FSC
www.fsc.org   FSC® C007785

First edition published 2002
Second edition published 2008
Third edition published 2012
This fourth edition published 2016

This book may contain links to both internal and external
websites. All links included were active at the time the book
was published. SAGE does not operate these external
websites and does not necessarily endorse the views
expressed within them. SAGE cannot take responsibility for
the changing content or nature of linked sites, as these sites
are outside of our control and subject to change without our
knowledge. If you do find an inactive link to an external
website, please try to locate that website by using a search
engine. SAGE will endeavour to update inactive or broken
links when possible.

Library of Congress Control Number: 2015949706

British Library Cataloguing in Publication data

A catalogue record for this book is available from
the British Library

ISBN 978-1-4739-1901-3
ISBN 978-1-4739-1902-0 (pbk)

At SAGE we take sustainability seriously. Most of our products are printed in the UK using FSC papers and boards.
When we print overseas we ensure sustainable papers are used as measured by the PREPS grading system.
We undertake an annual audit to monitor our sustainability.

Contents

List of Checklists and Figures   vii
About the Authors   ix
Acknowledgments   xi
Companion Website   xiii

I   THE STARTER KIT   1

1   Introduction   3

2   How to Learn, How to Study   17

3   Make University Positive   35

II   THE SURVIVAL KIT   49

4   How to Survive Academic Reading   51

5   How to Make the Best Notes   65

6   How to Be Creative and Visual in Your Learning   79

7   How to Be Analytical and Critical   93

8   How to Be Reflective   105

9   How to Get on in Groups   115

10   How to Harness a Digital You   127

III   THE BIG ASSESSMENT TOOLKIT: CRACKING ASSESSMENT   145

11.1   How to Make Sense of Your Course   147

11.2   Probably the Most Important Thing on Writing You'll Ever Read   153

11.3 The Ten Step Approach to Better Assignments 167

11.4 How to Reference and Avoid Plagiarism 181

IV THE BIG ASSESSMENT TOOLKIT: ASSESSMENTS – HOW TO EXCEL 189

12.1 How to Write Great Essays 191

12.2 How to Produce Excellent Reports 207

12.3 How to Deliver Excellent Presentations 225

12.4 How to Run Your Own Seminars and Workshops 241

12.5 How to Write a Brilliant Dissertation 251

12.6 How to Revise for and Pass Exams 263

V THE EMPLOYABILITY KIT 281

13.1 PDP and HEAR: Knowing Who You Are, Becoming Who You Want to Be 283

13.2 How to Move on … and Get that Job 295

Bibliography and Further Reading 309
Index 317

List of Checklists
and Figures

Checklist

Study Tips   14–5
Essays   205
Presentations   239
Exams 278–9

Figures

1.1	Personal Skills Review	8
1.2	Six Steps to Success	11
2.1	An example of a learning contract	30
2.2	Blank 24-hour timetable – plan	31
2.3	Blank 24-hour timetable – review and improve	32
2.4	Course events and deadlines timetable	33
2.5	Term plan timetable	33
2.6	Weekly Plan timetable	34
3.1	Projected income and expenditure for academic year	46–7
4.1	Keep index card records	56
5.1	Cornell notes template	70
5.2	Concept map template	71
5.3	Pattern note template	72
5.4	Mindmap of pattern notes	74

6.1	Ideas map: why should we be creative?	81
6.2	Brainstorm of 'Evaluate the usefulness of pattern notes to a student'	83
7.1	Critical Thinking Wordle™	94
7.2	A beginner's guide to critical thinking	97
7.3	Challenge crossword puzzle	100
7.4	Preparing a question matrix	102
7.5	Question matrix on 'Evaluate the usefulness of positive thinking to a student'	103
7.6	Our notes on one of John Hilsdon's sessions on critical thinking	104
8.1	Example of a student's learning log on 'How to survive academic reading'	112
8.2	Reflective learning template – use for logs or blogs	113
10.1	Mindmap – using a computer and researching online	136
10.2	Delicious – an example of social bookmarking	139
10.3	Evaluate your sources	141
11.2.1	The free write tool in action	159
11.3.1	The assignment journey	176
11.4.1	Should I reference?	184
12.1.1	Developing a plan or structure for your essay	194
12.1.2	An example of an essay plan or structure	197
12.1.3	The Paragraph conversation	203
12.2.1	Types of report	209
12.2.2	The ideal report	210–1
12.2.3	Reports vs essays	216
12.3.1	Structure of a presentation	228
12.5.1	The classic dissertation structure	253
12.6.1	Exams checklist	278–9
13.1.1	The reflective cycle	290

About the Authors

Tom Burns and **Sandra Sinfield** are co-authors of *Teaching, Learning and Study Skills: A guide for tutors* and *Essential Study Skills: The complete guide to success at university* (fourth edition).

Tom Burns, always interested in theatre and the arts and their role in teaching and learning, led the Hainault Action Group setting up adventure playgrounds and devising Community Events and Festivals for the local community. Whilst still a student Tom set up and ran the first *International Dario Fo Festival* – with symposium, theatre workshops for students and local people and full dramatic performances by the Fo-Rame theatre troupe of *The Tiger's Tale* and *The Boss's Funeral*.

Sandra Sinfield has worked as a laboratory technician, a freelance copywriter, an Executive Editor (*Medicine Digest*, circulation 80,000 doctors) and in the voluntary sector with the Tower Hamlets Research and Resource Centre and with the Islington Green School Community Play written by Alan, *Whose Life is it Anyway?*, Clarke and produced at Saddlers Wells.

Together Tom and Sandra have taken a production of John Godber's *Bouncers* on a tour of Crete music venues, written and made a feature film (*Eight Days from Yesterday*) and produced teaching and learning courses and materials in a range of settings. Their *Take Control* video won the IVCA gold award for education – and has been embedded in an online study resource (*Six Steps to Success* – http://learning. londonmet.ac.uk/epacks/soccer/).

Tom Burns and Sandra Sinfield are both Senior Lecturers in Education and Learning Development actively involved in the Association for Learning Development in Higher Education (www.aldinhe.ac.uk). Most recently they have developed the student-facing *Study Hub* (www.londonmet.ac.uk/studyhub) and the staff-facing *Take5* website and blog (http://learning.londonmet.ac.uk/epacks/take5/), the latter of which is designed to seed, share and support staff engagement with engaging and innovative learning, teaching and assessment practices.

Working in the Centre for the Enhancement of Learning and Teaching at London Metropolitan University, they continue to develop learning, teaching and assessment innovations with a special focus on engaging praxes that ignite student curiosity and develop power and voice.

Acknowledgments

As always a very special thank you goes to our families for their love, support and encouragement, and to all our students across the years, without whose engagement and energy none of this would have been possible.

In particular special gratitude goes to **Andy Mitchell**, LondonMet graduate, freelance editor and designer, for acting as a critical friend to the emerging manuscript and who produced many of the book's illustrations and accompanying downloadable resources and **Chloe Noble**, Literature Undergraduate, artist and freelance designer, who has shared her blog with us and who produced the artwork introducing the different Parts of the book. A big thank you also to **Jennifer Dixon**, **Perry Campbell** and **Tanya Pinnock**, who allowed us to print extracts of their work.

And finally, extra especial thanks this year to the following friends and colleagues who have taken the time to write an open letter to our readers with their advice, encouragement and guidance and who have shared their insights and their resources with us:

Sandra Abegglen Course Leader Education and Social Policy, School of Social Sciences, London Metropolitan University.

David Blundell Principal Lecturer and Programme Leader for Education, School of Social Sciences, London Metropolitan University.

Hugh Clarke and Fitzgerald Douglas Counselors, Student Services London Metropolitan University

Kate Hoskins Reader in Education, School of Education, University of Roehampton.

Maureen Kendall Senior Lecturer, Faculty of Life Sciences and Computing, London Metropolitan University.

Chris O'Reilly Formerly of LondonMet and now freelance Web Designer and Educational Technologist.

Neelam Thapar Head of Careers and Employability, Student Services, London Metropolitan University.

Cécile Tschirhart Head of Learning and Teaching, The Cass, Faculty of Art, Design and Architecture

London Metropolitan University.

Renzo Veschini Schools, Colleges and Widening Participation Officer, External Relations

London Metropolitan University.

Companion Website

Essential Study Skills is supported by a wealth of online resources for both students and lecturers to aid study and support teaching, which are available at https://study.sagepub.com/burnsandsinfield4e

For Students

- **Printable handouts and checklists** serve as handy chapter companions as you work your way through the book
- **Selected journal articles** give you free access to scholarly journal articles chosen for each chapter to expand your knowledge and reinforce your learning of key topics
- **Web links** direct you to relevant resources to deepen your understanding of chapter topics

For Lecturers

- **Corresponding chapters** from Burns and Sinfield's teaching book: *Teaching, Learning and Study Skills: A Guide for Tutors*
- **Web links** catered to lecturer specific needs, direct you to additional online readings

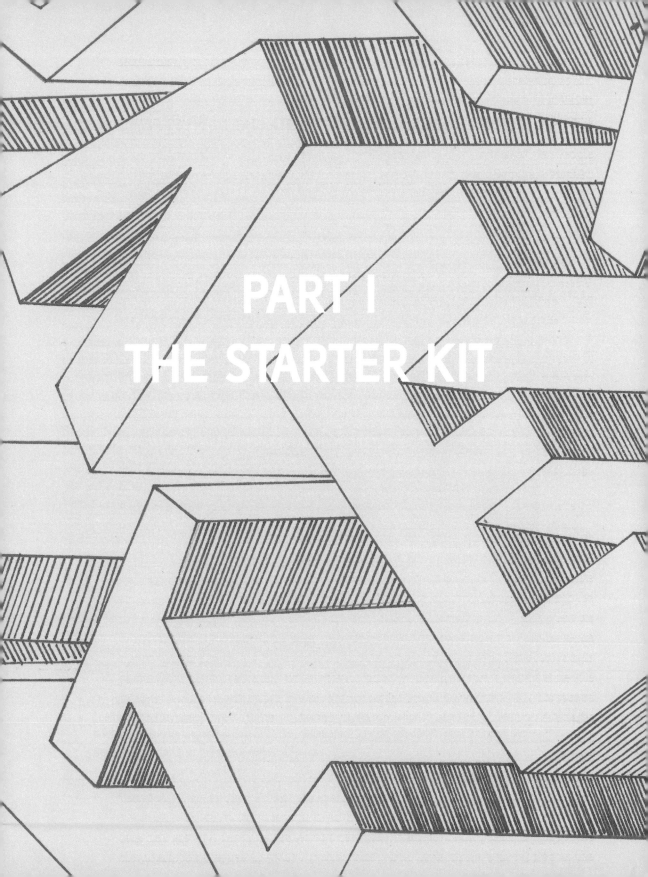

PART I
THE STARTER KIT

1
Introduction

Coming to university can feel great – you're excited – you're joining a whole new group of people and a whole new way of life … But you also feel apprehensive, under-prepared and nervous – we're here to help with that.

' This book really sets students up to succeed! **'**

- Introduction and welcome   4
- Web support   5
- Make a friend, write a blog   6
- Using this book   6
- Each chapter looks like this   7
- Personal skills review: strengths, needs, hopes and fears   7
- What our students have said about coming to university   9
- Six steps to successful study   10
- The six steps   11
- Summary   14
- Activity: the checklist   14

Introduction and welcome

Welcome to *Essential Study Skills: The Complete Guide to Success at University* (ESS4). This book is designed to help you become a more effective and happier student by uncovering some of the mysteries of university life and revealing the 'what, why and how' of learning, studying and succeeding at university as quickly as possible. We also suggest that university is more than studying – and to get the most from university we suggest that you embrace all that your university offers you – different people, new friends, clubs and societies.

Both of us, the authors, were the first in our immediate families to go to university and whilst we found aspects of university life strange, difficult or alienating, we managed to really enjoy ourselves, both as students, and by getting involved in the students' union (SU), by going to the film club, by hanging out in the canteen and chatting to people, by watching bands and by writing for the student newsletter. Because of all of this we learned more, grew more and enjoyed our studies as well.

Life at university is more fraught now than when we were students: there are loans to take out, enormous fees to take on board, you're worried about the cost to yourself and your family – and the job market is unpredictable: you may just want to study hard – never lifting your head out of your books. In these troubled times, this book is designed to help you understand how to succeed at university; but we are going to suggest ways of enjoying university as well. We look at all the different things you will be expected to do as a student – from independent learning to group work, from essays and reports to presentations and seminars, from dealing with your hopes and fears to being successful in creative, analytical and critical thinking – with tips and strategies for how to do them well. We also look at how to make university a positive experience that can change your life in wonderful ways.

It may take some time to work through the book – but you will be a happier and much more successful student if you invest a little time learning how to make the most of university.

Style warning

We have tried to be user-friendly, speaking directly to you without over-simplifying or, worse, being patronising. But this is difficult. There is no one writing style or way of explaining university life that will work for everybody, we hope it works for you.

Book warning

Becoming a successful student is a little like learning to drive. You would not expect to just read a book on driving and leap into a car ready to whizz up the motorway. You would expect to have many, many driving lessons; you would practise and practise to get it right. Hopefully you would see your driving instructor as a critical friend, there to give you advice – and guide you towards being a better driver … We hope that that is the role of this book for you. We do pass on successful techniques and suggestions; but they have to be put into practice – again and again. This is not a quick fix. We cover techniques that will need practising and refining to work for you. We also suggest ways of getting involved in university – from becoming a peer mentor to joining the gym or getting involved in the social side of university life – that may feel like distractions that will get in the way of your studies – but these are important too and we heartily recommend that you make time for these as well.

Out of your comfort zone

It is hard to change, but being a student requires that we do change – otherwise why bother going to university in the first place? Embrace change as a positive. Be prepared to get involved with university – to make new friends and do new things. Be prepared to shed unsuccessful study strategies – and to put the time and effort into developing new, perhaps uncomfortable ones. Reflect on and critique your own practice – and, when at university, try to take feedback from tutors as good advice designed to help – not to put you down. Be prepared to make mistakes and learn from them.

As human beings we learn by trial and error, by having a go, getting it wrong – then having more and more goes until we get it right. As we get older, this feels uncomfortable: we feel foolish or embarrassed. Yet, if we can get over those feelings, if we can force ourselves out of our comfort zones, and consciously decide to take risks, make mistakes and improve, everything else gets better. There are only two big mistakes:

- to be so frightened of making mistakes that we do nothing
- not to learn from our mistakes.

Web support

This book has been written with a companion website where we have put vidcasts, study packs, resource links and much, much more. Check out the website (https://study.sagepub.com/burnsandsinfield4e/) to see what we have for each chapter of the book.

We have also built the Study Hub, a website for students at our own university, and you are very welcome to use that as well – and to join our Study Chat Facebook group in which we post study advice and guidance throughout the year:

Study Hub website: http://learning.londonmet.ac.uk/epacks/studyhub/

Study Chat Facebook group: www.facebook.com/LondonMetStudyChat

Make a friend, write a blog

Learning is multi-modal, that is, we learn with many senses, in many ways and by using many strategies and resources. We learn by listening, watching, making, doing, reading, talking, writing and drawing – and we cover all these things. You can read this book – and then explore the web for additional reading and online tutorials – and we hope that you do that. At the same time, we have tried to make this book as comprehensive as possible – your complete guide to success at university.

We will ask you to discuss things quite a lot throughout this book – talking is really good active learning. Don't worry if you haven't got a university friend just yet – but do look out for one.

Even if you do have a classmate who is a friend – we suggest that you use Facebook, Twitter and other online spaces to talk through and reflect on your learning. Set up a new blog and use that to make useful notes on your student journey. See also Chapters 8 and 10 which also discuss blogging your learning – from slightly different angles. Use or read student blogs or student video diaries and see what other people are writing about out there. A quick online search for student study blogs takes you to many examples to choose from.

To get the most from this book, we will want you to get involved by reading actively, making short notes and by writing about what you have learned. As we suggest in the title to this section – the best advice of all is to start your own blog, and blog about your learning. Telling others is a great way to reinforce our learning for ourselves.

Using this book

This is a book that you can work through step by step but it has also been designed so that you can dip into different sections when you feel they will be useful to you. The trick is to know what you want from each section of the book at any particular time.

Each chapter looks like this

Each chapter in this book has an overall theme and whilst there might be some slight changes in the presentation of material, certain things will recur throughout the book. Typically there will be:

- aims that state what we think the chapter will achieve
- an introduction to and presentation of information – coupled with, variously:

  - things for you to find out and activities for you to do
  - questions to answer
  - student and staff quotes
  - queries, discussion and commentary

- further reading and guides to resources, including online resources and work packs
- a summary that draws the chapter together and to a close
- tips and end of chapter activities.

TIPS

- Before you start reading a chapter – think first: what do I know? What do I need? This gets you tuned in for success.
- Work through each chapter with notepad and pens at the ready. Make notes of the good stuff. Get involved with the activities.
- When you have finished a chapter, make the learning conscious: reflect or self-test: what do I know now? What would I tell someone else? Then blog it.

Students: "It opened up different strategies, learning strategies, and now I don't feel inferior."

Examiners: "This changes students' lives, not just their study skills."

Course
leaders: "The effect on our students was like stardust."

Personal skills review: strengths, needs, hopes and fears

In this section we ask you to reflect on your own strengths and needs – and to think about what it feels like to come to university. Before you have a look at comments shared by some of our students – have a quick brainstorm, then answer the questions in our personal skills review. Don't think too much about your answers. This is not about getting it 'right', it's about responding spontaneously.

- What are my strengths?
- What is it about me that has got me to university?

Now – answer these questions:

1	How do you feel about yourself as a learner at the moment? Are you good at learning? Are you good at studying?
2	How positive do you feel about being a student? How committed are you to developing your study skills? What are you prepared to do to improve? How much time and energy are you prepared to put in?
3	How organised are you? (If you have brought up a family or juggled work with a hobby or family, then you are used to organising your life. This is a useful, transferable skill.)
4	If you have studied before, did you have set times to work? Do you have a place to study – a room, a desk, a table? Have you got an overall approach to studying? Do you feel you have successful strategies overall? What do you need to enable effective study?
5	What reading do you do at the moment? Are you happy with your reading skills? What do you think you need to make you a more successful academic reader?
6	How confident do you feel about using the library? Can you do successful online searches? Have you used journals or e-journals yet? What do you need here?
7	Do you make notes when you study? Are you happy with your notes? What do you do with your notes? What do you need to learn about notemaking?
8	What sorts of writing do you do at the moment (e.g. letters, blogs, emails, tweets, texts)? Have you written essays before? What sort of marks did you get? Are you happy with that? What do you want to get from the sections of the book that cover academic writing?
9	Have you ever had to make a presentation to a group of people? (A talk of a set length to a specific audience, usually on a specific topic.) How did it go? What do you feel about the idea of having to do presentations on your course? What do you want to know about presentations?
10	Have you revised for and sat exams? How did it go? How do you feel about your memory? How do you feel about exams? What do you need to know about revision and exam techniques?

FIGURE 1.1   Personal skills review

How do you feel now? The questionnaire outlines the sorts of things you will need to do to study effectively – you cannot write an essay, for example, if you cannot organise your time, make useful notes or read academic texts. Hopefully you have gained a better picture of your own strengths and some of the qualities that you have already that will help you succeed. The rest of this book will take you through these processes in even more detail, so that you understand them and get the opportunity to practise and reflect upon them. You should also have an idea of some areas that you might like to work on – follow those up.

If your university runs a Personal Development Planning (PDP) system (see Chapter 13.1) – make notes on this skills review and put them in your PDP file: what strengths did you identify? What areas are you going to work on?

What our students have said about coming to university

No matter how much you wanted to go to university, once you get there, you will typically experience an emotional rollercoaster: you may be nervous – you may be excited. You are looking forward to all the people and experiences – and you are terrified that you will not make any friends, and that you will not cope with the work. We have captured some of the things that our students have said to us about what coming to university felt like for them – have a look and see if any of their feelings match your own – and be reassured – all these feelings can be dealt with: they, we, you can survive and do well.

I'm not sure that I'll find enough time to study. I'm not organised and I know that I'll have to be if I want to work, study and maintain my family and friends.

I'm apprehensive about how my studies will affect the rest of my life. Being a student is going to have a dramatic impact on my life, I can see that. But I wanted to do this course – so I'll have to work out how to make it work.

I find it hard to concentrate for long periods.

My memory isn't as good as it used to be.

I haven't written an essay for ages and I'm anxious about putting pen to paper …

I'm worried because English isn't my first language; my daughter is better at English than I am and she has said that she will help me. She also thinks that I'm being very brave studying in English – which makes me feel strong instead of foolish.

I'm worried that I'll find it hard to cope with the difficult reading. I wish I could read faster. I have heard that academic reading does get easier with practice – I certainly hope so.

(Continued)

(Continued)

I'm not very good at spelling. I'm never sure when to use a comma or a full stop. I've forgotten all the rules of grammar.

I'm going to use the spell checker on my computer. I've also heard that you need to build up your own dictionary of all the new words and names that you're learning. I've already bought a small exercise book to do this.

I hated school – why on earth did I think I could cope with university?

I am worried that the work will be difficult and I won't be able to understand it; but I am going to try to be brave and learn from my mistakes. I'm going to ask questions if I don't understand what's going on.

Do you recognise any of these feelings? Are any of these you? How do you feel now after reading all these? Sharing our fears can show us that fear is normal – and solutions are possible. A quick antidote to a quivering mass of fear, though, is to start to think positively about your way forward; so we conclude this first chapter with a look at the six steps to successful study. Read through that next section – making notes of all the tips, tricks and advice and make notes of what you are going to do with that information.

Six steps to successful study

If you are in halls, make friends with the people there. If you are in a student flat, make an effort to integrate and make friends on your course. If you live at home, make sure you spend as much time in the university as possible: it's about being there! It's about being with the other students!

Are you the first in your family to go to university? Are you an international student worried that you won't fit in? Are you leaving home for the first time and homesick? Are you angry that you are not leaving home? Are you feeling old, thinking that you are unlikely to make friends – or worried that you're too young and inexperienced to do well? Well you are not alone. No – seriously – everybody tends to feel bad about their student selves. Everybody else looks like they know what they're doing – and you're the only one who looks, sounds and feels like a fool. This is not true. Mostly we feel this way because it's natural – everybody does; sometimes we feel this way because we have not consciously learned how to study and learn. The next chapter explores that in more detail. In the meantime, here is a quick guide to successful study.

The six steps

Our work suggests that there are certain approaches to study that promote engagement, active learning and success. We call these the six steps to study success, SOCCER, and they inform this book. For a quick overview, read the sections below and think about how you can put them into practice in your studies.

1	Study techniques can be learnt – good students are made, not born
2	Overview is vital – everybody needs the big picture
3	Creativity is essential – and can be developed
4	Communicate effectively – in the correct form
5	Emotions rule – dealing with the whole you is crucial
6	Review – without reflection there is no learning

FIGURE 1.2   Six steps to success

1 Study techniques can be learned – good students are made, not born

It is all too easy to think that we are not 'cut out' for studying. Bad school experiences can make people believe that studying is not for them – they are not good students. But why should you know how to study effectively? If you wanted to be a firefighter or a farmer or a chef or a carpenter you would know that you would have to learn how to be one. If we think of studying like this it can become easier. All the way through this book we will look at the constituent study and academic skills that can help you to succeed. In terms of developing your study techniques consider:

- the Survival Kit section, which explores the key study and academic skills that you need to really do well at university
- the Big Assessment Toolkits, which explore firstly how to approach assignments – and secondly how to do well in the different sorts of assignments you are set at university.

 Why didn't they tell us this before? I left school feeling like a complete failure – but it was just that I didn't know how to learn. These techniques have given me such a boost. I feel really confident now.

2 Overview is vital – everybody needs the big picture

Whilst it is true that we tend to learn things in pieces, one step at a time, this is helped if we have the big picture first – if we know how the subject will be covered. It's like a jigsaw puzzle, it is much easier to put the pieces together if we have the picture on the box. Similarly, if we understand how universities work and how our courses have been put together, we will be able to achieve more, more swiftly. Have a look at:

- The Big Assessment Toolkit: How to Make Sense of Your Course

 I really hated school; not knowing what was going on and why. Using the 'overview' has made all the difference. I'm now on top.

3 Creativity is essential – and can be developed

There is a lot of 'common sense' about being a successful student – it is common sense to be well organised, to make time each day for study. There's nothing wrong with common sense, we know students who have gained good degrees with common sense and sheer hard work. However, if you want to do that little bit more, if you want studying to be a little bit easier and more interesting, then a touch of creativity is needed.

If you give back to lecturers what they have told you, if you just use their examples and read the books that they recommend, then you will be a strong, average student. To get a little further you have to be creative, you have to go somewhere or think something different. How can you do that? We discuss creativity generally, and explore creative ways to approach assignments and notemaking. We take you through techniques that encourage a different or more original approach to your studies. Look at:

- The Survival Kit sections:
  - How to Make the Best Notes
  - How to Be Creative and Visual
  - How to Be Analytical and Critical

- The Big Assessment Toolkit: Probably the Most Important Thing on Writing You'll Ever Read

 At school I was told to go away and get a job in a shop (sorry shop workers!), that I would never be able to learn anything. Putting colour and pictures into my university work has made all the difference; now I get As for my assignments.

4 Communicate effectively – in the correct form

 They used to write things like 'there's no introduction' or 'there's no conclusion' on my essays. But no one ever told me what these were – or why they wanted them. Now I only have to worry about my ideas, I know how to present them.

Just as we cannot 'know' how to study, we may not 'know' what an essay, report or presentation is. These things have specific shapes to them (what), they have specific purposes (why) and there are tried and tested ways of approaching them (how). In order to help you develop successful assessment techniques, we discuss effective communication in the context of essays, reports, dissertations, presentations and seminars. See:

- The Big Assessment Toolkit: Cracking Assessment – The Ten Step Approach to Better Assignments
- The Big Assessment Toolkit: Assessments – How To Excel

5 Emotions rule – dealing with the whole you is crucial

Studying and learning are seen as 'brain' activities: cognitive and intellectual, but they are 'body' activities as well: we can learn by doing and making – as well as by reading and writing; and for most of us studying can be fraught with emotion also. When we first start a course we are apprehensive, nervous or even terrified. If we do not admit our own emotional responses to university issues, we cannot address them, and we will never be able to benefit from our positive responses or overcome our negative ones.

Check out what our students have to say about positive thinking on our Study Hub website:

- http://learning.londonmet.ac.uk/studyhub/positive.html.

In this book, see especially:

- The Starter Kit: Make University Positive

 You ask what the first day was like? I was het up, frightened, terrified ... I thought 'Why the hell have I done this to myself?' I just wanted to run away ... Oh I love it now, I don't want to leave!

6 Review – without reflection there is no learning

Learning is process and learning is active, it involves an active selection of what to learn and how to learn it, it involves self-testing and review. Throughout the book we will be examining different memory and revision strategies, including reflective learning logs and Personal Development Planning. We also want you to reflect and self-test after every chapter – and to explore and reflect on how you learned what you did. Learning and remembering are not necessarily automatic or simple, but we can learn how to do these effectively and we have structured the book to reinforce this. To explore this in more depth go to:

- The Survival Kit: How to Be Reflective
- The Big Assessment Toolkit: How to Excel: How to Revise for and Pass Exams
- The Employability Kit: PDP and HEAR

I love doing my learning logs, it makes me make sense of what I'm doing. If I didn't do my logs, I don't think I'd understand anything at all.

Summary

To set the context for ESS4, we have briefly introduced ourselves – and introduced the book itself – making suggestions as to how to use ESS4 successfully. We moved on to consider some of the emotional dimensions of being a student – reassuring you that you can survive your feelings, but emphasising that you will need to shift outside of your comfort zone in order to make the most of university – to grow.

Coming to university can be unsettling and change can be uncomfortable; we looked at some typical hopes and fears about becoming a university student. If you also have some of the feelings written about in this chapter – we hope it reassures you – you are not alone. Fear is normal, but there is usually something we can do about our fears – and in that light, we introduced you to the six steps to study success. We have argued that good students, like you, are made, not born. If you build SOCCER into your study habits every day, you will make real progress.

Activity

The checklist

- ☐ **Enjoy being a student.**
- ☐ **Help your family and friends realise how important being a student is to you.**
- ☐ **Have a regular place to study – when you sit there your body will learn to work.**

- Move out of your comfort zone – make mistakes and learn from them.
- Concentrate for 15 minute blocks at first and build up.
- Work for half an hour every day
- Make some time to study every week day. Turn off your phone, don't answer the door. Focus.
- Write something every day – your reflective blog?
- Develop your memory (Chapter 12.6).
- Discover if you like working alone – or with other people.
- Discover if you like working with noise or quiet.
- Discover if you like working in the morning, afternoon, evening or night.
- If English isn't your first language join an academic English class.
- Buy an English dictionary, a subject dictionary and a dictionary of sociological terms.
- Buy an exercise book and make your own subject dictionary.
- Write new theories, words and phrases on Post-its and stick them up all round your home. Take them down when you know them.
- Prioritise, make lists, use a diary, use a 24/7 timetable.
- Sometimes be very organised … Sometimes sit amongst a pile of work and plunge in.
- Enjoy studying, do not see it as 'work'.
- Use deadlines to keep you on track.
- If unhappy with your spelling, punctuation or grammar, buy a simple grammar book and use it.
- Keep a small notebook with you. When you have a bright idea or insight, write it down.
- Find a friend, get a study partner, use online discussion boards, set up your own blog and write about your studies and your learning.

'And you go, yes, and it really spurs you on!'

Access the companion website to this book and find helpful resources for this chapter topic:
https://study.sagepub.com/burnsandsinfield4e

2

How to Learn, How to Study

We're not born knowing how to study – these learning and studying strategies will help you make the most of the study aspects of university.

- Introduction 18
- Past learning experiences 18
- What is learning? 19
- Harness a multi-sensory approach to learning 20
- Studying: when, where and how 21
- Independent learning 25
- A beginner's guide to taking control of your studies 26
- Summary 29
- Further reading 29
- Activity: two key things to do right now: learning contract and timetables 29

Introduction

In this chapter we bring together arguments about learning with an exploration of how to study – and how to study at university. We begin by asking you to examine your past learning experiences – and consider a multi-sensory approach to learning and how to harness this. We explore when, where and how to study – with a focus on how universities organise their teaching and learning; assessment is tackled in Chapters 11 and 12. As always – think: what do I know? What do I need? How will I harness this information to promote my active learning and study success?

Past learning experiences

Before moving on, we'd like you to think back to your own past learning experiences. In particular, think about the conditions that helped you to learn – and the things that got in the way of your learning. Make brief notes to answer the questions below – then read what another student has said.

- Think back to a previous successful learning experience. It does not have to have been at school – it could be learning to drive or sky dive. Why was it successful – why did you learn?
- Now think back to an unsuccessful learning experience. What was it? Why did little or no learning take place?
- Looking over these good and bad experiences of yours – can you sum up: 'Things that help learning to happen' and 'Things that prevent learning'?
- If you wish, use your notes to free write quickly on 'Things that help me learn – and things that stop me from learning'.
- Once you have completed your own thoughts, compare your thoughts with those written by another student, below.

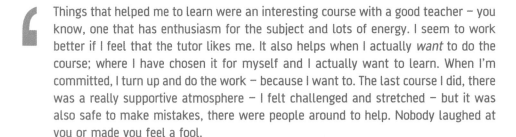

Things that helped me to learn were an interesting course with a good teacher – you know, one that has enthusiasm for the subject and lots of energy. I seem to work better if I feel that the tutor likes me. It also helps when I actually *want* to do the course; where I have chosen it for myself and I actually want to learn. When I'm committed, I turn up and do the work – because I want to. The last course I did, there was a really supportive atmosphere – I felt challenged and stretched – but it was also safe to make mistakes, there were people around to help. Nobody laughed at you or made you feel a fool.

The worst learning experience I had was at school. I had to be there – it was compulsory – but I never really saw the point of it. I just felt so powerless all the time. I never knew what we were doing or why or when or how. It was a nightmare and one of the reasons that I left school the minute I could!

Do you recognise some of yourself in the responses? What might this tell you? One thing we can see is that if we are going to be successful when learning, then we must want to learn: we must be interested and motivated.

On the other hand, what seems to stop people from learning is feeling unmotivated, confused, unhappy, fearful and powerless. These are some of the reasons that compulsory education does not work for some people.

TIP

Whenever you start to study, sit down and write your own personal goals for that course. Put them on Post-its and display them over your desk. Cut out pictures that represent your success to you and stick these up also. Use these to keep you motivated and interested.

What is learning?

Learning is not about the empty student coming to university to be filled with knowledge and wisdom – though some people might wish that it was! Learning is active and interactive; it is a process. Learning involves engaging with ideas – and engaging with other people as they engage with ideas (Wenger-Trayner, 2014). An early author on study skills, Devine (1987), describes learning as a series of processes:

- gathering new ideas and information
- recording them
- organising them
- making sense of and understanding them
- remembering them
- using them.

Learning is about gathering new ideas and information – engaging with and acquiring information from classes, lectures, seminars, tutorials, discussions, practical activities, reading (textbooks, journals, newspapers and more). It is notemaking – recording what is important. We encounter information in many forms, in many places and at different times – we have to reorganise the information to make sense of it for ourselves and remember it. Finally we have to be able to use the information – we have to be able to discuss it with other people and use it in our assignments. Learning also changes us, once truly learned something cannot be unlearned – we have crossed a threshold and become someone slightly different (Land, 2010).

- Before you can forget your lecture or class, don't rush home, go to the canteen and talk about it.
- Get a study partner or form a study group: discuss lectures and seminars. Discuss your reading.
- Write before you know or understand it all.
- Discuss your writing.

Harness a multi-sensory approach to learning

So learning is active and social and it also involves all the senses. If you went to a Montessori primary school, you would already have been encouraged to see, hear, say and do in order to learn effectively; for we learn some of what we see, we learn some of what we hear, we learn when we speak or discuss (when we say) and we learn when we do (when we make something or engage in an activity) – but it is argued that we can learn most when we see, hear, say *and* do. Here we explore visual (sight based), auditory (sound based) and kinaesthetic (touch, feel or movement based) learning.

- *Sight*: to learn by seeing, enjoy learning by reading and by watching television, film or video. Enjoy watching your lecturer and seeing how they convey information – how they show you what is important. Use pictures in your learning and revision activities: draw cartoons and pictures to illustrate your points, draw pattern notes, put in colour, and put in memory-jogging cartoon images or visuals. (See also Chapters 5 and 6.)
- *Sound*: to learn by hearing and speaking, enjoy learning through listening and joining in discussions. You will learn as you explain things to other people. Make audiotapes to support your learning using songs, rhymes and jingles that you write yourself as learning and revision aids. Tape yourself and sing along. Talk yourself through your assignment.
- *Feel*: to harness the kinaesthetic, enjoy practical learning activities, from making something, to performing a science experiment to role-playing. Make charts and patterns of the things you want to remember – role-play ideas or act them out in some way. Care about your subject – find meaning and value in your course.

Activity

Watch, listen, learn: Barbara Oakley has given an interesting TED Talk on 'How to learn' (https://youtu.be/O96fE1E-rf8). Watch the video and make notes whilst thinking, 'How will I use this information to become a better student?' Reflect: How much of the information did I hear? How much did I see? How much of it did I feel was right?

Studying: when, where and how

 I'm a mum, I work, I've got my parents to look after … I guess I'm organised!

Studying is more formalised learning – and it tends to be hard work. We are going to explore when, where and how to study and provide you with very practical advice and tips.

When should I study?

 I know we are supposed to start work weeks before the deadline, but I usually start two or three days before.

Many students do not start work until a deadline really frightens them – they need the hit of adrenalin to get them over their study fears and into working. The trouble is that whilst adrenalin is great for getting you out of a burning building – it does not help you develop the depth and breadth you need for university level thinking and writing.

 The best tip I ever got was to do at least half an hour's work each day. This has put me on top of all my studies … And usually once I start I get a little bit more done and I feel so much better.

I know what I should do, I really know … but I just can't face it.

Studying can feel unbearable, un-do-able, like climbing a mountain. But there is more than one way to face a mountain. For some a mountain is so large and danger-ous that they are afraid of it. For some a mountain is an exciting challenge. For some a mountain is just a thing to be tackled sensibly one step at a time. If you normally fear or dread your assignments – change the way you see them. Adopt a 'one step at a time' approach. Look at assignment questions at the beginning of a course. Think about the question before lectures and classes and before you start reading. Break the question down into manageable chunks. Read about one 'chunk' at a time. Write one paragraph at a time – then revise and improve as you do more reading.

 I never seem to feel like studying.

Nobody leaps out of bed in the morning going, 'Wheee – this is the day that I tackle that huge assignment!' So do not rely on feeling like studying. You have to make the time to study – you need a system. Every university student has to work out for themselves just how much time they are prepared to give to their studies – but it should be 35 hours or more each week. You have to decide how much work you are prepared to put in, to get the results – the grades – that you want. Study five days a week – plan and use your time – even when you don't feel like it.

When planning out your time think about:

- *Best time of day?* Are you a morning, afternoon or evening person? Try to fit your study times around your maximum performance times. Work with your strengths.
- *Travel time*: reading on the bus or train is a really effective use of time.
- *Friends and family time*: your studies are important – but most of us would like to have friends and family still talking to us when our studies are over. Help them to help you be a successful student.
- *Housework time*: we need to keep our homes at least sanitary. Watch out though – housework and all chores can become excellent excuses for not working. They become displacement activities – sometimes it feels as though it is easier to completely re-build the house rather than write an essay!
- *Paid work time*: these days we need to earn money whilst we study – we have to work – and still fit in 35 hours of study each week. Sometimes universities help by fitting lectures and other classes into one or two days a week. Beware – this does not mean that all your studying can fit into two days a week! Remember you have to give 12 to 16 hours to classes – and another 20 or so hours to independent study – *each week*. If you cannot do this, you will be in trouble.
- *Rest and relaxation time*: studying is hard work – it can also be very stressful. It is important to get sufficient rest whilst you study and it is useful to build stress relief activities – dancing, exercise, gym, meditation, massage, yoga – into your timetables right at the beginning of your studies.

TIPS

- **Find paid work at your university – this helps you be there more.**
- **Join your university gym – use it at least once a week.**

- *Prioritise time*: make lists and prioritise tasks. Keep a diary – note when you are going to read; note which assignment you are writing – when.

- *Study timetables*: timetables give you a strong guide to your work – if you keep to them. But more than that, without timetables you may feel that every time you are not working you ought to be studying. You may not do that studying, but you worry – and this exhausts you. Eventually it may feel that your whole life is work, work, work. Something will have to go – and it could be your studies! Use the timetables at the end of this chapter – plan when you will study – and when you will not study.

Where to study

Everyone deserves a nice place to study, but real life is not always like that; sometimes we just have to adapt to what we have and make it work. Here are some tips about making a study space work for you.

- Negotiate a space with family or flatmates. Creating a study space helps everyone in your life – including you – realise just how important your studies are.
- A good place to study needs light and air – you need to see and breathe – but does not necessarily have to be a completely quiet place. Work out what works for you.
- You will need space to lay out your work, pin up your timetables, deadlines and notes. Have your textbooks out and open.
- Pin up all the new words that you are learning, immerse yourself in your learning.
- Do not tidy your work away. Having your work visible keeps it alive in your mind whereas putting it all away can give the impression that you're finished.
- Have pens and pencils, also highlighters, a stapler and staples, paper clips, correction fluid, Post-its, coloured pens – and all sorts of different sizes of paper. Play around with materials and colour, get an injection of energy and enthusiasm.

Practise being positive: 'Now I am working', 'I enjoy being a student'. Avoid those old negative thoughts: 'I don't want to be here', 'This is too hard'. Negative thoughts have a negative effect – positive thoughts have a positive effect. Give 100% whenever you sit down to study. Act as if you and your studies are important – they are – so are you.

What other students have said:

It felt really good having my own study space. It made me feel like a real student.

I felt that at last I could settle down to some real work.

I felt a bit frightened at first – you know? Like now I couldn't put it off any longer! I'd have to take it seriously.

Sometimes I use my space to sort of trick myself into working. I think, I'll just sit there for a minute ... Next thing I know I've been working away for an hour and I feel really good.

I felt guilty at having to cut myself off from the kids. It just felt so selfish. I have to work really hard at still giving them some time.

I used to get so frustrated; it was like every time I sat down to work they would start demanding things from me. Now we all sit down to work at the same time – even if they are just crayoning or reading a storybook. This has helped us all feel better.

I still like going to the library to work – but it's great having a proper place for my stuff at home. It really does help.

Experiment with working at home, in the library and when you travel – being a commuter adds hours of study time to your week, if you use it. But whether you want to work in a library or on a bus, you will also need a study space at home.

TIP

If you have children, try to make a family study time – so you all work together.

How to study

University is supposed to be a full-time occupation – using up to 35–40 hours of your time per week. You are supposed to be studying and learning full time, through lectures, seminars, tutorials, the virtual learning environment (VLE) and through your independent study. Here's how:

The lecture

One lecturer plus a large group of students – can be 150 or more. The lecturer is an expert, a researcher at the cutting edge of the subject. The lecturer gives a short-cut to key information – and successful students make notes – and use those notes to seed further reading, thought and writing. Always prepare before you attend a lecture. Always think – what is it about? What do I know already? Why this topic? How will it help me with my assignment?

The seminar

A seminar usually consists of a lecturer plus 10–30 students. A seminar is supposed to seed your thinking and develop your ideas through discussion – it is active learning. Join in the discussions. Prepare beforehand: read, watch or write what you are supposed to.

Learn seminar survival strategies: know how to present your opinions assertively, not aggressively; learn how to interrupt the person who never stops talking; and learn how to draw out quiet people who may actually have much to offer. Don't worry whether people are making friends with you – you make friends with other people.

The tutorial

A tutorial is like the seminar but with one tutor to four or five students. There is definitely no hiding place in a tutorial. You will have to be prepared and you will have to join in.

The VLE

Universities include virtual, blended or e-learning experiences as part of their teaching and learning practices. Find out how your course is going to be delivered – and how to make the most of it. Even though the information is 'virtual' – the work is still real – and the learning is still social and interactive.

–TIP–

Be prepared to join in with online conversations about the work. If you are expected to post comments or blogs in the VLE – do so; and remember to read and 'like' the comments left by your peers – be supportive, encouraging and friendly. See also Chapter 10.

Independent learning

In the UK we 'read for' our degrees – that is, our thinking and learning is seeded by lectures and seminars – and then we are expected to read and read and read. There is much emphasis on independent learning. That is, you will be expected to follow up ideas in various ways, including reading around a subject, on your own and on your own initiative. For more on academic reading, see also Chapter 4.

–TIP–

Be an interdependent learner: have a study partner or group.

A beginner's guide to taking control of your studies

This whole book is designed to get you studying in more successful ways, but here are some very practical things to do right now.

Want it: you will not learn anything unless you want to. Know what you want from each course that you are studying. Know how your life will be changed when you reach your goals.

TIP

Write your goals on Post-its and stick them up in your study space. Write your learning contract (below) for each course, module or unit that you do.

Get the overview (Chapter 11.1): read and understand the aims and the learning outcomes. Know what you have to do and learn to pass your course – and how you will be assessed.

Epistemology: every course has its own theory of knowledge – what counts as argument and evidence – its epistemology. Make sure you know the what, why and how of all your subjects. Read the journals to get a model of how to argue and write in your subject.

Be positive: just as an athlete will perform better if they think they can win – so a student will learn more if they can adopt positive attitudes; if your motivation runs low, act like a successful student, believe that you can succeed.

Pace yourself: work for an hour – take a break. We concentrate best in 15-minute bursts. When we study we have to get into the habit of regularly recharging our mental batteries to wake up our brains. We can do this by:

- taking a short rest
- changing what we do
- making the task very important
- making the task interesting, stimulating or more difficult.

Prioritise time: be strategic – do first the assignments that carry the most marks or whose deadlines are coming first.

Use time: we know students who sit down to study – out come the pens and paper – they get rearranged. Out come the books and the highlighters – they get rearranged. They go for a coffee. They go for a glass of water. They put one lot of books away and get out another set. They look at the clock – oh good! An hour has passed – they put their materials away. But they have done no work. Before you study – set goals. Afterwards – reflect. Make the learning conscious.

Worry about one assignment at a time: put up a set of shelves in your brain. Put all your different worries on the shelves. Learn to take down one thing at a time and give it your total concentration. When you have finished with that, put it back on the shelf and take down something else.

Be active: listen/read actively, asking questions as you go. What does it mean? Do I understand it? If not, what am I going to do about that? How does it connect with what I already know? How will I use it in my assignment?

Review actively: at the end of each study session – reflect on what you have read or heard.

TIP

Write a blog post at the end of every day.

Study partners and groups: for many, study is best when undertaken actively, interactively and socially; this is where a friend, study partner or a study group can be invaluable.

Don't end on a sour note: try not to end a study session on a problem – it is demotivating and it can make it that little bit harder to start studying again. Use a study partner, friend or online discussion space to talk it over.

Relaxation and dealing with stress: make time to rest, relax and let go of stress. When we are stressed our body releases cortisol – a hormone that has a direct impact on the brain causing the cortex to shrink – and adrenalin – the flight or fight hormone. The combination of these hormones eliminates short-term memory and produces the narrow, tunnel vision necessary for fight or flight. This might save our lives when escaping from a burning building, but works against us when studying where we need breadth and depth of vision.

TIPS

- **Make a note of the problem and sleep on it – sometimes the solution comes to you when you wake up. But don't lie awake fretting all night; this does not solve the problem and you have made everything worse by losing sleep and gaining stress.**
- **Join the gym. Take up yoga. Practise meditation.**

Organisation and time management: if you are now feeling overwhelmed by all your responsibilities as a student, try this five-step plan to tackling those worries – and getting things done:

1. List everything that you need to do: this may feel like a really bad idea and that you'll be even more frightened; but the opposite is true. Once you write the list, and you can see the reality of the 'problem', it becomes more manageable and less overwhelming.
2. Divide each big task that you have to do into smaller steps. So do not just put down: 'write essay'. Break it down: 'brainstorm question', 'read up on ...', 'write a paragraph on ...', etc.

3. Organise your big list into things that must be done now; soon; later.
4. Do one of the *now* tasks immediately and cross it off. You will instantly feel more calm and in control.
5. Prioritise your list and put it into a 'to do' order.
   (With thanks to our colleagues at Reading University.)

Still procrastinating? You have to be organised – you have to be methodical – do not procrastinate – just do it! Try this activity suggested by Michelle Reid of Reading University. Work with a group of friends, especially if they are fellow students. You will need Post-it notes and pens.

Activity

The time sponge

Everybody takes one large Post-it and writes their biggest time sponge at the top (a time sponge is anything you find yourself doing instead of working – checking your phone, messaging friends, etc.).

Everybody passes their Post-it to the person on their left. You all read someone else's time sponge problem and write a possible solution.

Pass to the left again and write another solution to another problem.

Keep going until you have run out of space on the Post-its.

Everybody takes a turn to read out the problem on the Post-it they have been left with – and the various solutions offered.

Everybody says one thing they will now do differently after listening to all the sponges and solutions.

When planning your time – think about these:

- *Study timetable*: this is a 24/7 timetable (24 hours a day, seven days a week) that covers how many hours per day go to non-study and how many go to your studies. It is where you can plan which subjects to study and for how long. It takes some trial and error and experiment to get this right – so do give it that time.
- *Assignment timetable*: this is a record of all the assignment deadlines that are coming up either in a term, a semester or across a whole year. Fill in deadlines and pin it up on your wall and place a copy in your folder and diary. Never let a deadline take you by surprise.
- *Exam timetable*: similar to the assignment timetable, this is a record of all the exams you will be taking. Note dates, times and locations. It is all too easy to turn up at the wrong time, on the wrong day and in the wrong place!

- *Revision timetable*: at the appropriate time, each student should devise their own revision timetable where they work out when they are going to test their knowledge and practise for the exams that they are going to sit

Photocopy the timetables below: experiment with using them to help you focus on your work and get the most from your time.

Summary

We have looked at learning and considered when, where and how to study; some authors call this SHAPE: style, habit, attitude, preference and experience. The trouble is that we may stay with unsuccessful study habits even when they do not work, just because they are that – a habit or a preference. None of the good practice in this chapter will mean anything unless and until you put the ideas into practice. Until you push through your discomfort and learn new, successful practices.

Further reading

BBC Scotland's Brain Smart website: www.bbc.co.uk/scotland/brainsmart/.
Devine, T.G. (1987) *Teaching Study Skills*. Newton, MA: Allyn and Bacon.
Wenger-Trayner, E. (2014) Key note at ALDinHE Conference, Huddersfield University, 2014.

Activity

Two key things to do right now: learning contract and timetables

1 Write a learning contract

Reflect on what you have read so far and write a brief learning contract saying what you want from your course: what you're prepared to do to achieve your goals, what might stop you, and what's in it for you (what will change about your life when you achieve your own goals).

- What I want from this course is …
- What I'm prepared to do to make this happen is … (Use the six steps to success like this … Build on my visual strategies like this … Visit the library … Write for half an hour every day …)
- What might stop me is … (Note the issues in your life: work, family, friends … How might these affect your studies? What are you going to do about that?)
- What's in it for me (WiiFM) is … (Knowing WiiFM can help motivate you on those cold, wet days when it feels too hard to get out of bed …).

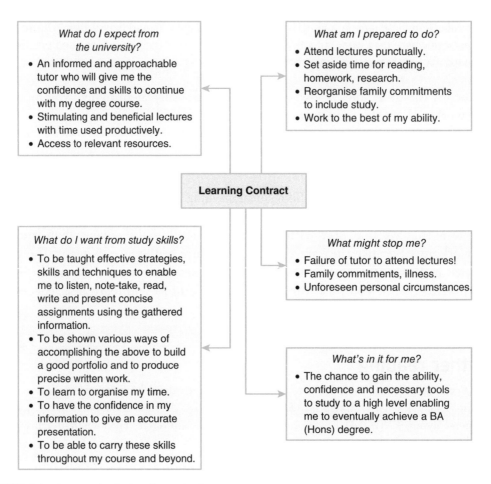

What do I expect from the university?

- An informed and approachable tutor who will give me the confidence and skills to continue with my degree course.
- Stimulating and beneficial lectures with time used productively.
- Access to relevant resources.

What am I prepared to do?

- Attend lectures punctually.
- Set aside time for reading, homework, research.
- Reorganise family commitments to include study.
- Work to the best of my ability.

Learning Contract

What do I want from study skills?

- To be taught effective strategies, skills and techniques to enable me to listen, note-take, read, write and present concise assignments using the gathered information.
- To be shown various ways of accomplishing the above to build a good portfolio and to produce precise written work.
- To learn to organise my time.
- To have the confidence in my information to give an accurate presentation.
- To be able to carry these skills throughout my course and beyond.

What might stop me?

- Failure of tutor to attend lectures!
- Family commitments, illness.
- Unforeseen personal circumstances.

What's in it for me?

- The chance to gain the ability, confidence and necessary tools to study to a high level enabling me to eventually achieve a BA (Hons) degree.

FIGURE 2.1   An example of a learning contract

2 Fill in your timetables

Take some time to complete the following timetables – and experiment with them – see how to use them to organise and motivate yourself.

TIP

We have put in *two* blank 24/7 timetables – complete one as a *plan*; complete the other as a *review*. Then decide how you will need to adjust your plans to be more successful.

Filling in the 24-hour timetable:

- Fill in the first one, indicating when you expect to work, sleep, do chores and so forth. Think about the time that you have left. Put in times for study and relaxation. Think about it – are you being realistic? Make sure that you are not under- or over-working yourself. Run that programme for a few weeks.

- After a couple of weeks, review your success in keeping to the study times that you set and in achieving the goals that you had in mind.
- Change your timetable to fit in with reality. Use the second blank timetable for this.
- Remember to do this every term, semester, year.

Time	Monday	Tuesday	Wednesday	Thursday	Friday	Saturday	Sunday
1.00							
2.00							
3.00							
4.00							
5.00							
6.00							
7.00							
8.00							
9.00							
10.00							
11.00							
12.00							
13.00							
14.00							
15.00							
16.00							
17.00							
18.00							
19.00							
20.00							
21.00							
22.00							
23.00							
24.00							

FIGURE 2.2   Blank 24-hour timetable – plan

Time	Monday	Tuesday	Wednesday	Thursday	Friday	Saturday	Sunday
1.00							
2.00							
3.00							
4.00							
5.00							
6.00							
7.00							
8.00							
9.00							
10.00							
11.00							
12.00							
13.00							
14.00							
15.00							
16.00							
17.00							
18.00							
19.00							
20.00							
21.00							
22.00							
23.00							
24.00							

FIGURE 2.3   Blank 24-hour timetable – review and improve

Events and deadlines				
Write down the dates of the following events each term:				
	Course 1	Course 2	Course 3	Course 4
Course title				
Exam(s)				
Essay deadline(s)				
Laboratory report deadline(s)				
Seminar presentations				
Field trips/visits				
Project report or exhibition deadlines				
Bank holidays or other 'days off'				
Other events (specify)				

FIGURE 2.4   Course events and deadlines timetable

	Term plan – what is happening over your terms/semester?						
	Monday	Tuesday	Wednesday	Thursday	Friday	Saturday	Sunday
Week 1							
Week 2							
Week 3							
Week 4							
Week 5							
Week 6							
Week 7							
Week 8							
Week 9							
Week 10							
Week 11							
Week 12							
Longer term deadlines:							

FIGURE 2.5   Term plan timetable

Keep a weekly plan: key events and activities each week							
Week Number:	Monday	Tuesday	Wednesday	Thursday	Friday	Saturday	Sunday
8am							
9am							
10am							
11am							
12 noon							
1pm							
2pm							
3pm							
4pm							
5pm							
6pm							
7pm							
8pm							
9pm							
10pm							
11pm							
12 midnight							
1am							

FIGURE 2.6   Weekly plan timetable

3
Make University Positive

University will involve hard work – lots of it … but it is so much more than that. To really get university – you need to get out there, make friends and do stuff. Join clubs and societies, become a peer mentor, get involved in the students' union. This is not frivolous. Make time for this – in many ways it is what going to university is all about.

- Introduction   36
- Believe in yourself   36
- Feel the fear … and do it anyway   36
- Take responsibility – be positive   39
- Positive things to do at university   40
- Places to go and things to do   42
- Summary   45
- Activity: positive things to do   46

Introduction

> When I ask other students if they have anyone to study with, they tend to say they don't know anyone in their subject as they have massive lectures and prefer to make friendship groups in halls instead. I can't emphasise enough how important it is to get to know people on your course ... if all else fails, become a peer mentor. It develops your confidence – you get to meet and help new people. I've not looked back!

Being at university is not just about studying your subject and gaining a qualification that will help you get that better job. More than that, interacting with a diverse group of people of different ages, classes and nationalities is a wonderful, rare opportunity for expanding your horizons and for personal growth. Joining clubs and societies and writing for the students' union magazine or helping out with the radio gives you the chance to develop yourself in ways that you can't possibly imagine before you go to university. It goes beyond qualifications to developing personal friendship groups and special interest networks that change your life forever. Throughout this book we stress how helpful it is for you to make friends, to form study partnerships and study groups as part of your active and interactive learning strategies. In this chapter we explore how to get the most from university with a focus on the personal, human and social aspects of being a student. The bonus is – these are all things that will actually get you that job that you want (see also Chapter 13.2).

Believe in yourself

Being a student can be scary, especially as some of the things that we worry about will actually happen. We will have to understand the subject and make those notes. We will have to write those essays and give those presentations. Even so, worrying never helps us to cope with life – it is exhausting and actually makes life harder. This section looks at positive thinking – offering the proposition: think positive – believe in yourself – and you will improve your life, not just your life as a student.

Feel the fear ... and do it anyway

> They say that the only things we end up regretting are the things we didn't do. It's true, I've made some terrible mistakes – but I'd rather have had the experience than not.

The overarching theme of most positive thinking books is that fear boils down to a lack of self-confidence and a lack of faith in ourselves. We fear things because we believe that we will not be able to do them well – we will not cope. But consider the things that we do achieve as human beings. We managed to learn our language, and if our home is bi- or multi-lingual, we learned more than one. If we are able-bodied, we learned how to walk, run, dance, play sport. If we are not able-bodied we have learned how to adapt, adjust and do the best we can. We managed to go to school and survive that. Many of us then went on to get jobs – maybe even raise families. All of these activities and many more we did eventually take in our stride – no matter how much we feared them beforehand.

Overall, we tend to be much more resilient than we give ourselves credit for. In the end, whatever life chooses to throw at us – we cope with it. Sometimes, we even cope spectacularly well. All we tend to do by doubting ourselves is actually make it more difficult to cope – not easier. It is not life that we need to fear, saying no to life is the problem. All we do when we listen to or give in to our fears is to damage our own lives.

Why do we experience fear?

> I was 40 years old and someone gave me a pair of roller skates – I was delighted. I kept the skates at my mum's so that I could skate around the streets there ... One day, my skates were gone. My mum had given them away in case I hurt myself ... I was speechless. What sort of an idiot did she think I was?

But, you might argue, surely this fear is there for a purpose? If not, where does it come from? Why do we have it? Evolutionary, cognitive and popular psychology all have something to say in this debate. The evolutionists explain that we have evolved from animals where to be on unfamiliar territory is to be in danger – so fear is normal when on new ground – the issue is not the fear, but how we react to it.

Cognitive psychologists discuss the complex interplay of personal, environmental and behavioural factors – family, class, gender and ethnic group – that influence how we will feel in any given situation. In terms of being a student, if we are from a group that traditionally does well in education, it will be easier for us to see ourselves also doing well; whilst if we are from a group that traditionally does not succeed in education, it will be easier to see ourselves as failing. This does not mean that we cannot succeed, it means that we must put more effort into believing and knowing that we can succeed.

Popular psychologists, Susan Jeffers for example, argue that we are accidentally taught fear in the way that we are brought up: mind how you cross the road; don't go climbing that tree; don't go too fast. When people say these things to us they are really just expressing their fear: I don't want anything bad to happen to you. But what we hear, and internalise, is that they think that we are inadequate. In this atmosphere it is difficult to embrace 'having a go', learning by trial and error – seeing the positives in the inevitable mistakes that we must make.

But I'm not really an academic

A fear of making mistakes is particularly harmful if you are a student but you do not feel like a student – if you are in an academic environment and you do not feel like an academic. This is often called 'impostor syndrome' and everybody tends to experience it – in new jobs, in new situations and on new courses. If this describes how you are feeling right now, put effort into overcoming your own negative feelings. You are a student. You have been accepted onto a degree programme. If you are interested and motivated and if you work hard you can succeed. You will grow into the role of an academic.

TIP

Make sure you have one friend or relative who really does believe in you. Spend time with them!

Re-framing fear

We have argued that fear, whilst uncomfortable, is a perfectly natural and normal response to life – especially to new or unfamiliar situations. What we can do is change our response to that fear. Fear does not have to mean that we have to run and hide under the duvet; it can mean something completely different. Here are some new ways to look at fear: see if they help you at all.

- *Fear is good:* fear is okay, it is part of growth and doing new things. Fear does not mean, 'This is not for me!'; instead fear means that you are doing something new, you are facing a new challenge, you are taking a risk – you are being human. Thus, when we feel fear we should celebrate the fact that we are growing and changing. This is a good thing, not a bad one.
- *Fear affects everyone:* fear really does affect everyone and realising that we are not alone in our fears can actually help. Everyone feels fear when on unfamiliar territory. Everyone experiences fear when they do something new. Realising that we are not alone in our fears can take away the stigma of fear, it does not mean that we are cowards, just that we are human. Once we accept this we can move on.
- *The only way to get rid of the fear of something is to do it* ... the quicker the better. You know that this is true. You can spend months worrying about something, and then it

takes two minutes to do it. Let's get rid of those months of worry – do it now: you know it makes sense.

- *It is easier to face fear than to live with it*: it is easier to do what we fear than to keep living with the fear. The more we give in to fear the more fearful we become. So, every time you decide to face a fear, remind yourself that this is not a hardship – you are taking the easier option.
- *It takes practice*: re-framing fear in these ways may not come naturally to you. However, with practice you will find that you can face fear differently, and it will make a big difference – especially to the way that you face the challenge of being a successful student.

Take responsibility – be positive

> You know what, this did work for me. I gave up my job for an exciting project – and it failed. It cost me so much I lost my flat. This was my nightmare – jobless and homeless! I stayed on my friend's sister's couch … Miserable and feeling like I need to be punished. Someone gave me Jeffers' *Feel the Fear … and Do It Anyway*. Hah! I thought – but I found some work, I found somewhere to live. I'm back on my feet. I wouldn't have missed those experiences for the world. They've made me who I am now *and* – whereas I was a bit of a scaredy cat before – now I know that nothing can defeat me!

One big successful strategy is for you to take responsibility for succeeding at university. We all know that neither society nor nature is fair: class, ethnicity and gender do affect our life chances – a hurricane can destroy a home. But, if we keep blaming everyone else for what happens to us, we end up being trapped; when this happens we are the ones that suffer – no one else.

This is really important as a student. Look at your course, look at the work that you have to do – and say, I am responsible for doing the reading, making the notes, getting my work in on time, for getting good grades … Make those timetables, do the reading, discuss the course with your friends, write for half an hour a day … and the work will get done.

And, just as we can re-frame fear, changing the way that we talk about the world will make a difference. Say, 'I am looking forward to that module …' and 'I've heard that one is really difficult – if I do well, that's impressive!'

If you see life as a problem, if you talk about the world as a series of negative experiences … then life is hard for you. Imagine starting a new job – would you see that as a wonderful opportunity to meet new people and face new challenges? Or do you see it as hard work, with horrible new people and a difficult journey? How are you thinking about university? Say, I'm really looking forward to going to university. I'm really excited about my course.

And what about being a student? Just think about all that reading, all those lectures, all those essays and presentations. NOOOOOOOOOOOOOOOOOOOOOOOOO! It is so easy to think of studying as an imposing mountain of hard work and struggle – a series of exhausting problems. But, being a student can be a great time in your life – a time when you can think and learn; when you can make new friends and try out new opportunities; a time to flourish. Say, I'm working through that assignment one step at a time. And, I've started to make some great new friends …

Once you start using positive statements – I can … I am powerful … This is a great opportunity – it is important to keep going. You probably had a lifetime of the little negative voice telling you, 'You can't!' A couple of positive statements will not kill that off.

Some people write their positive statements on cards and stick them around the house – by the bed, on the bathroom mirror … You can even put a positive state-ment on the screen saver on your computer. We've got 'joy' on ours. Joy gives a quick boost when it appears – making it easier to get back to work. Take steps to develop your positive thinking and your self-belief as you immerse yourself in your studies, it will make a big difference to how you feel.

TIP

If you feel that this is a good idea – but you want to find out more – try a positive thinking book. We like Susan Jeffers' _Feel the Fear … and Do It Anyway_.

> I always practise positive thinking on my way to do a presentation. I can feel my mouth get dry – and all those butterflies … But I just keep saying, I can do it, I can do it … It works for me.

Positive things to do at university

> I had to live at home – and I hated it. Everything was changing – my world turned upside down and sideways – but my parents couldn't see any of this. Luckily, in my last year, I got a flat with friends from my course – that was so much better.

You may be the first in your family to go to university – or be an international stu-dent living in a strange country for the first time – you may just feel guilty about how much money all this is costing. Whatever the reason, many students feel that they have a duty just to knuckle down and get the work done, but you still have a duty to yourself to get the most out of university. Make the time to be with the people at university and to get involved in everything that is going on – this is what will make the real difference to you as a person.

Whether you live at home or in halls, get to know the people on your course. Do not rush off home the minute a lecture has ended. Do social things with other students – be the one to invite someone else to go for a coffee or to join the gym. Talk with them about your course and about everything else that you normally talk about. Invite people to a weekly study group in a social learning space. Be in the university for about 30 hours a week – that way, you will do the reading, you will discuss what you are learning … you will actually be a student!

TIP

If you are living at home, help your family and friends understand what you are doing and why. Reassure them that you still have some time for them. Tell them what you are going through – and how they can support you.

Make the most of your students' union

I know many parents who are students. These are the guys who dash off after lectures – who make no friends – who get isolated and miss out big time. It's important for them to get to know people and start making friends during the first few weeks. If they have child responsibilities, they've got to remember that being a student is full time and full on. They need child care for about 30–40 hours a week – for all the time they should be in university. They need to be free to 'be a student' and get to know people and feel comfortable.

Find your students' union offices and visit them. See what sorts of things they do and how you can get involved. Our SU has a wonderful president who believes in our university and in our students. He is a powerful voice for us – and in the process he is developing his own confidence, his own profile and his own skills. He will do well and go far in life, not just from his degree – but from his experiences in the SU and in the life of the university.

Students' unions have a practical purpose; they can represent students on university committees and fight for your rights if they have to. They also have social purpose: they are the ones responsible for the clubs and societies – and for entertainment, a student magazine, website, radio or TV station. All of these things are vital parts of student life. Offer to help with something – get involved in a small way at first and you will find that your isolation disappears and you really enjoy being an active student.

Become a peer mentor

It has really boosted my confidence with my own knowledge of the course and helping the students is incredibly rewarding.

Many universities have peer mentoring or student ambassador programmes. This is where students help other students, their peers, in some way or other. This can include everything from being a 'meet and greeter' in Welcome Week, where you help new students to not feel so lost or out of their depth, to becoming a writing or study mentor where you help students with their assignments in some way.

Become a peer mentor or student ambassador as soon as you can. We learn best when we teach someone else – and we become less self-conscious when we put someone else's concerns ahead of our own. Peer mentoring at university is the best way to develop our own resilience and self-confidence – and this develops professional, personal, interpersonal and communication skills – great for you, great for your CV, great for getting a good job (see also Chapters 13.1 and 13.2).

I have gained increased self-esteem, awareness of other people's worlds, improved communication skills by talking about my study and I improved my own skills and new experiences for my CV.

Places to go and things to do

Universities can be wonderful – but they can also be confusing and challenging places – typically there will be many support systems in place to help all students make the most of their time at university. This is a quick list of places to go and things to do to become more confident and more successful at university. Read the list – and do something with the information … but first, a message from a student counsellor.

The counsellor says

Universities have thousands of students all coming to study – and it may come as a surprise to know that there is such a thing as a student service. We take the emotional dimensions of your academic life very seriously. You gave everything you have to get your grades and then made a great choice to attend university and become a graduate. You may even be proud that you are the first in your family to complete this next step. Along the way, there may be tough times that could affect your personal or academic performance but they are not where the journey ends.

At student services, we do not know what your dreams or your goals are but we can certainly help you to develop a clearer vision of what you want to accomplish. We have supported thousands of students to overcome their challenges, improve their experience, achieve their degrees and improve their classification. The majority of students – male and female – who have used our service say that counselling is a very supportive, valuable and life changing experience.

Your emotions bind you to the best bits of student life and sometimes the awful reality is, things can get out of your control or go wrong and begin to impact on your studies – anything from anxiety, depression, loss of motivation, procrastination, relationship problems, sickness, sleep problems and even death in the family, the list goes on and on ...

Okay! So where can you find us and what can we do for you? Student services are often located in learning centres and appointments can be booked face to face or online at any stage of your learning experience. Student services can be seen and heard at inductions, Fresher's Fairs and other road show events. If you need to talk, we also offer confidential one to one counselling sessions and facilitate personal development workshops such as maximising your potential, stress management, presentation skills, motivation, goal setting, mindfulness, mental health awareness and time management. We look forward to seeing you on your journey.

Personal and/or academic tutor

Your personal and/or academic tutor gets to know you as a person and as an emerging academic. This is the person who can advise you if things are going wrong – or who can write that glowing job reference if things went very well. However, they can't do this if they have not met you.

---TIP---

Go and see your personal tutor before a problem arises.

Subject librarian (Academic Liaison Librarian)

The subject librarian is a specialist in his or her own right. They have knowledge of your subject, they may have put course materials and study resources online for you and they will be able to direct you towards useful books, journals and websites.

---TIP---

Find out when your librarian is holding a help session – and go there. Ask them about the books, journals and websites that will be most useful to you.

Learning and writing development and support

Most universities have some form of learning and writing development help – go there and use their courses, resources and help sessions to help you get that good degree.

 I just wanted to tell you that your Preparation course had me hit the ground running. I'm on track for a first class degree and it's due to the help I got before I even started!

If you missed your university's pre-sessional courses, don't despair because courses and workshops typically run during semester time, too. Check out the university website to see what is running, when and where. And don't just think about study skills and writing support – many offer maths and IT sessions also – be there or be square.

Students' union

The students' union runs the clubs and societies that serve your extra-curricular needs. If you really want university to work for you, join a club or society – stretch yourself, do something different, go outside your comfort zone – and get involved in your SU. Ricky Gervais, the comedian, became a success not just because of his degree, but because he was involved in the entertainments side of his SU.

Student support services

Universities typically offer chaplaincy, careers advice, counselling, dyslexia support, disability support, financial advice, peer support, volunteering and work placement opportunities … Find out exactly what yours has and how you can use student services to help you make the most of your time there – here's a quick rundown:

- Careers: have up-to-date information on career opportunities, job requirements and how to plan and prepare curriculum vitae (CVs). Make an immediate appointment with the careers people – we are talking in your first year here – not three weeks before the end of your degree programme. Find out what employment opportunities are open to you, now. Get advice about how best to tailor your degree programme to the sort of career you are likely to take up. If you are on a modular degree programme, this will help you choose the best modules for the career that you want. (See also Chapter 13.2.)

TIP

Start collecting information for your final CV the moment you read this. Have a folder (paper-based and/or online) where you keep key bits of information about yourself:

- jobs you have done, your responsibilities and how you developed
- courses that you have taken and how you have utilised the information learned
- modules that you took – and how they fit you for a specific job
- practice gained at group work, presentations and mentoring – and how that will fit you for the job that you are seeking ...

Go through this file every so often so that you always keep it up to date. (See also Chapter 13.1 on PDP and HEAR.)

- Work placement or volunteering: the work placement or volunteering officers are the ones who find placements for you whilst you are still on your degree programmes. Once you know what career avenue seems best for you, organise a work placement (where you are paid) or volunteering (which is unpaid). Find out how to get a placement in the best place for you. This is the key way of finding out whether or not you actually like the work. This gives you great experience to use both in your degree and in your CV – and if you make a good impression you may even find you have a job lined up before you finish your degree.
- Counselling services: counsellors offer confidential help with study, personal or social problems. We have hinted that being a student is not necessarily easy – so find out what counselling support might be available at your university. There is no stigma or shame involved in getting support when you need it.

TIPS

- Check out whether your course also has a work placement module – and sign up for it. The experience will be invaluable, you will meet and impress potential employers – and you will definitely have useful information for your CV.
- If you find that you are having problems adjusting to being a student, if you are homesick or if you feel overwhelmed by things – go and see the counsellor.
- Remember – do something with this information!! Who are you going to see? When? Why? Make notes!

Summary

It is easier to give advice on these topics than to take it. But all the advice here is gleaned from what students have told us about what worked for them – and what worked for us when we were students struggling to make sense of university. Do put into operation some of the strategies we have suggested above – they do work and they help break the ice and get the ball of positive friendships rolling.

Activity

Positive things to do

1. Positive thinking:

   - If in doubt – get a positive thinking book and put the ideas into practice. Check out our positive thinking web advice: http://learning.londonmet.ac.uk/epacks/studyhub/positive.html. (For a quick route there – do an online search: London Met + Study Hub + Positive Thinking.)
   - Become a peer mentor – there's no better way than helping others to develop your own self-confidence and self-esteem.

2. Worried about money?

   - Use the projected income and expenditure checklist, below, to work out your income and outgoings. Take control of your finances.

Income	£
Loan/grant/bursary	
Family support	
Job	
Other	
Total yearly income	
Monthly income	
Expenditure	**£**
Rent or mortgage	
Water	
Insurance (e.g. contents, phone)	
Electricity	
Gas	
Phone/mobile/internet	
TV licence	
Car tax	
MOT	
Car servicing and general maintenance	
Parking	
Food	

Toiletries	
Newspapers/magazines/coffees	
Books/stationery	
Miscellaneous course costs	
Laundry	
Public transport/Oyster card	
Clothing	
Sports/hobbies	
Christmas/birthdays	
Holidays/trips	
University ball/socialising	
Other	
Total yearly expenditure	
Monthly expenditure	

FIGURE 3.1   Projected income and expenditure for academic year

Deduct total yearly expenditure from total yearly income to work out your surplus or shortfall.

Access the companion website to this book and find helpful resources for this chapter topic:

https://study.sagepub.com/burnsandsinfield4e

PART II
THE SURVIVAL KIT

4

How to Survive Academic Reading

Okay – so you are worried about the reading – that just makes you normal. We're not born knowing how to tackle a university textbook or journal ... This chapter is designed to sort out academic reading for the worried student – with very practical guidelines about how to manage your reading throughout your time at university.

- Introduction   52
- Reading: key ideas and people   52
- Attitudes to reading   53
- A beginner's guide to reading (QOOQRRR)   54
- Practical strategies to use right now   57
- A quick note on plagiarism   58
- Make reading fun   59
- Online resources to support academic reading   60
- Summary   61
- Activity: find the library   61

Introduction

> With the web, I'm surfing websites, on YouTube, engaging in Instagram, Facebook, Twitter, LinkedIn ... And I still didn't know how to read for university!

In the UK you are not *taught* your degree, you *read for* your degree: that is, you are supposed to read to learn for your degree. Yes, you are given information in lectures, classes, seminars and tutorials, but this will never be 'all you need to know' on a subject. You are supposed to build on what you are told – and you do that by reading. Lots of it.

Reading is hardest when we first start to study a new topic. Everything feels new and uncertain. You don't know what the subject is *about* – or what is important. You're not sure who to read – or why. You don't know whether to read something really difficult or to 'cheat' and try something easy ... and you're worried that it will only get harder. That's why reading makes so many people – not just you – uncomfortable.

> I don't know what I'm reading or why. I hate this.
>
> So what on earth does 'Read around the subject' mean then?
>
> What are the basic things that I ought to know and understand? Who are the people that I ought to read?
>
> How much of my reading list must I cover?
>
> Can I use Wikipedia? The tutor says no – but it's so helpful!

The secret to successful reading is to know what you are reading – and why. And, no matter how bad you think you are at academic reading, know this – as time goes on, whilst the texts (books, chapters and articles) themselves get harder – because we start to know more, the reading itself becomes easier.

─TIP─

Read with the assignment question in mind. Share the reading with your peers. Keep a notebook of *all* your reading. Read Wikipedia – but don't *only* read Wikipedia.

Reading: key ideas and people

> I sat there reading this critical theory book on Hardy, and I said to my mate, 'I don't understand any of this!'. Luckily for me he said, 'Don't worry, you will'. If he'd said anything else, I might have given up – but he was right.

The first reading you do at university is designed to introduce you to the key ideas, people and principles of your subject. After that you will move on to the more difficult ideas and theories – and you will be expected to use what you read when you answer your assignment questions. You should always read more than one source on a topic – and weigh up what the different people say.

For example, if this is the first study skills book that you have ever read, this subject might be new to you. But if you now pick up another study skills book and go to their section on reading, you will be able to see what they write. If it is different from this, you might ask yourself why. This might prompt you to look at yet another study skills book to see what they say – and so on.

This is the basic principle of academic reading. You start reading to gain an understanding – you then develop that by reading more and by reading what different people have to say on the same topic. You start to notice arguments for one point of view – and arguments for a completely different point of view. You engage analytically and critically with all your reading and you develop your knowledge and understanding as you bring the differing arguments together in your own mind. This is where your writing comes in. As you read, start writing potential paragraphs for your assignments – trying to bring different arguments together, for example:

 Burns and Sinfield (2016) argue that academic reading is … However, Bloggs and Brown (2011) make a case for reading as …

Attitudes to reading

 That week when you did that reading session I hated that and I was really uncomfortable the whole lesson … because I was so unsure and not confident and, as I looked round, everyone seemed to be getting on with it and I thought I don't know what the hell they want me to do.

And you know as soon as you're in that position, you can't learn anything, you can't take anything in. Things were being said, and I couldn't understand. And I was sitting with a couple of people who seemed to know what it was all about and I thought 'Oh crikey'. You know? And it was awful. It was horrible. I didn't like that at all.

Do you recognise these feelings about reading? It would not be surprising if you do, most of our students find reading a difficult, time consuming puzzle: they are not sure *why* they are reading, they don't understand *what* they are reading and they don't know *how* to read and use an academic text. All this prevents us from engaging successfully.

One of the best ways to understand the point of the reading is to start writing. Right at the beginning of your course, look for a difficult essay question on one of the more difficult modules. Yes – really – try something difficult first. Write out the whole question and give yourself just *ten minutes* to free write an answer. Free writing is where you write non-stop without correcting what you are writing – without trying to get it 'right' – you are just having a spontaneous 'go' (see Chapter 11.2).

Obviously what you write will not be 'the answer' – you do not know enough yet – but now you know what to look for when you read – you are reading to find the missing bits in your writing and in your thinking.

Free writing assignments right at the beginning of your course will help the whole course make more sense. You will know what you are listening for in lectures – you will know what you are looking for when reading. The sooner you start your assignments, the sooner you are reading with a purpose.

> Free writing every week meant that I understood why I was reading for the first time!

A beginner's guide to reading (QOOQRRR)

> I was thinking about all those books on that booklist. I was thinking I had to read every single one of those books and I didn't know how I was going to manage that so I thought I'd just bluff it a bit you know.
>
> But later on I found from you that I didn't need to do that. When you did that bit about reading – about books. I mean I wasn't aware that I didn't know anything about that first page bit, about this is the author and this is when it was published and this is where it was published. I didn't know any of that. I didn't have a clue because books have always been really alien to me you know?
>
> And when you showed us about looking in the index and looking in the contents and then finding the bit that interests you and then going to your first paragraph and reading the first few lines and seeing if it's what you want. I found that really valuable.

We have argued that you need to know why you are reading for it to make any sense to you at all. Here we are going to elaborate on that with an active and interactive reading strategy designed to help you make the most of all your academic reading.

We have summed it up as QOOQRRR: question, overview, overview, question, read, re-read and review.

Q: Question – think first: what do I already know on this subject? What do I need from this reading?

O: Overview – your course: read your module aims and learning outcomes – read the assignment question: these all tell you why you are reading!

O: Overview – the book, chapter or journal: this will tell you what you are reading!

Q: Question – So, in the light of all that, ask yourself: *Why am I reading this, now?*

R: Read the text actively and interactively – marking it up as you go. Underline, highlight, circle key words or points – make notes in the margin: who would agree or disagree? What does it remind you of? Where will you use the information?

R: Re-read your own annotations and marginalia – now you are ready to make your key word/key point notes.

R: Review your notes – are they any good (are they sourced: author (date) *title*, place of publication: publisher)? Can you use them? What will you now read or write?

QOOQRRR in more detail

First, *question*: ask yourself, what do I already know on this topic? What do I need to find out? Survey or *overview* your module handbook again: what is the assignment question? What are the module aims and learning outcomes? These tell you *why* you are reading.

Then, get the *overview* of the text you are reading – what is it about? You should always know *what* you are reading before you start: read the author and date – is this the right person to read? Is this text recent enough? Check out the contents page – are you going to read one chapter or more? Why? Check out the index at the back (this is the list of useful words in the book – and where they are mentioned – the page numbers) – are the key words from your question in there? On what pages are they mentioned? Read those first.

If reading a whole chapter: read the introduction and the conclusion – these sum up a chapter or an article, they tell you what it's about. Read the first sentence of every paragraph – these outline what each paragraph is about. Once you have gained the overview of your course and the overview of the text – pause and *question* again: so, why am I reading this, now? You are now ready to read actively – with clear goals in mind.

Read through the text actively and interactively marking it up as you go. That is, underline key words, circle things, make notes in the margins. Reading is *not* passively absorbing the ideas of other people – it is asking questions, interrogating, arguing with what you are reading. It is a conversation – and like all conversations, it works better if you join in as well. So as you read you are asking: what is the point here? Who would agree or disagree with this? Where might I use this in my assignment? Who else would I refer to, to back up this line of argument? And as you do that, you make notes and scribbles to record this conversation. At this point, do not make your 'take away' notes – they will be too detailed – just make notes on the text (your text – not a library book!).

Once you have been through once, *re-read* your own scribbles, notes, annotations and marginalia – have a good think about them, and make your key word notes – remembering *why* you are reading. If you are reading because you have started a whole big new topic that you do not understand, you might want to summarise the whole thing – and lots of notes might be useful. Fine. But if you are only looking for ideas for one paragraph of one essay, you may only need to pick out a couple of ideas to use – and really, really short notes will be enough.

Once you have finished making your notes, *review* them and check whether they are useable ... Then write something – read something else.

TIP

This strategy may feel slow and time-consuming – but it saves time in the end because it is so focused and productive.

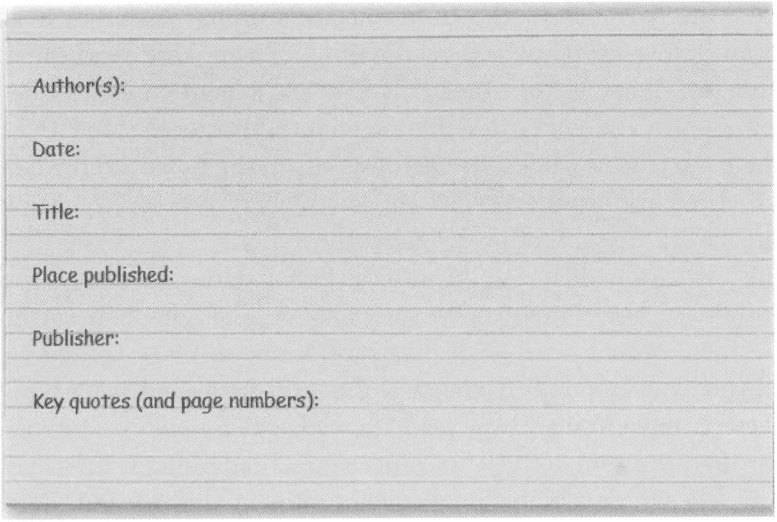

Author(s):

Date:

Title:

Place published:

Publisher:

Key quotes (and page numbers):

FIGURE 4.1   Keep index card records

Remember referencing! Always record the author, date, title, place of publication and publisher when you read. Put the page numbers for quotes. Make *index cards* of everything you read – you may use the text again in another essay.

Practical strategies to use right now

One of the most powerful things I ever learned to do was to photocopy chapters – and write all over them as I was reading. I really felt in charge – I took control of my reading. Everything changed when I did that.

Academic reading is hard work and requires concentration, time and effort. So when you are going to read, get prepared mentally and physically. Here are some effective reading tips and strategies. As always, as you read through this section ask yourself how knowing that will help you as a student – make notes to remind yourself:

- Have everything you need to hand: dictionary, key texts (printed off or photocopied); pens, pencils, highlighters; notebook for new names, words and concepts; index cards and note-paper for your references and key word notes.
- Have the lighting and sound tuned to your study preference.
- Have water and fruit available to keep you energised.
- Make sure you will be undisturbed. Unplug your landline, switch off your mobile. Do not look for a disturbance to get you out of reading!
- Work at your 'best' time of day. In-depth reading is hard work and should be done when you are at your most alert. Work for an hour – and take a break.
- Set clear goals for each reading session: brainstorm – what do I know? What do I need? Which part of the question will this help me with? Use the QOOQRRR active and critical reading system.
- Read analytically and critically, engage with the text. Ask yourself questions about what you are reading. Do you understand it? Could you sum up the key points in a few words? Can you analyse it? Can you see what argument is made? What evidence is being offered? Who would agree or disagree? How can you use the information in your assignment? Annotate (obviously *not* the library books!).
- Read beyond the reading list – remember if you just give back to the tutor what they gave to you, you will get an average grade.

---TIP---

Use a variety of reading resources: books (printed and electronic: e-books), journal articles (printed and electronic: e-journals), academic websites, reports and conference papers, abstracts.

- Read people who 'agree with' you – but also read the opposition as well. Academic writing requires balance – and argument. Your academic reading requires that also.
- Keep a record of what you are reading. As soon as you sit down with a text, record the author, date, *title*, location of publication (where it was published) and publisher (A (D) T. L:P). Make this an instinctive act that you do not even need to think about. If you use material from your reading without giving the reference you will be accused of plagiarism – even if this is an accident.

TIP

Record everything you read onto *index cards* and file them. Put the source (A (D) T L: P) at the top; summarise what the text was about; capture a couple of good quotes – with page numbers. Doing this means that you can use source material in more than one module and on more than one assignment. *Use a referencing resource*: www.notting ham.ac.uk/nmp/sonet/rlos/studyskills/harvard/resources.html.

A quick note on plagiarism

Plagiarism means kidnapping – and if you do not give your sources when you write you are in effect kidnapping someone else's work and passing it off as your own. Plagiarism is a major academic offence for which you can fail a module, be suspended from university – or even have your whole degree annulled.

Well, I read it, I agreed with it and now I've put it in my own words – it's mine now. I don't have to give sources then, do I?

Yes you do – the ideas still came from someone else. And anyway, you are supposed to be giving sources – you are not supposed to be making it all up – you are supposed to be using and acknowledging the knowledge-claims of your subject.

If you are worried about plagiarism, read our section on How to reference and prevent plagiarism (Chapter 11.4) – and use our online Preventing Plagiarism resource. In this there are student views on plagiarism, a tutorial and exit tests so that you can check out that you have understood it. Web search: LearnHigher Preventing Plagiarism Course or find it here: http://learning.londonmet.ac.uk/TLTC/learnhigher/Plagiarism/.

Make reading fun

When reading, do have an assignment question in mind – and try to have some fun as well – we learn more when we can play with ideas. Try some of these:

- After reading, make a *collage* of the key ideas in the chapter or article. If asked by your tutor to present your reading to the class, use your collage as a poster to help you remember and discuss the key ideas.
- Instead of writing about your reading – make a *visual summary.* Draw a diagram or picture of the text using as few words as possible. As you struggle to capture the ideas in pictures you will find that you are really struggling to understand and learn what you are reading.
- Build a *reading dossier* or a *reading notebook* not for one assignment but *over the whole of your degree programme.* Make or buy a series of sketchbooks and each week write about what you have read, why you read it, what it made you think about, what you now know about your subject, how you now feel about your progress/knowledge/ assignments …
- Vary your reading entries by sometimes drawing what you think – or adding pictures from newspapers or magazines. Make this space as creative as possible. Make it a place or thing that you want to use. When you have to write assignments, your reading dossier should provide plenty of source material – and it should be easy to use because you have invested feelings in it as well as thoughts.

TIP

Blog these.

- Don't forget to construct your own *subject dictionaries.* As you study new material you discover new words, concepts and phrases, so note these. Make your subject dictionary a key study and revision aid for yourself. Take control of your learning.
- Use Wikipedia – but don't only use Wikipedia!!

 Have you considered why we students read Wikipedia? It's not just because it is a source of information, but also because it can narrow down the topic and focus the research. Obviously this means that if the subject has not been covered in depth or is missing elements, it can throw a student in completely the wrong direction. It can also send the reader to some very suspect sources. This is what you ought to be telling us!

Online resources to support academic reading

> There is a correlation with stock usage and e-resource usage. Those who achieved a first borrowed on average twice as many items as those who got a third. (University of Huddersfield: www.daveyp.com/blog/archives/1370)

Explore these online resources and see how they help you to understand the reading process and develop your reading strategies. Why not blog, Facebook or Twitter your positive thoughts about them to other students?

- *Evernote* allows for a portable, messy, private online notemaking space: www.evernote.com/
- Or try *Cornell* notes: http://coe.jmu.edu/learningtoolbox/cornellnotes.html
- Or *visual notes*: www.visual-literacy.org/periodic_table/periodic_table.html#
- Have you thought about making notes on a *Prezi* website? http://prezi.com

Making *outlines* can help us understand and remember our reading. Try the following:

- **Webspiration Classroom – from the creators of Inspiration, a wonderful graphic organiser that now allows for online collaboration and one of the best visual outline creators on the web: www.mywebspiration.com/**
- **Quicklyst – a free user-friendly site for creating outlines. Quicklyst also integrates with a search engine and dictionary for enhanced note taking. Study queues can be made as well: www.quicklyst.com/**
- **Knowcase – create collaborative outlines with this easy to use site that features a drag-n-drop interface: http://knowcase.com/**
- **Thinklinkr – a real-time collaborative outline creator that has a nice built-in chat feature to engage in project development: http://thinklinkr.com/**
- **Checkvist – a great collaborative online outliner that has an abundance of features such as gmail/browser integration, mobility, and nice import/export features: http://checkvist.com/**

And, with thanks to Alice Gray, if you want to develop *speed-reading skills* try the following resources:

- **Short Burst Learning** – to find your current reading speed: http://speed-reading-cd.shortburstlearning.com/reading-test.htm
- **Doyle, D. (2010) Glendale Community College: Self Pacing Methods** – for five useful methods: http://english.glendale.cc.ca.us/methods.html

Summary

In the UK we are not taught our subjects, we read for our degree – and thus special reading strategies are useful and necessary. We have looked at the what, why and how of academic reading – offering guides to online support – and our own QOOQRRR reading strategy. We hope that you now feel a little better about reading – and that you will put these strategies into practice right now.

Activity

Find the library

Even in a digital age, reading starts with the library. Find your university library. Find where the books for your subject are kept. Make a habit of spending some time there every week. Notice the books that are available on your subject and dip into them. Have a look at the books that are available on other subjects as well. If you are studying sociology, you might find useful material in the psychology section of your library; if studying literature, you might try some quantum mechanics, get creative – mix it up a bit.

- *The Counter Loans section*: there are never enough books to satisfy all our students. Therefore, universities have a special mini-library within the library proper. This is where all the essential reading is usually kept – and you can actually get your hands on it because these books are only allowed out for an hour or two. Use this area. Tip: If there are books that you need that are always out on loan, request that at least one copy be placed here.
- *Books and e-books*: become aware of the most up-to-date and useful texts on your subject. Get used to picking these off the shelves and having a quick look in the index – what is in the book? Can you make a few quick notes now – or will you have to read it later? When? Put a date in your diary. What e-books are available for your course? When are you going to access these to make notes for your assignment?
- *Journals and e-journals*: the most up-to-date books are always several months old by the time they are actually written and published – to keep up to date with your subject read the latest journals.

Find your subject librarian and ask them to recommend the best journals and e-journals for you. Make a habit of reading them. When reading don't just look at the information and ideas, look also at how arguments are constructed, how articles are written – this will be a model for your writing.

Now – complete our library checklist:

Books

Find the part of the library that houses the books for your subject.

- My books are ....
- The Dewey decimal number is ....

Journals

- My physical journals are kept ....
- Two journals I could be reading:

  - Journal One ....
  - Journal Two ....

- E-journals I can access include: ....

Newspapers

The newspapers are kept ....

Counter Loans Area (CLA)

My CLA with key texts is ....

I can borrow texts for .... hours and for .... over the weekend.

Study Areas

What facilities does your library offer?

- My library offers quiet Study Areas ....
- My library offers group Study Areas ....
- My library has a canteen ....

Workshops

Some libraries contain student help workshops – does yours?

- My library does/does not have workshops.
- They are located ....
- Opening times are ....

Review

Three things I like about the library:

1. ....
2. ....
3. ....

Access the companion website to this book and find helpful resources for this chapter topic:
https://study.sagepub.com/burnsandsinfield4e

5

How to Make the Best Notes

Nothing is as empowering as active notemaking – it fundamentally changes the relationship between you and the information you meet. Make memorable notes and you dramatically increase your success – here's how.

- Introduction   66
- Notemaking: what, why, how?   66
- Why notemaking?   67
- A beginner's guide to ideal notes   68
- Linear notes   68
- Cornell notes   69
- Concept maps   70
- Mindmaps   71
- Pattern notes   72
- A beginner's guide to pattern notes   73
- The revision cycle   75
- Summary   76
- Further reading   77
- Activity: first lecture questions   77

Introduction

When we first started teaching, we saw students who took down every word we said – now we see students making no notes at all. Neither of these strategies is useful. Writing it all down is too passive, you end up trapped by the way that other people think and with so many notes that you will never read them. No notes means that you are not engaging with the lecture or class at all, you will forget everything, you might as well not have been there; at worse, you become totally dependent on your lecturer's PowerPoint slides. Notemaking helps you take control of information for yourself, it is fundamental and one of the most empowering things you can learn as a student. We are going to explore notemaking by making a case for notemaking as a thinking process and as part of your active learning.

Notemaking: what, why, how?

We want to begin this chapter with a small brainstorm. When brainstorming, just write down what pops into your head – do not try to get things 'right', just try to capture your immediate responses. So, before you move on to reading about notemaking, spend a few minutes preparing yourself by brainstorming 'notemaking':

- Why do we make notes?
- When and where do we make notes?
- How do we make notes?

Take a moment to compare your responses with those of some other students:

- **Why do we make notes?**

  To remember – I make shopping lists and lists of things to do.

  To use the information, for example in my essays and exams.

  To recall key points.

  To understand what I am learning.

- **When and where do we make notes?**

  I take notes at work, especially in meetings.

  In lectures, seminars and tutorials.

When I'm reading – I'm not going to remember it all, am I?

In the middle of the night in bed – no seriously. I often wake up and think of a really good point for my essay. So I keep a pad and pen by the bed so that I don't lose the thought.

- How do we make notes?

Well, I write my notes down – I know other people who tape theirs.

I take down too much information, I really hate my notes.

I take down key words, but I sometimes forget what they mean.

I make rough notes and do a shorter version later.

How does your brainstorm compare to the ideas shared by other students? What do you now think? The point of a brainstorm is to get our brains ready for action. A quick brainstorm before a lecture or before we read tunes the mind into the subject, we are ready to focus … So – now that you have completed your own brainstorm and shared the ideas here – think: what do I want from a chapter on notemaking? Now you should be tuned in and ready to get the most from this chapter.

Why notemaking?

Taking notes – that you understand, so not just notes, but good clear notes – in class can actually save time. You are in class anyway so you are not wasting time doing them. If you combine class notes with doing 30 minutes to an hour's research directed by the notes, you do not spend endless amounts of time looking down false trails, and you do get lots of relevant info quickly.

A good notemaking system allows you to capture, re-order and understand information (see also Chapter 2). Coupled with an active revision cycle, notemaking allows you to actively select and remember useful information. Making notes puts you in control of your own learning – this is engaging and powerful. Active notemaking helps every student think for themselves and gain a voice within their own education. A good notemaking system also saves you *time* – you do not have to re-read all of those PowerPoints or listen again to every lecture – you review your key word notes.

A beginner's guide to ideal notes

There are many different notemaking systems that people use, but they tend to break down into two main formats: some sort of linear (line-by-line) system or some sort of non-linear or pattern system. Whatever your system, all good notes should have:

- *Source*: if lecture – title, lecturer's name, date; if text – author, date, *title*, place of publication, publisher.
- *Headings*: capturing key sections of the talk/chapter.
- *Key words*: key points, examples, illustrations, names, new ideas – *not* everything.
- *Some structure*: things that make the notes easy to navigate – patterns, numbering, arrows, highlighting, etc. – things that link the notes to the course aims, outcomes and assignment.
- *Mnemonic triggers*: things that make the notes memorable – cartoons, colour, illustrations – the Von Rostorff effect – we remember that which is bizarre, funny or bawdy (Palmer and Pope, 1984).
- *Further reading*: people or articles to read – noted and highlighted.
- *Connections*: some indication of how the notes could be used in your assignment.

Are your notes like this? Read on.

Linear notes

Linear – line-by-line – notes are the most common form of notemaking adopted by students and university staff. Typically it involves making lists, perhaps with bullets, numbers, highlighting and/or underlining used to identify key or important topics. This notemaking form is neat and has an instant logic and appeal. The danger is that it is very passive and you can be trapped into the argument and evidence used by the subject. This is the notemaking form most likely to promote conscious or unconscious plagiarism (see also Chapter 11.4: How to reference and avoid plagiarism).

The problem with linear notes

Many students would feel that they had got 'really good' at notemaking if they ended up with pages and pages of information. There would be a very reassuring feel to having captured everything. However, there are many problems with linear notes:

- You take so many notes you feel swamped by them.
- You take so many notes that you never use them again.
- If you cannot write really fast, you panic and miss even more of a lecture.
- If you leave things out you can feel like a failure.

- It is an exceedingly passive form of notemaking – you are not working on the information, you are recording it like a photocopier.
- You do not need to be able to think to make linear notes, but you do need to think to be able to learn.
- All the information looks the same, which makes it very difficult to recall specific points of information.
- It is a monotonous way of learning – it is boring and it only engages a small part of the brain, which is not a good thing.

Cornell notes

 When my students tried Cornell notemaking, they found that they wanted to research further – they wanted to do more. With linear notes they just copied from the PowerPoint slides and that was it.

Cornell notes are similar to linear notes in that they too have a linear form. However, the Cornell system is intrinsically more active than the straight linear format, requiring the notemaker to engage both analytically and critically with the notes that they make.

Typically in the Cornell system, the notemaker divides their page in three: one column is for the collection of notes; one is for summarising information into key words or phrases; the final part of the structure is for writing a brief summary of or critical commentary upon the notes. It is here that the notemaker can reflect on the information gathered – and think about what they should now read or do to follow up the ideas in the lecture.

TIP

Write: I will use this information in my assignment like this ...

The key benefit of this strategy is that it encourages us to understand why information is important and why we have noted it. It encourages critical reflection and the making of sense, meaning and connections. It puts our own understanding and participation at the centre of the knowledge construction process.

| Course: |
| Date: |

Main points	Notes
Summary	

FIGURE 5.1   Cornell notes template

Concept maps

When you make a concept map, you produce a graphical, hierarchical representation of key concepts. You are supposed to note the relationships between concepts or sub-concepts in the way you draw connections between them. C map tools or software can be found online (http://cmap.ihmc.us/) – and are useful if you want to make notes on your laptop.

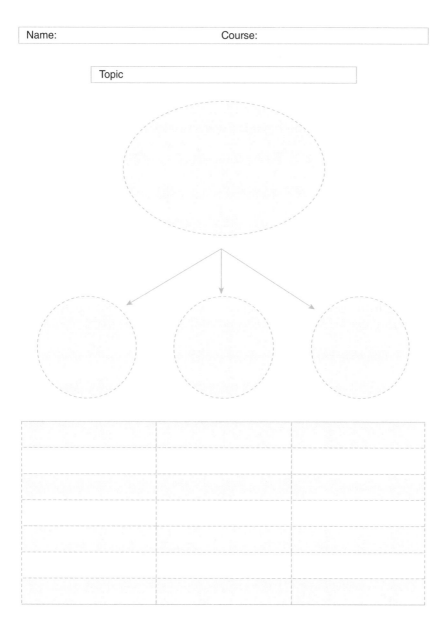

FIGURE 5.2 Concept map template

Mindmaps

Mindmaps are perhaps the most familiar non-linear notemaking format. Sometimes described as spidergrams or nuclear notes, these non-linear notes are encouraged by Tony Buzan (Buzan and Buzan, 1999) as an active and creative way to both generate and capture ideas.

The idea with the mindmap is to put the central topic in the centre of a diagram. The notemaker builds the diagram by drawing out subsidiary lines with ideas linked to the main theme – adding colour and pictures to make the notes distinct and memorable. Buzan's advice is to only ever put one word on a line – this aids in-depth thinking and understanding. Mindmapping as a process is literally more engaging because it harnesses our logical and our creative capacities.

Pattern notes

Pattern notes are the name we give to any non-linear format – and this is the one that we recommend most strongly. The pattern note format is more flexible than Buzan's strict one word per line mindmap – and when used it becomes both a notemaking and a learning tool. As with the mindmap, the idea is that students select and connect information for themselves – where this very selection/connection

Name:

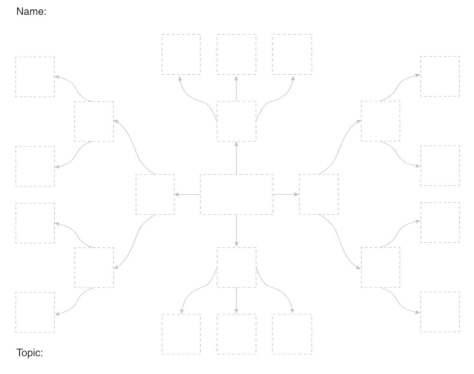

Topic:

FIGURE 5.3   Pattern note template

process is itself an active learning strategy. Pattern notemaking allows the formation of a set of unique pattern notes each time you work.

Typically when making pattern notes, it is important that we build in our own mnemonic (memory) triggers – typically small cartoons that illustrate the ideas in some way and that are funny or bizarre so as to trigger deep memories. In this way each set of notes becomes unique and memorable. Making pattern notes encourages us to play with ideas and become transformed by them in the process:

> As soon as one can no longer think things as one formerly thought them, transformation becomes both very urgent, very difficult and quite possible. (Foucault, 1988: 154)

Or, as our students might say:

 I still say notemaking can save people time. Even if they do not follow through all the 'proper' processes, it will still help to narrow down the amount of research needed.

Patterns are best

The advantages of pattern notes are:

- Instead of taking down masses of possibly useless information, you select only that information that will be of use to you.
- They produce a summary of information in short notes and you are inclined to re-use notes that are manageable.
- You do not need to be able to write quickly, you just need to practise selecting useful information.
- Selecting and arranging useful information keeps you actively engaged with your information and hence you learn more.
- You can make your notes interesting and memorable with colour and cartoons.
- Each set of notes looks unique – this also helps to make them memorable.
- Building mnemonic triggers – colour, pictures, diagrams and unusual things – into your notes engages the whole brain into your learning and therefore you understand and learn more.

A beginner's guide to pattern notes

When making key word notes from lectures and from your reading there are several stages that you can go through – the trick is to remember that you can draft and re-draft notes. You do not need to get them right first go.

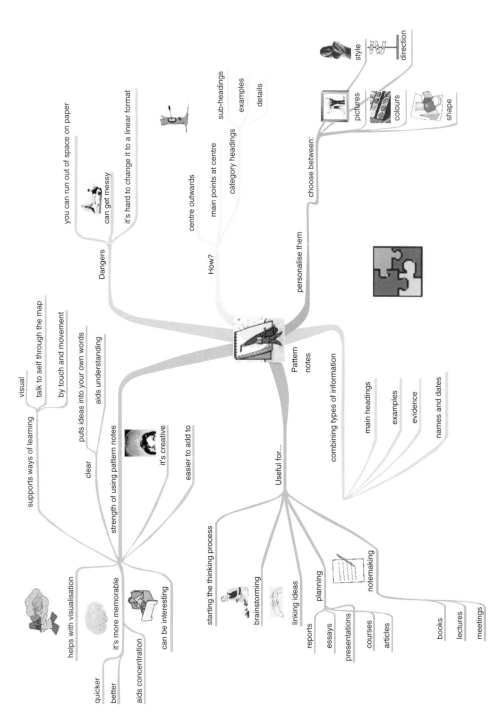

FIGURE 5.4 Mindmap of pattern notes

- *Prepare*: get an overview of the lecture or chapter before you start. With books, read the beginning and end of chapters. With lectures, you should get the sense of what the lecture is about from your syllabus or scheme of work.
- *Brainstorm*: once you know what the lecture or text is about, then brainstorm. Identify what you know on the topic and what you need to find out. Your assignment question will help you here.
- *Goal set*: work out the information that you want to take away – an overview, key points, key names and dates, key quotes. Remember to look at your assignment question!
- *Be active*: with your goals in mind, engage with the lecture (or a text) in an active way – searching for and identifying key words, points, etc.
- *Draft*: put the key points down in a 'rough' way first. With a book, we have suggested that you make notes on the text itself (Chapter 4). With a lecture, you might put the title in the centre of a piece of paper and draw points away from the title. If things connect directly to the central topic, branch them off. If they connect with each other, draw them off from the sub-branches.
- *Review your rough notes*: decide what you need to keep and what you do not need. Think about how to connect ideas with each other. Think about how to make the notes memorable – what picture or cartoon will you draw or cut out from a magazine to glue on?
- *Construct your final key word pattern*: add colour, pictures and diagrams to illustrate points and to act as memory triggers.
- *Revise*: review your notes regularly to commit them to your long-term memory.
- *Do something*: talk about the lecture; compare notes with someone else; read something; write something. Do not file your notes away – pin them on your wall; add to your wall notes every time you read. After every class, review your notes regularly – add to your wall notes, talk, read, write.

The revision cycle

There is no point making notes if you do nothing with them or nothing about them. We forget 98% of what we encounter after just three weeks if we do not test our memory – if we do not revise. This revision cycle builds memories in your brain and commits information to your long-term memory where you need it. After every lecture:

- Make a shorter more dynamic version of your notes. Put in pictures that are funny, bawdy or bizarre to stimulate your memory.
- A day later spend two minutes actively recalling your notes – plug memory gaps.
- Do this two-minute active recall again a week, a month and six months later.

Use your notemaking as a place to play with the ideas that you are encountering and learning. Illustrate your notes – use lots of colour – buy or make beautiful sketchbooks and draw amazing images ... These are not frivolous suggestions. The more you play and engage and think about the ideas – the more you will learn. Enjoy your notemaking – have some fun.

- *Play with it*: there are many, many different ways of arranging notes in patterns – from concept maps to mindmaps and beyond. Go to: www.visual-literacy.org/periodic_table/periodic_table.html#.
- *Module patterns*: buy an A1 pad and build up a pattern note of every module that you do. Add to your module pattern week by week.
- *Paragraph patterns*: when preparing for an assignment put key words from the assignment question onto different sheets of A1 paper; after every lecture or your reading add new points to the different paragraph patterns. Free write paragraphs using these notes.
- *Module walls*: if you can, use the walls of your home to help you study. Put different module questions on different walls. When you come home from a class, when you have read something new, add notes of the information to the module pattern on the wall. You literally immerse yourself in your learning. More than that – when you look from one module wall to another, you can see the links between the different subjects you study. This is excellent, productive learning.
- *No-stress notes*: make pattern notes of television and radio programmes – this is great practice without the stress of it being vital for your study success. Visit other people's lectures and make pattern notes in those. Again there is no stress – just practise.
- *#ESS4*: why not make pattern notes for each topic in this book? This will definitely give you the practice that you need to get started.

Summary

We have examined notemaking as part of active learning and argued that a good notemaking strategy helps you both record and learn information. We have explored and illustrated different linear and pattern formats so that you can eventually choose the system that best suits you. We particularly wanted to make a good case for pattern notes so that you felt persuaded to develop them for yourself. So now it is up to you.

Further reading

Buzan, B. and Buzan, T. (1999) *The Mind Map Book*. London: BBC Publications

Gibbs, G. and Makeshaw, T. (1992) *53 Interesting Things to Do in Your Lectures*. Bristol: Technical and Educational Services

Palmer, R. and Pope, C. (1984) *Brain Train: Studying for Success*. Bristol: Arrowsmith

Activity

First lecture questions

What have you done with or about your first lecture? Please answer and think about the following questions:

- Did you make notes? What have you done with the notes?
- Why not shorten them to key words and pictures and stick them up on your wall at home? Take them down when you have learned the material.
- Why not review your notes and write a short piece along the lines of: How I will use this information in my first assignment? (Of course – this means you have to read the assignments. For all your modules! Yes you do!)
- Have you discussed the lecture with anyone yet? Why not ask someone to have a coffee with you – and discuss the next lecture that you go to?
- Have you followed the lecture with any reading? What did you read and why? What have you done with your reading notes?
- Have you followed the lecture with any writing? Why not brainstorm the assignment question and free write a bad answer to it? (See also Chapter 11.2.)
- Have you blogged about what you did, why and how much you learned? If not – why not try?

Now – do this for every lecture!

Access the companion website to this book and find helpful resources for this chapter topic:
https://study.sagepub.com/burnsandsinfield4e

6

How to Be Creative and Visual in Your Learning

To really shine, to have some fun, to go that one step further, everyone needs to build creativity into their learning.

- Introduction   80
- A beginner's guide to brainstorming   82
- Draw-to-learn: why we should be visual   84
- Image mediated dialogue   88
- Summary   91
- Further reading   92
- Activity: three creative things to do   92

Introduction

> I went for a job interview and was asked to give as many uses of a pen as I could think of in two minutes. I had to be really creative, on the spot!

6 If you have not tried creative techniques before, we will be asking you to change or adapt your learning style. And, as always, you might find that change uncomfortable. No one likes to be uncomfortable, even more so perhaps in the educational context where for so many of us everything already feels so strange and uncomfortable. Try to reassure yourself that the discomfort will pass, and that the benefits in terms of improvements in your ability to study and learn – and in the grades that you will get for your work – will more than compensate you for the discomfort that you are experiencing.

Some people believe that you are either born creative or you are not – the same way that much of education is predicated upon the belief that you are either born a good student or you are not. But just as we argued that everyone can rehearse successful study techniques and thus learn how to be a successful student, so we argue that everyone can learn creative learning styles and with practice become more creative. A really influential voice in this area at the moment is Ken Robinson.

Robinson argues that the world needs people who can respond to complexity in adaptable, resilient and creative ways. He criticises much of the education system for actively stifling creativity; however, we can find and develop our own creative aspects. If we do this we move from enduring our lives to enjoying our lives; and, we argue that if you do this as a student, not only will you better enjoy your studies, you will be better fitted for the world of work when you gain your degree.

How can I be creative?

Why should we be creative?

Common sense.

5 If you become trapped into using information in the way that other people have used it, you are in danger of producing assignments that only give back to the tutor what s/he has said and what s/he has recommended that you read.

Obviously this is neither active nor significant learning. But it gets worse. Something that just passively parrots-back information to the tutor will at best only gain you an average grade. It is also really boring for the tutor. Imagine the tutor with 150 assignments to mark, all of them only giving back what s/he has used in the lectures? Only citing the books that the tutor recommended?

It is the essay that has gone somewhere different, that has found an original example or illustration, that has put ideas together in an original way that will catch the tutor's eye that will make them smile. And oh what a relief from reading those 149 other essays that all say the same thing! Thus at this very practical, common sense level, it is good to be creative.

One justification that we would like to offer for creative learning also touches on the notion of active learning – or the lack of it.

Without a creative approach the student is in danger of remaining a passive learner, only using information in the way that other people have used it. Because they have not used a creative notemaking system, but have passively recorded what others have said, and the way that they have said it, these students get trapped into other people's thought processes.

Carl Rogers, humanist, psychologist and teacher, addressed this by emphasising that significant learning takes place when students reach out for what they want and need when learning.

Active and significant learning.

4 We argue that creative approaches can help you to identify what it is that you want and need from your course. Yes, you will still have to read those set texts – and you will still have to frame your answers in certain way: you will have to get to grips with academic practice. But getting an original angle on a question; seeking out original things to research and read; and then recording information in your own original and creative way – will help you to make the course your own.

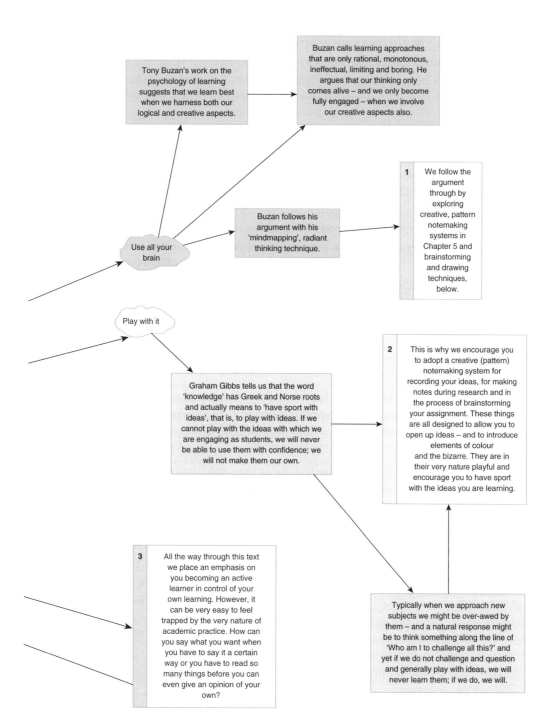

FIGURE 6.1 Ideas map: why should we be creative?

Creative and visual thinking can turn studying into something that you enjoy rather than endure. It stretches and develops you and really does improve the quality and richness of your learning. Sadly, whilst we all have the capacity to be creative, this is not necessarily valued or developed by the education system (Robinson, 2006, 2009). We would like you to feel positive about being creative when you study, so we have gathered a few arguments together in Figure 6.1. Read them through and see what you think – and then move on and work your way through the rest of the chapter – remembering to put all the ideas into practice; nothing will change for the better unless you do something differently.

A beginner's guide to brainstorming

> Creativity is about approach. Changing the process – where or how you get your information is another creative approach. For example, in my sports course I went to the local leisure centre and interviewed the manager. From that I got a contact for the local council. The information the council supplied transformed my assignment – and it gave me a real buzz knowing I had used my initiative successfully.

Brainstorming is a creative approach designed to open up thinking – and help us think differently about our studies. When brainstorming an assignment topic, for example, brainstorm all the key words in the question and allow as many ideas as possible to float into your mind. The trick is to respond immediately and not to censor your thoughts. Sometimes a thought might appear silly, irrelevant or frivolous. It may be that the thought seems odd, with no place in an academic context. Yet just that silly or odd thought could lead you on to a really bright or original idea that will make your assignment clever, even unique. When our work has that spark of originality, when it is that bit different from all the other assignments that are dropping onto a tutor's desk, then we may gain the attention of the tutor – we may even gain a higher mark.

Try this brainstorming strategy with one of your assignments and see how well it works for you. The trick with an assignment question is to brainstorm every single word in the question.

1. **Write the whole question in the middle of a really large sheet of paper – A1 or flip chart paper is best.**
2. **Do not abbreviate the question. Any word that you do not write down is a research avenue that you do not explore – this could well mean marks that you have thrown away.**

3. Look at all the words in the question. Circle or underline the key words.
4. Write anything and everything that comes to mind when you look at a word.
5. When you have finished, move on and do the same to another word. Keep this up until you have tackled all the words in the question.
6. Then go round again – even more ideas might pop out.

Cross reference your brainstorm with the module aims and learning outcomes – brainstorm those words as well. Make sure you leave nothing important out of your thinking or your research.

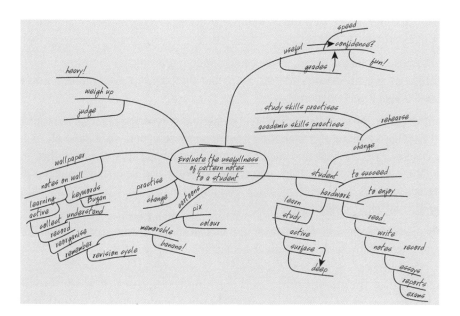

FIGURE 6.2   Brainstorm of 'Evaluate the usefulness of pattern notes to a student'

- Brainstorm topics with a friend or a study partner.
- If you get stuck – use the critical thinking questions on each part of the assignment question: who, what, why, where, when, how – what if, so what, what next? (See Chapter 7.)
- Practise ten-minute brainstorms with every question in your module/course handbook. Choose to answer the question that gave you the most interesting brainstorm.

Draw-to-learn: why we should be visual

On my first day of art class in elementary school, I died a little inside. It doesn't seem like a big deal in retrospect, but at the time it was soul-crushing.

I was sitting at the long wooden table with my classmates, filled with excitement. I already enjoyed drawing, coloring, and creating, so I figured this would be my favorite class. Our first assignment was to fold a sheet of paper in half and draw a person on it. No other directives or instructions, just draw a person. Great. I got this. I took my time, paying attention to every detail. Face. Clothing. Appendages. Hair. Yes! What a work of art. I sat in awe of my creation.

For the next half of the assignment, we were told to flip our papers over, and the teacher would now show us the correct way to draw a person. Circles. Rectangles. Ovals. Measuring. Erasing. Re-drawing. Erasing. Erasing (for some reason I could never get those blasted erasers to work, they just left gray smudges all over my paper).

We then opened up the paper, so we could see both drawings at the same time, and the teacher explained to us why and how our first drawing was rubbish, and the second drawing was phenomenal.

What would possess a person to make a career out of crushing children's creativity? And how boring would this planet be if we took these people seriously? All four of my children love drawing, and each have their own unique style (and yes their own way of drawing a person!). They also enjoy exploring new techniques, and learning different methods. But I couldn't imagine telling them that there is a right and wrong way of creatively expressing themselves.

(Taken with permission from: https://thedadosaur.wordpress.com/2015/07/30/theres-more-than-one-way-to-draw-a-person/.)

Drawing is one of the most under-used learning techniques or academic literacies. Perhaps because most of us stop drawing when we leave primary school, it becomes something that we do not do. Instead of being enjoyable, drawing makes us feel vulnerable, silly, inadequate or foolish. But drawing can be an intellectual activity that helps us analyse, reflect upon, investigate, explore, understand and communicate about the world, our experiences and our studies.

We focus a lot on visual thinking in this chapter to help you get creative – and lose your fear of drawing. Visual thinking is much more than accurate, representational drawing; we can use drawing to help us think, to reflect, to experiment, to explore, to understand and to communicate. Once we allow ourselves to draw, no matter how 'badly', we start to think in deeper and richer ways about ideas. When we draw what we are learning, we learn more, not least because in doing so, we have to translate words, ideas, theories and concepts that we hear or read into images that we see – and that process is in itself a form of analytical and critical thinking and it promotes deep learning.

This section of the chapter explores a range of visual thinking practices – please play with them all – see how rich they are. If you are really interested in discovering more of the theory of drawing as thinking and learning – please explore the ideas on Brighton University's Visual Practices website (see Further Reading, below).

Draw a learning journey

 When you told me what we'd have to do in your class, I wanted to leave – but it was too late ... I'm so glad it was too late. The creative approaches were a revelation – and that assignment got me my best grade ...

Draw a story board or timeline that shows how you got to be at university. Put in pictures that represent key moments or turning points in your life. Reflect on your journey to university. Then draw a story board or timeline of how you see yourself succeeding at university. Make this as creative as possible – draw your goals and visions. Pin this picture over your desk to inspire you when you get frustrated or stuck. Free write a quick self-evaluation to start off your PDP or CV file (Chapter 13.1) … you will only get better!

Academic Pictionary

Choose a word or term or concept from the course you are studying. Instead of explaining that concept to someone else in words, draw a diagram or picture that represents the word for you. Show it to another person and see if they can guess what you were trying to say. Then discuss it.

TIP

Develop a range of symbols for the key topics that always come up in your lectures and the reading; use those as a shorthand in your notes.

Draw your notes

> There was this group of students working with young people on a drawing project … and it was so cool because they all *used their overalls as their notebooks!* They would draw pictures on them. Write notes on them. Paste things onto them. It was amazing – and I've been wanting to do that myself ever since.

After reading a chapter, do not write anything – just *draw* a representation or diagram of all the information that was in there – use stick figures and bubbles and cartoonish attempts at drawing – do not go for perfection! Use one side of a piece of paper – make that paper any size that you want. Use as many colours as you like and be as imaginative as possible with your images. Reflect on how well you now understand that reading/lecture.

Picture your lecture

> I remember that class, it was years ago now – but I've never forgotten it because that was my first picture-only notes session. He started with, 'What is history? If you see a hedgehog dead in the road, you might think – "That's history!" …' So I drew a flat hedgehog lying in the road and I was away … Unforgettable.

Go to your next class or lecture and make notes only in pictures – write no words at all. If worried that you will miss important information this way, pair up with a friend and make sure that you compare notes at the end. When we have done this, these notes are always the ones that we remember for the longest time.

Draw your essay

In Chapter 11.2 we write a lot about overcoming writing blocks by developing various free writing techniques – we do this because we want you to lose any fear of writing that you may have – and to get into a writing habit. But, free writing is not the only creative way to think about your essay – and not the only way to engage with the ideas on your course – you can get visual with it as well.

Warm up your drawing 'juices' by putting cartoons in your notes to make them more memorable (Chapter 5); by drawing the theories and concepts that are important to your course; and by making 'picture only' notes. Once you have done this, you might like the creative challenge of starting your essay by drawing it first. There are several ways that you could approach this – here are a couple:

- *Make a rich picture*: have the question in front of you – and a large piece of paper – and fat, colourful felt tip pens. Read the question – pick up a pen – and start to doodle images that illuminate or illustrate the key words in the question. Change pens – change colours. Make sure that you doodle something in response to all of the words in the question. Go round and doodle again … Think about drawing lines or nets or arrows that link pictures and ideas together. Step back – *describe* and then *analyse* the picture that you have created – saying how it has responded to the question – and how you might now answer that question.
- *Story board the essay*: choose an assignment question and brainstorm it – releasing lots of key words and phrases – releasing more questions – but no answers. After the brainstorm, think about characters, images or motifs that might be appropriate to tell the 'story' of the question. Using your characters and motifs, on separate pieces of paper, tackle each of the key words or phrases you have produced, one at a time. Draw a small doodle, sketch a rough illustration or produce a rich picture (see below) in response to each one. Organise the different pieces of paper to tell a story – your essay storyboard. Reflect – is this the story of the answer to your essay? What will you now read or do to help you answer the question?

Collage your project or essay plan

Make a habit of collecting pictures from newspapers and magazines so that you always have a store of images. As you can make collages of your reading (Chapter 4), so you can use collage as a brainstorming activity to get you started on an assignment.

So, when you want to get started on a new project, use your magazine images to create a collage. With your question in mind, choose pictures that seem to represent the question, parts of an answer, your own beliefs or thoughts on the topic at that time … The important thing is to have the general topic or question in your mind as you select all the different images that seem in any way relevant.

Once you have a good collection of images – and maybe a few key words – and still thinking of your topic or question, choose pictures and words apparently at random … combine the images you have chosen by placing them onto a large sheet of paper in a way that feels good or makes sense to you. Then sketch it the way that it is so you retain a representation of this 'first draft'.

Now take the various pieces and glue them onto another sheet of paper or onto a board, anything that is to hand – and that feels good in this process. This glued down version of the collage may be exactly the same as your first draft – or it may differ slightly – it does not matter as long as you are still happy with it. At some point – stop. Make the decision that the picture is now complete.

Finally, reflect on the picture that you and your unconscious have created. First, write a detailed, literal *description* of what is in the collage. Then *analyse* that description – saying why or how your collage 'answers' the question. You should now be ready to work on your assignment or project.

Index card collages

Develop your creativity by producing a daily collage. Get a stack of large index cards and some liquid glue. Keep collecting those magazines. Every morning, or once a week, sit down with a magazine, the index cards and the glue. Tear or cut out pictures, words, small icons that appeal to you. Use them to produce collages on as many index cards as you can. Keep these collages to help you overcome writing blocks (Chapter 11.2), to help you with qualitative research (Chapter 12.5), and to use in image mediated dialogue (below).

TIP

These processes not only help to unblock you when stuck – they also help you to see things in fresh and energising ways. Here's how we did it: http://lastrefugelmu. blogspot.co.uk/2013/06/artmooc-week-2-fantastic-art-and.html, or search for lastrefugelmu + fantastic art.

Image mediated dialogue

Don't know where to start a difficult assignment? Pull out your stack of index card collages. Write out your assignment question. With the question in mind, select just one collage that seems to speak to the assignment question. Write a literal description of what you can see in your collage. Then write a short analytical piece on why the collage answers the question for you. Review all your writing. You should now be able to start writing your assignment.

Pictorial reflective journal

 At the end of our project we all had to produce one quilt piece that summed up the learning for us. We could sew onto our quilt piece, we could print directly onto our square of fabric ... or make a collage on it ... Some people knitted things and sewed them on – others stuck things on their fabric square – whatever we wanted. At the end all our pieces were sewn together into a friendship quilt of the module. It was a great experience – and the quilt is still hanging in the university hall.

Create a beautiful, illustrated learning journal, where you reflect very visually upon all of your learning on your course. Some people buy quite expensive and beautiful sketchbooks from art shops – others make their own sketchbooks with cardboard and string and various different sorts of paper; this gives each book a wonderful and special feel.

TIP

Do an online search for 'Make your own sketchbooks' if you want to be inspired.

In your sketchbook draw a picture, paint something or create a collage every day or at least once a week reflecting on what you have learned. Annotate your illustrations if you want – but definitely form the pictures first. After a while, think about how this form of reflection has deepened and enriched your understanding of your course. At the end of your course you will have a wonderful and inspiring visual record of your time at university that you will want to show your family and friends … that will give you happy memories of your studies for many years.

No, no, no – I really can't draw!

If your response to the visualising and drawing ideas suggested above is captured in our sub-heading: *no, no, no* … then try these short drawing activities. Remember – the idea is not to be a brilliant technical artist – it is to liberate your drawing self so that you become happy with whatever sort of drawing you are capable of. You use this freedom to liberate your creative self. Given that this will get easier with practice, why not try drawing regularly – say for five or ten minutes every day? You can do this in private if you are self-conscious, but we have found that doing these things with other people is more fun.

Five drawings in five minutes: read the following list and draw a picture in response to five of the words for one minute each: Asymmetric, beautiful, colourful, detailed, edge, far away, geometric, hidden, inside, joint, knot, look up, miniscule, number, opening, pattern, quirky, reflection, sensuous, texture, underneath, view through, wall, you choose. Keep these drawings in a little exercise book and just enjoy them – or see how you can use the drawings in your notemaking, learning and revision practices.

Oval doodles: draw ten ovals, the same size – now in two minutes, doodle on them so that they are all different. Do this every day. (Both of these ideas proposed by Eileen Adams at an Access Art Sketchbook conference, 2011).

Blind drawing: blind drawing is not drawing with your eyes closed – but drawing whilst looking at what you are drawing – but not looking at your drawing paper. So, settle down and just start looking at and drawing lots of different things. *Enjoy* how strange and wonky and quirky they look. Feel released because these pictures cannot look 'real' – but they may look good in some other way. To start blind drawing: settle down to draw something – make sure that you can see it easily, but it is more difficult to look at your paper. Really look at what you are drawing all the while you are drawing it. Try to really see it – but do not look at your paper – and do not take your pen or pencil off the page. Be bold, move your pen or pencil back and forth across the page as you draw what you are looking at. When you think you have drawn all of the thing you are drawing – stop – look at your picture. Be happy with it no matter how strange it looks. Do this often. Become happy with your strange and quirky drawings.

Foot drawing: like blind drawing, foot drawings release you because they cannot look 'real' – but they can look interesting. I think you can guess the rest: get a drawing or painting implement that you can hold with your toes ... find something to draw – look at it really closely, really *see* it – then draw it – badly – but with fun and spirit.

Daily watercolour: buy yourself a small watercolour set with at least one brush. Sit down every morning for about ten minutes and paint a watercolour ... of your room, your desk, the cat or dog, a pencil pot, a chair ... Just relax, focus on enjoying the watercolouring. Pin up your water colours around your room – be happy with them as they are.

Blind draw plus daily watercolour: start the day with a quick blind draw – and then watercolour that. This is a bit like 'colouring in' which has recently become really popular as a stress release, relaxation technique. There are loads of 'colouring in' books being produced for adults right now – and they are selling in their millions. Save your money. Blind draw – colour in ... relax.

100 pieces of paper: get 100 pieces of paper, choose a maximum of five drawing, making or painting implements or resources and give yourself a set time (three weeks?) to draw or paint on all of your 100 pieces of paper. Do not throw any away. Review your drawings after some time has passed. You will be surprised at how much you like them – and how much you like the ones that you would have thrown away if you allowed yourself to be a critical judge as you went along. Give them to your friends as presents. (Taken from Laura Frantz in Paper Monument, 2012)

Rich pictures and diagrams: when starting on a new topic, let yourself think about it by drawing a picture or diagram of all that the topic means to you. The following link takes you to some small Systems Thinking and Practice (Diagramming) tutorials: http://systems.open. ac.uk/materials/T552/. These constitute different draw-to-learn activities including spray diagrams, rich pictures, systems maps, influence diagrams, multiple cause diagrams, sign graphs. Explore all the tutorials – and use the strategies in your thinking.

Read Chloe's blog: Chloe Noble realised that many of her fellow students did not make visual notes because they thought that they could not draw. Chloe produced some simple lessons on shape drawing that show beyond any shadow of a doubt that anyone can be visual, because *you don't have to draw to make visual notes*: https://noblechloe.wordpress.com/first-year-learning-logs/visual-notes/who-says-you-need-to-be-able-to-draw-to-make-visual-notes/.

Visual learning: Pauline Ridley from Brighton University has put together a whole website focusing on the role of drawing in learning and research: http://about.brighton.ac.uk/visual learning. Please explore this website and use the ideas in your own studies. Pauline has also produced *Drawing to Learn* booklets that can be downloaded from her visual practices website: http://about.brighton.ac.uk/visuallearning/drawing/ – use these to help you to be a more creative and more successful student.

Find and do an art-related MOOC: once you stop telling yourself that you cannot draw, enrol on an art MOOC (massive open online course). The first one we took was 'Introduction to art: concepts and techniques'. Each week we were introduced to new ideas in art – and then put them into practice. We had to upload pictures of our art attempts for other people to review – and we had to give feedback on other people's art. The effect was stunning not just on our 'art' – but on our self-confidence and creativity. If you are interested in seeing what we did – you can search our Last Refuge blog (search for lastrefugelmu). Our posts on the first #artmooc start here: http://lastrefugelmu.blogspot.co.uk/2013/05/artmooc-introduction-to-art-concepts.html.

Get even more digital: check out this 'padlet' of artefacts that were all made on the same topic – e-learning and digital culture: http://padlet.com/nurmih9/fe6dqg43g5dt. Be inspired. Then go to Alan Levine's '50+ web ways to tell a story' wiki space and use some of the tools there to create animations or comic books of your notes: http://50ways.wiki spaces.com/. Good luck.

Summary

I started the daily watercolour after hearing about it on Desert Island Discs. I did it to tackle stress at work. Each morning I would get in early and spend about ten minutes doing a quick drawing and watercolour. It didn't matter how awful my pictures were – I just kept going. It was life-changing. Not only did I get to actually sort of like my quirky watercolours – I found that my self-confidence grew. Without realising it, I started to feel better about myself – and happier. I recommend this to everybody now!

This chapter has explored ways to bring some creative and visual practices into your learning process. We learned when we can play with ideas – but sometimes we need permission to play — most of us definitely need permission to play with drawing … We opened with a focus on brainstorming – but the majority of the chapter detailed a range of draw-to-learn techniques to adopt and build into your study practices. All of these have developed our creativity and our self-confidence – and our students have told us that these creative practices have changed their lives – and their grades. Some students have said that they now enjoy their learning for the first time. We hope that by now you are trying out some of the strategies outlined above. Why don't you blog about them? You might find as Chloe did that helping other people become more visual will help you to become more visual – and hence you will become a happier, more creative and more successful student.

Further reading

Dadosaurus Rex Blog: https://thedadosaur.wordpress.com/.

Paper Monument (ed.) (2012) *Draw It with Your Eyes Closed: The Art of the Art Assignment*. New York: Paper Monument. Available at: www.brooklynrail.org/2012/08/art_books/draw-it-with-your-eyes-closed-the-art-of-the-art-assignment (accessed 15 October 2015).

Ridley, P. *Drawing to Learn* booklets and Visual Learning website: http://about.brighton.ac.uk/visuallearning/drawing/ (accessed 15 June 2015).

Robinson, K. (2006) Ken Robinson says schools kill creativity (speech). Available at: www.ted.com/talks/ken_robinson_says_schools_kill_creativity (accessed 15 June 2015).

Robinson, K. (2009) Changing education paradigms (speech). Available at: www.ted.com/talks/ken_robinson_changing_education_paradigms (accessed 15 June 2015).

Activity

Three creative things to do

1. *Brainstorm your assignments*: go to one of your module/course handbooks – choose between three and six questions – allow yourself ten minutes per question and brainstorm. Reflect on the brainstorms and the process.

2. *Rich picture it*: once you have brainstormed one or more essay questions, now draw your brainstorms – letting images flow through your pen in response to the words that you have produced. Step back – describe your drawings – analyse them – how do they answer the question?

3. *Make index card collages*: buy a stack of large index cards and make a collage on every one of them. Use these collages to help you approach a difficult assignment. Use these to generate responses if conducting a qualitative research project.

Access the companion website to this book and find helpful resources for this chapter topic: https://study.sagepub.com/burnsandsinfield4e

7

How to Be Analytical and Critical

One difference between college and university is critical thinking – at university you are expected to be analytical and critical at all times. This chapter explores analytical and critical thinking – with very practical strategies to adopt such that you become an effective and critical student.

- Introduction   94
- A beginner's guide to critical thinking   95
- Critical questions for reading and writing   98
- Challenge yourself   99
- Flawed logic   100
- Summary   101
- Activity: use the question matrix   101

Introduction

I kept being told that my work was too descriptive – or that I'm not being analytical or critical enough ... But no one told me what these mean!

Critical thinking is often placed at the very heart of what it means to be an academic, a professional in the workplace and a student. Critical thinking is the art of making clear, reasoned judgements based on interpreting, understanding, applying and synthesising evidence gathered from observation, reading and experimentation (see: www.criticalthinking.org/pages/defining-critical-thinking/766). One of the key purposes of university, it is argued, is to develop analytical, critical and sceptical abilities: rational ways of viewing and analysing information, knowledge-claims and the world. The student is supposed to use their university time to develop their abilities to evaluate the arguments and evidence that they encounter – and to know the reasons why they have made the judgements that they have. In this way we understand our courses, the reading and our assignments – we know what we are writing and why. This involves nurturing a critical *attitude*: a habit of approaching the world in a questioning and critical way. We move beyond purely instinctive, emotional or belief-based responses and develop the *habit* of analysis, interpretation and evaluation.

TIP

This is a core employability skill, good for the CV – one of *the* main skills employers want from a graduate.

FIGURE 7.1   Critical thinking Wordle™

Well, you might say, that's all very well, but I just came here to learn business or history or science – what has this got to do with me? As an engaged learner in control of your own learning, you are not just consuming ideas – you are *engaging* with them. You have to evaluate and discriminate between different ideas and different bits of research that you read and that may make different claims. All the different and contradictory arguments cannot be true – you have to make up your own mind about what you believe and why. You have to know how to use the evidence to justify your point of view or position … you have to justify your answers to assignment questions. Analytical and critical thinking strategies enable you to do that well.

A beginner's guide to critical thinking

> When I did my first sports management report in the second year – on Islington Tennis Centre – I had all sorts of trouble identifying the theory at first. Later, when our results came through the main feedback was that I needed to make better use of theory – and be more critical.

I keep six honest serving men

They taught me all I know

Their names are what and where and when

And who and why and how. (Rudyard Kipling)

Kipling's quote refers to the six key questions that any good journalist should ask when investigating a story. They help the journalist move from description to analysis: from being a passive observer of an event to an active and engaged critic. Here, being a critic or being critical does not mean finding fault – which is the common sense or everyday meaning of the word – but means weighing up the evidence, looking at all sides of the story and drawing reasoned conclusions. This process is designed to help us move from a sort of passive gullibility where we believe anything that we are told – or that we read – to active engagement so we decide for ourselves – using the evidence.

So criticality is supposed to move us from the norm of accepting one person's account or one perspective or one point of view – to a norm or habit of looking at all sides of the story – and drawing our own conclusions that we could argue for in our assignments – offering solid evidence to prove our arguments.

As a student, it is really useful to use the journalism questions when encountering new ideas, information and knowledge. Get into the habit of always asking:

what is this about? Who wrote it, why, when, where? What impact did it have when it was written? What impact or relevance does it still have now? Why? To whom? How will I use this in my assignment?

After exploding the question to find different resources, I critically analyse the materials found with the five 'W' and 'H' method. I then use them to write, which means an assignment should contain who, what, when, where, why and how reasoning.

Don't stop at the journalism questions!

John Hilsdon, from Plymouth University, shared the Kipling poem with its six journalism questions: who, what, why, when, where and how; but he argues that a good student should go further and deeper than that. He suggests that on top of the six journalism questions, we get into the habit of also asking: What if …? So what …? What next?

- '*What if?*' asks, 'What if it were different?' For example in an essay on 'The causes of homelessness' – ask, *What if it were unacceptable in our society to have homeless people?* If we ask this, we might now think that it is not really okay for there to be hundreds of homeless people on the streets. We might start to think – *Why is it acceptable? What could be done differently?* Asking different questions can make us see things differently; it stops us from accepting things as they are: we become more critical.
- '*So what?*' asks us to sound out the implications and to judge the evidence generated by our what if … questions: *If it were unacceptable to have homeless people then … what? What are the implications for society? What would we in this society have to do differently to change this? And – what are the implications for this essay that I am writing?*
- '*What next?*' asks us to think through the implications and draw conclusions about the new information that we have gathered by using our other questions – in reality, that is, in the real world in which we live – and in our assignments. The new questions that we have asked should force us to think differently – and this should prompt us to draw different conclusions and find different answers to our initial assignment question. Asking: *Is there somewhere where it is unacceptable to have homelessness? How do they achieve that? What does it 'cost'? Is this cost more acceptable than the cost that our society pays for having homeless people? How can I weave this into my essay?* – should mean that we find and think about new information or ideas, which makes our work richer and deeper.

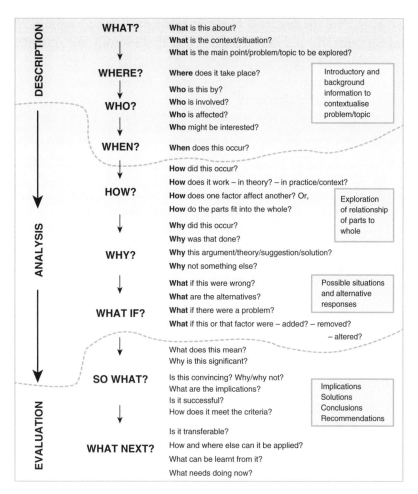

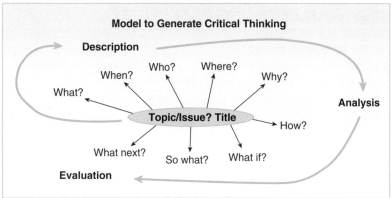

FIGURE 7.2   A beginner's guide to critical thinking

Source: Reproduced with permission from www.plymouth.ac.uk/uploads/production/document/path/1/1710/Critical_Thinking.pdf

All these questions are designed to get us thinking around a subject, thinking in depth, thinking critically and analytically – and this extends our understanding.

 I now break all my assignments into sub-questions. This is followed by free writing, which I do apply to my assignments.

TIP

John Hilsdon developed a range of critical thinking resources for staff and students, and we have reproduced his questions cycle to help you move from *description* to *analysis*. If you want to go a bit deeper into this topic go here: www.plymouth.ac.uk/ uploads/production/document/path/1/1710/Critical_Thinking.pdf, or search online for *critical thinking + Plymouth*.

Critical questions for reading and writing

Just as we can apply a critical questioning approach to our assignment questions, critical questions can also help us to shape our reading and our writing. The tip is to make the process a habit – something that we do without even having to think about it.

READING TIPS

When reading – for every paragraph you read – ask critical questions:

- What is this paragraph about?
- Where is the author 'coming from'?
- How does this impact on their argument?
- What evidence are they offering? How valid is it?
- Who would agree with this? Why?
- Who would disagree with this? Why?
- How could I use this in my assignment?

Reading in this critical way means that you are actively engaging in an analytical fashion with information as you go. This is a very good thing!

When writing – for every paragraph you write – answer the critical questions that a reader might ask:

- What is this paragraph about?
- What exactly is that?
- What is your argument?
- What is the evidence – and what does it mean?
- How does this relate back to the question?

When writing, try to answer those questions as you go – this helps your writing to be analytical and critical. As always, we recommend that you do not try to answer all the questions at once; leave gaps as your write – knowing that you will review and revise your work. So, as you write, try to answer those questions, but write *blah* or *need an idea here* when you run out of ideas – and follow that up with more reading. Writing to answer those questions gives you structure, you can 'go with the flow' and avoid writing blocks – and you can read more to fill those gaps later. Adopting this approach means that you will find yourself constructing critical, argumentative paragraphs. Drafting and re-drafting gives you the time and space to read more – to review and improve your writing.

As with any type of work, practice makes perfect. To be a good writer one must practice writing. I have learnt a valuable lesson here and I am now more aware of what is expected from me. I have come to appreciate how to analyse and be critical of the resources I use for my assignments.

Challenge yourself

Students wrestle with critical thinking – here's something that one of our students sent us:

I was thinking about this topic, critical thinking. In order to become a critical thinker one must be honest and deal with your own assumptions, prejudices and pre-conceptions … The word 'challenge' popped into my head. A student must challenge themselves in order to become critical thinkers. I produced this crossword for you:

CHALLENGE
Being Critical

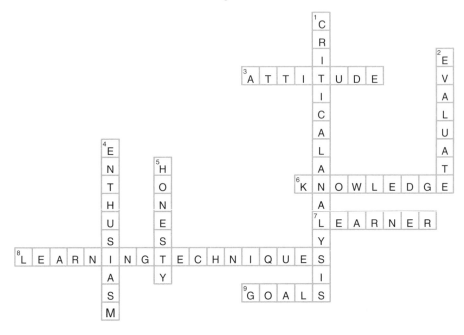

ACROSS

3   You need the right one of these to be critical
6   You will develop this over time
7   It helps to be creative
8   You need to develop these to be critical
9   Set these for each assignment

DOWN

1   Be more critical
2   You must do this in order to make a judgement
4   Be curious and engage with the material
5   Appraise your own prejudices

FIGURE 7.3   Challenge crossword puzzle

Flawed logic

 I really like the *yourlogicalfallacyis* website.

When we study and encounter new ideas and knowledge-claims, we have to look out for false arguments and logical fallacies – things that look okay at first glance, but that crumble when you really interrogate them. We need to be aware of these when we are reading – and when we are writing. The 'yourlogicalfallacyis' website provides examples of flawed reasoning, false premises, inappropriate comparisons, drawing conclusions on too few examples and false cause and effect. Check out this website and all the different examples of false reasoning and flawed arguments that they offer – this will provide you with another excellent set of tools with which you interrogate ideas when you encounter them in your reading – and it will help you to avoid constructing your own flawed or false arguments in your own writing.

┤TIP├

See https://yourlogicalfallacyis.com/appeal-to-authority – and use the navigation arrows to investigate all the examples of flawed argumentation that they offer.

Summary

In this brief chapter we have linked analytical and critical thinking to active learning habits. We explored in detail how to use the extended journalism questions to help you approach ideas, knowledge-claims and arguments with scepticism and a critical eye. Applying the nine questions (who, what, where, when, why, how, what if, so what, what next) is a practical way to apply critical thinking to help you unpack your assignment. When you turn an assignment into a question matrix (see below), you generate questions to investigate and answer on your way to answering a whole assignment question. Although this can feel like 'yet more hard work', smile – do it with good grace – it will develop your understanding and improve your grades! We also demonstrated how to read and write with a questioning approach; putting these strategies into practice will make you critical as a habit – and this will save you time in the long run. Finally, we recommended the 'yourlogicalfallacyis' website which demonstrates the ways that bad arguments can look convincing. Exploring this site will give you yet more tools with which to analyse and criticise that which you see, read and hear. This chapter is deceptively short. Do not be fooled by that. These strategies will radically alter the quality of your research, your thinking and your writing. It is now up to you to try these things for yourself and see.

Activity

Use the question matrix

We have argued that you can use the nine questions, the question matrix, to open up a question – and to think more deeply and widely about your assignment questions. A big problem with assignments is that when we see a question, we think we need to produce an answer. This often leads us to think 'small', making snap judgements and not really investigating a topic in depth.

This stops us from seeing the potential breadth and richness of our assignment questions – and it means that we will not discover enough information to produce a decent answer. When generating our smaller questions it is useful to apply the journalism questions: five Ws and an H plus the extensions, What if...? So what? What next? – to each part of the assignment:

- Who?
- When?
- What?

- Why?
- What if...?
- How?

- Where?
- So what?
- What next?

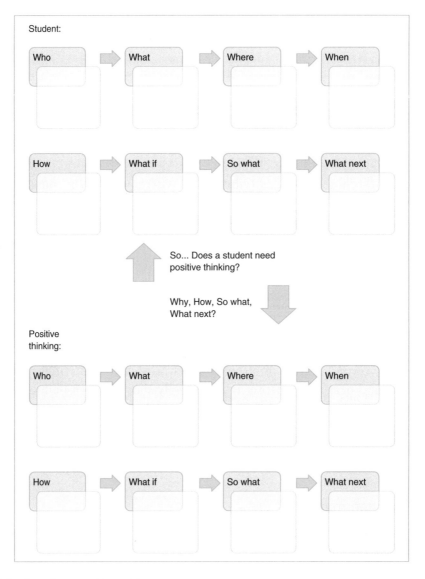

FIGURE 7.4   Preparing a question matrix

Prepare a question matrix

Now we would like you to take a few minutes to put this questioning approach into practice. Use the nine questions above to unpack the question, below, using the question matrix template in Figure 7.4. Then compare your results with our example (Figure 7.5).

- Write the whole question out in the middle of a very large sheet of paper.
- Underline the key words.
- Write questions for all the key words.
- When you have finished compare your version to ours.

The question:

Evaluate the usefulness of positive thinking to a student.

We suggest that you spend five or ten minutes on this before moving on to compare your effort with ours.

How do you feel after your first attempt at generating more questions – rather than answers?

Many students we know do find this approach intimidating at first. All it seems to do is produce yet more hard work. It feels exhausting – and they return to the method of looking at a question and just writing a quick answer – even though this has never worked well for them before. Old bad habits can be comfortable and familiar; they feel easier – even if they don't work.

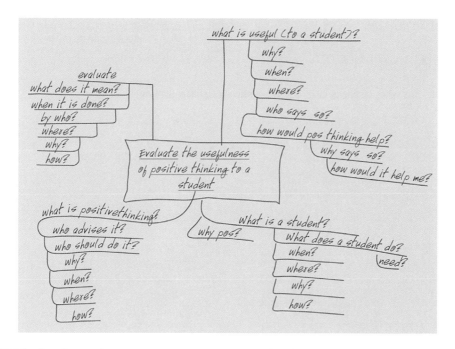

FIGURE 7.5   Question matrix on 'Evaluate the usefulness of positive thinking to a student'

If you want to develop into a successful student – you need to push through that old discomfort barrier that we keep writing about – and make changes. You do need to grasp the nettle of hard work (yes – now we sound like those nagging teachers that you hated at school!) ... But remember your positive thinking, too (Chapter 3). Try to avoid seeing this as yet more hard work. Smile – and say to yourself, *This is what I can do to do the job well.* Now try this approach on some of your real essay questions.

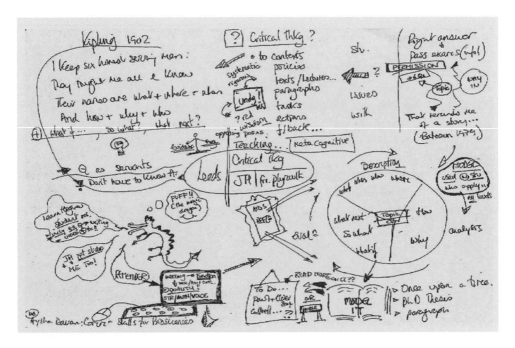

FIGURE 7.6   Our notes on one of John Hilsdon's sessions on critical thinking

8
How to Be Reflective

Without reflection there is no learning – it is as simple as that. Reflect and make your learning conscious – self-test to check that you have remembered – or you forget everything you have heard or read or seen.

- Introduction 106
- What is reflective learning? 106
- Beyond the revision cycle 107
- Why be reflective? 107
- How: keep a reflective learning diary 107
- A beginner's guide to reflective learning 108
- Case study: Chloe's blog 111
- Summary 111
- Activity: get blogging 112

Introduction

Welcome to this reflective learning section where we focus on the learning log and blog. As you have gathered by now – this is not the only section on reflection in this book. We ask you to revise after every study session – to revise your notes in order to remember them, and to revise your own progress in your PDP and CV files. This form of reflection and self-testing is essential if we are to learn anything at all. Learning is not random. We need to take control of our learning by active goal setting – active learning – and active reflection.

This chapter looks particularly at the learning log and blog – you may also want to re-visit Chapter 2: How to learn, how to study; Chapter 5: How to make the best notes and especially Chapter 13.1: PDP and HEAR. Whilst these chapters are separate, their message is uniform: in terms of successful academic practice, reflection is something that you should be actively engaged in, for without review, there is no learning. In this chapter we are going to suggest that you keep a reflective learning diary or blog to make your learning more effective and successful.

What is reflective learning?

Reflective learning involves a process of thinking over what you have done – of making your learning conscious – of actively revisiting and testing what you have learned. It is part of the active learning that we practise throughout this book. With each chapter we ask you to think about what you need from the chapter itself – to set your own goals. Within each chapter we present information – supported by activities, questions and discussion that are all designed to get you to engage actively with the information. After the chapter we want you to actively review the learning that has taken place for you: *What did I want from this? What have I gained? Where and how will I use what I have learned?* And right here in this chapter we suggest that you blog about your learning, because telling others what you have done is the best way to revise and learn yourself. All the evidence on learning emphasises that no matter how active all your other learning practices are, without this active reflection, there will be no learning. In this chapter we are going to explore how to formalise this active reflective learning in a learning log or blog.

TIP

Check out this blog post on how to learn – make notes of the new information there, and on how you will use it to develop your study practices – then blog about it: http://bigthink.com/neurobonkers/assessing-the-evidence-for-the-one-thing-you-never-get-taught-in-school-how-to-learn.

Beyond the revision cycle

Active revision equals successful study – it is as simple as that. We hear students complain about being asked to reflect on their learning – it feels like doing it all again – it feels like hard work. But if this is not done, then no learning has taken place. All those hours sitting in lecture theatres – all those hours reading – and wasted. Now that is what we call hard work – hard work is wasted work – because without revision, nothing was learned in the first place:

- Without a revision cycle we forget 98% in three weeks.
- Revision starts from day one – and should be ongoing. We need to actively choose what to learn from every lecture, seminar or piece of reading.
- This is different from exam revision – which means revising to pass an exam; this is learning for life (though if you do want to know how to revise for and pass exams, see Chapter 12.6).
- A reflective learning log or blog is a form of reflective writing that will help you to understand, learn and write about your course material.

Why be reflective?

Ongoing review of what you are learning – and why – puts you in control of your own development. This is essential for your learning and pragmatically it will enable you to produce your assignments. This is why more universities are encouraging students to produce learning logs or blogs – or to engage in PDP (Chapter 13.1). It is not some exquisite form of torture devised to make your life miserable – they are hoping to demonstrate in practice that when you actively reflect – you do learn more … but this only works if you engage with some level of enthusiasm. Don't just go through the motions. Reflective learning is for you – not the university. Set your own goals, reflect on what you have learned and take control of your own learning.

How: Keep a reflective learning diary

Your reflective learning diary, log, journal, sketchbook or blog is your own analytical, detailed and yet concise record of your studies. The process of completing this diary allows you to test your own learning as you make it active and conscious; this improves the quantity and quality of your learning.

Writing your diary should follow swiftly upon a study session – and the writing itself should be purposeful and concise. As said, we have had students complain that it feels like doing all the work again. But in many ways – that is the point.

By reflecting on a study session, you are quickly doing all the work again – and thus you are learning it. Without doing this activity – you will forget it. So, although it may feel frustrating – it is learning. and without it you might as well not have bothered going to that lecture or that class.

Most recently we have asked our students to do this active reflection in a blog – using an online writing space like WordPress (https://wordpress.com/) where you can create your own website for free. We want students to make their learning conscious in words and pictures – and we hope that they will also read each other's blogs and comment upon them. This encourages deep reflection. It also encourages dialogue between learners so that the learning becomes social and interactive. Our experience is that when students do this, not only do they learn more – they also develop their ability to write about what they learn – and therefore their assignment grades radically improve.

The structure outlined in the beginner's guide to reflective learning below works with our students; once you have tried it, re-shape it so that it takes the form or shape that works best for you.

TIPS

- Keep a diary or a blog for each module that you do.
- Spend a few minutes after each study period – a class, lecture or independent study – completing your journal.
- When completing your learning diaries – make conscious what you remember – follow up what you didn't understand.

A beginner's guide to reflective learning

This reflection has ten parts: what, why, learned, illustrations, reaction, successes and problems, link to assignment, reading, writing, and goal setting. It does not have to be a rigid thing – experiment until you find a structure that best meets your needs and suits your learning approach.

Write your diaries in beautiful notebooks that inspire you to use them – on blog spaces that you have customised to reflect who you are (see also the section on blogging to learn in Chapter 10) – use notebooks for some modules and blogs for others.

Write briefly in short paragraphs – or use a pattern note format. The important thing is to be concise and focused. Use key words and phrases – and colour and cartoons to make them memorable.

- *What*: make *brief notes* of what you did – the lecture or seminar that you attended, the reading that you have done.
- *Why*: make brief analytical notes. Why did you do it? If a book, why did you read it? If a lecture or seminar, what was the lecturer trying to achieve? Why did they run that session? What did you want from it? How was it useful? What learning outcomes did it cover? What part of the assignment question is it helping you with? Know why you are doing something and you move from being a passive to an active learner.
- *Learned*: make brief notes on all that you think that you learned from the lecture, class or reading. These notes are where you make your learning conscious, it is an instant form of self-testing, which improves both the quantity and quality of your learning. When we do not do this we are in danger of leaving the learning behind as we walk away from that lecture or close that book. Make this section of your review detailed, but concise.

-TIPS-

- Think – what part of my assignment will this help me with?
- Write to make it interesting for your reader – this helps you take control of the material for yourself.
- Diaries and blogs get easier with practice – and develop your academic writing.

- *Illustrations*: think about what you have learned and try to draw it in diagrams or simple cartoons. This extra engagement with the ideas will help you understand what you are learning. Make your drawing unusual, funny, bizarre – and this will make it memorable. With blogs, you can upload photographs of your drawings or you can find images online that bring the ideas to life.
- *Reaction*: make brief notes on your emotional response to the activity – notice the affective dimension to your learning. This allows you to build a picture of yourself as a learner and as a student. This reflection allows you to notice what and how you like to learn, the subjects and topics that you enjoy – and the ones that you do not like so much. This means that you can choose modules and teaching and learning strategies that suit you. It might also help you choose the right sort of job for you (see also Chapter 13.2).

-TIPS-

- Be honest. You will not get a true picture of your own likes, dislikes and preferences if you paint a rosy picture of yourself.
- Use the discoveries that you make here to inform your subject choices – and your job choices.
- Use the information to help you refine your own learning style.

- *Successes and problems*: it is all too easy just to focus on our failings – so note your successes, too. What did you do well? What preparation had you done that made the session more successful or easier for you? What bits didn't you understand? Which bits were confusing or difficult? What did you do about that? How did you solve the problems that you encountered as you studied?
- *Link to assignment*: consciously think – how will I use this in the assignments? Make notes. Again – this is vital – without this sort of active reflection, you might forget why you were making those notes in the first place – you will not use the information in your assignments.
- *Reading*: what will you now read? Why? When? You are supposed to read about the theories and concepts that you hear about in lectures and classes. Evidence suggests that if you do the active reflection suggested here – you will see the point of the reading and actually do it. If you do not – you will not.
- *Writing*: what will you now write – a sample paragraph for one of your assignments? Get into the habit of writing briefly after every class. Obviously the log and blog are part of that writing. But it can also be good to draft rough paragraphs for the module assignments – gaps in the paragraphs show you what else you need to find out – they show you what to read.
- *Goal setting*: make brief notes about anything else that you will do next ... nothing will ever give you 'all you need to know' on a subject. Therefore, you should always be thinking: what next?

TIPS

- Make this reflective process a habit – just do it – do not waste time moaning and resisting!
- Make it creative and fun – enjoy writing for a reader – illustrate your online blog with photographs of your notes and other pictures.
- Produce a sketchbook of ideas, thoughts and learning – use a real sketchbook that you draw in and illustrate in many different wondrous ways.
- See the Visual Directions website for advice on reflective learning, sketchbooks and podcasts from staff and students – and beautiful images of what a journal could look like: http://cltad-web2.arts.ac.uk/cetl/visual-directions/
- We practise what we preach and write our own blogs: *Becomingeducational* on WordPress and *Lastrefugelmu* on Blogger – you are welcome to search them out and see how we do it!!

Without doing my review, I wouldn't even have understood the class, let alone remembered it!

Case study: Chloe's blog

Chloe Noble was one of our students this year. She initially really hated the idea of blogging her learning – in fact one of her first blog posts was called: Why I really hate blogging! However, as time went on, Chloe not only used her blog to reflect on her learning – she developed her blog into something wonderful and inspiring.

Chloe developed 'challenges' to issue to other students – we really liked her 30 day drawing challenge in which several students in our class took part – and which was used by students from around the world. Chloe started to put together video diaries for her future self – and she developed short tutorials teaching people how to draw: You don't have to be able to draw to make visual notes (https:// noblechloe.wordpress.com/first-year-learning-logs/visual-notes/who-says-you-need-to-be-able-to-draw-to-make-visual-notes/).

Chloe has produced one of the most inspiring blogs that we have seen – and it demonstrates some key things about being a successful student – you don't need to like the idea of something to be able to do it. You don't need to be automatically good at something to be able to do it ... You do need to overcome your own resistance. You need to get past seeing things only as a problem. Once you do that – you can do anything.

No matter how much you dislike the idea of blogging to learn – try to see the opportunities for you in it – and make it work for you. Here's a link to Chloe's blog: https://noblechloe.wordpress.com/.

Summary

An ongoing review system will allow you to make your learning conscious such that you revise and remember. Reinforce your active learning by using reflective learning diaries and blogs – where you enjoy writing about and illustrating your learning. This improves both the quantity and the quality of your learning and it will improve your academic writing and other assignments. This process should help you to notice any problems that you are having understanding or learning the material – so that you do something about that. You should also start to notice the subjects, situations and learning strategies that suit you best – which may help you choose a job that will actually suit you. Finally – if you really want to check whether it works – why not write a brief reflection on your engagement with every chapter in this book?

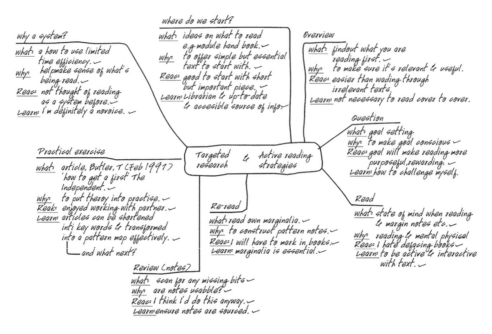

FIGURE 8.1 Example of a student's learning log on 'How to survive academic reading'

Activity

Get blogging

Use this reflective learning template to help you structure your own reflective learning logs or blogs. As you get used to writing and illustrating these, you will find that you start to adapt the template to your own style – but remember to always think about how a study session will be used in your assignments – and always illustrate your logs and blogs – this makes them memorable – and appealing.

Reflective learning diary or blog – template	
What	Make brief notes of what you did: the lecture or seminar that you attended, the reading that you have done.
Why	Make brief analytical notes: why did you do it? How was it useful? What learning outcomes did it cover? What part of the assignment question is it helping you with? Knowing why you are doing something helps you move from being a passive to an active learner.
Learned	Make brief notes on all that you think that you learned from the lecture, class or reading. Make it interesting for your reader. Be engaging.

Illustrations	Draw pictures or diagrams that illustrate what you have learned. Sketch funny cartoons to make the learning memorable. Remember – you don't need to be able to draw to make visual notes: https://noblechloe.wordpress.com/first-year-learning-logs/visual-notes/who-says-you-need-to-be-able-to-draw-to-make-visual-notes/
Reaction	Make brief notes on your emotional response to the activity: notice the affective dimension to your learning. It allows you to build a picture of yourself as a learner and as a student. It may help you choose the sort of job that suits who you are.
Problems/ solutions	If you encounter any problems understanding or learning the material – make a note – and make a note of how you solved the problem.
Link to assignment	How you will use the key information in that study session in your assignment? This is probably the most important thing you can do to promote active learning and study success!
Reading	What will you now read? Why? How will you use that in your assignment?
Writing	What will you now write? When? Tip: Start drafting rough paragraphs for your assignments way before the deadline.
Goal setting	Make brief notes about anything else that you will do next … nothing will ever give you 'all you need to know' on a subject. Therefore, you should always be thinking: what next?

FIGURE 8.2   Reflective learning template – use for logs or blogs

9

How to Get on in Groups

If you have issues with group work, or if you don't know how to succeed in *assessed* group or team tasks, then this chapter is for you.

- Introduction   116
- Study groups   116
- Assessed group work   117
- What is group work?   117
- Why groups?   118
- Advantages and disadvantages of group work   119
- SWOT your group work   120
- How to 'do' group work   120
- A business-like approach   120
- Belbin's group roles   121
- Adair's processes   122
- A beginner's guide to group work   124
- Summary   125
- Further reading   125
- Activity: use the ten stage approach − with an observer   125

Introduction

> I was going to drop out – I was so miserable. But I was doing a group project with someone and I couldn't let her down. I stayed to finish our presentation – and then I just stayed.

Group work can be brilliant or it can have you tearing out your hair. It is one of the most emotionally charged areas of university life. Feeling part of a good group can make university feel 'do-able' and having responsibility for your group can help you stay when you otherwise might drop out. This chapter explores some of the positives of personal, informal study groups – and moves on with a special focus on how to succeed at and reflect on *assessed* group work.

Study groups

Many people arrive at university feeling shy and alone. People like us write about making friends and getting a study group going and you just want to shout at us to leave you alone. Don't we know how shy you are – don't we know how difficult that is! But finding and making friends is the best way to make sure that you stay at and succeed in university. If you are shy – push through your shyness and reach out to make friends anyway.

One of the first things we do with our students is to get them into groups speaking with and listening to each other. We invest much time and energy in the first weeks of our course so that our students start to find out about each other and they start to see who in the class they like – or who shares their attitudes and values. They start to work out who could become a friend.

Gradually people find that they talk about the different lessons with another person. They find themselves discussing the assignments in the coffee shop. Our goal is that by week four of their first year at university, our students are forming their friendship and study groups so that they feel welcome in our class, they feel they belong in the university and they are able to support each other in their studies.

TIPS

- Even if your tutor does not specifically set aside time for you to get to know the other students in your class – make time yourself. Listen to people. Go for coffee with people. Smile at people and encourage them. Be the brave one who says *Let's go for lunch* – or, *Should we all go to the library together?*

- Make sure you have a study partner and a study group. Share the reading – discuss your assignments – critique each other's work. This is supportive, dialogic, collaborative learning – with all those big words, don't you just know that this is a good thing?

Assessed group work

So, we argue that your own informal groups will help you enjoy university more – and the collaborative talking, reading, thinking and writing that you do in your own groups will improve the depth and breadth of your learning and the quality of your work. On top of that, most universities build assessed group activities into their teaching programmes:

- because they believe in collaborative learning – we are interdependent beings and should recognise and build on that
- because group work offers support – social and academic. Tasks are easier when they are shared – and learning is easier when we discuss it with others
- because they are pragmatically preparing students for the world of work – if you cannot work with other people, you are unlikely to keep a job.

Whatever your university's reasons for asking you to engage in group work, see this as an opportunity and get the most from it.

Some people do see assessed group work only as a problem – it feels too difficult to get a task done when you don't know the other people in the group – and perhaps you feel you would not like them if you did know them. This is another good reason to make the effort to get to know your fellow students in the first few weeks of your course – and for you to start to make friends. It is easier to work with people if you already know and like them. As always, whatever your feelings, it helps if you adopt a positive approach: be prepared to make your groups work, whoever you have in the group with you. Whatever your group is like – be prepared to like and support *them*. To help you, we are going to explore the what, why and how of group work.

What is group work?

 I love group work. I enjoy working with other people – I like the camaraderie and I like the fact that I'm not on my own as usual.

A group has to have a membership of two or more people. There should be a sense of shared identity: you should all *feel* like a group with shared goals. You should feel a connection to and be able to interact with each other – with a sense that you can achieve your goals together.

Perhaps it is in these initial definitions that we have hit upon some of the problems with academic groups. How many people in an academic group do *feel* that sense of identity and interdependence? How many embrace the task and the sense of shared goals? How many resent and resist the whole group work process?

If the latter sounds like groups that you have been in – or that you are in now – what are you going to do to make your group feel and operate like a group? This is important not only because it makes the task more enjoyable, but also because, your group process may be assessed. You may be asked to reflect on the whole group work experience – and this reflection will be awarded a grade. This is not an opportunity to moan about the people who did no work and how much you hate group work – it is about how you worked as a group, roles that were adopted, problems that occurred and how they were solved.

─TIPS─

Make notes as you go along. Use the pyramid discussion – also known as think-pair-share to get started. When asked to start a group project, do the following:

- **everyone thinks about the topic on their own**
- **discuss ideas in pairs**
- **build ideas in fours**
- **only then get going on the task.**

Why groups?

Group work offers many advantages to students of all ages – yes, really. Group work can foster supportive, active learning giving you the opportunity to discuss ideas, collaborate with others, deepen your personal knowledge and develop your personal and interpersonal skills. Working with others means you share the workload; it really is easier to do all the reading if you share it out and discuss it.

When engaged in a group project, you can develop assertiveness rather than aggression; tact and diplomacy rather than bullying and hectoring; flexibility and compromise rather than intractability and stubbornness. You can learn to listen as well as to speak, to encourage others as well as to establish yourself – and to work co-operatively and collegially with a team.

All these things will help you get that job – if you have noted them, if you have collected evidence for your CV file. Another advantage of group work is that a good group offers social support that can break down the isolation often associated with being a student.

Advantages and disadvantages of group work

 They keep making us work in groups, but university is a competition – why should I help other people?

Of course, there can be disadvantages to group work. For one thing, many students are competitive and are chasing their own good grades. If a group activity is assessed, they do not want *their* group grade based on the effort – or lack of effort – of others. Thus they are incredibly resentful of those in the group who do not pull their weight, who do not turn up, who do not stay on track, who dominate or bully or distract, who stay silent, or who talk too much, who are not interested or committed. None of this feels satisfactory and it causes much resentment. But, every disadvantage can become an advantage if you work out how to resolve the problems that you encounter. So notice what is happening in your groups.

Notice the difficult situations that arise and how they are resolved. For example, if there are people who do not speak or don't turn up for meetings or do not contribute to the group task; instead of being angry and frustrated, try to discover the real problem – and see if you can find a solution. Take the time and trouble to find out what is going wrong for those other people. Ask them – talk with them. Be the helpful and friendly one – not only might this solve your group work problems, your own problems and worries will also diminish.

Be creative – if people are really too busy to come in to university for extra meetings on your group project, can you use virtual meetings or blogs to take your projects forward? Your attempts at finding solutions may not work, but that doesn't matter. That you recognised and attempted to address a problem is what will make you employable.

Put notes about your group activities – your problem solving and your project successes – in your CV file (Chapter 13). When applying for jobs, you will be able to *prove* that you are good at group work by giving examples from your time at university. It is the examples that you give – and the way that you tackled your problems – that will make all the difference in that vital job interview. And this refers to another 'why' of group work – it can and does prepare you for your future employment.

If you have to write a reflective account of your group work: make notes of your group sessions, your conflicts and resolutions, your strengths and weaknesses, the plusses and minuses of the experience.

SWOT your group work

SWOT stands for Strengths, Weaknesses, Opportunities and Threats.

- What are your group work strengths? What do you already like about group work and the way that you perform in a group? How are you going to build on your strengths?
- What are your weaknesses? What do you really dislike about group work and/or your own performance in groups? How are you going to tackle your own problems and issues?
- What opportunities are there for you in group work? What do you get out of your group projects? How have you managed to grow as a person and as a student through group tasks?
- What are the threats? What are you really worried about? What are you going to do about that? What is wrong with group work as far as you are concerned? What have you done to tackle your fears and overcome your concerns?

Once you have answered these questions, think about your answers – discuss them with a study partner: what do they tell you about yourself? How can you harness your responses to help you succeed in group work? Put notes in your CV file and read on.

How to 'do' group work

The best way to get the most from group work is to approach it positively, determined to get the most from it. If you really dislike group work, but have to engage in it, fake it to make it. Role-play being an active, positive student who enjoys group work. Do not sit there scowling and punishing the people in your group because you don't like group work – it's not their fault.

Another simple and very effective strategy is to choose your groups with care. Do not just team up with those people sitting next to you – or those nice chatty people from the canteen. Group tasks normally involve hard work: choose people who are as motivated, positive and industrious as you.

A business-like approach

Management theorists like Belbin and Adair have attempted to de-mystify group work so that businesses can run more effectively. Critics say that they offer rigid and inflexible descriptions which do little to help us either to understand groups or to perform better in them; however, we have found that students like using Belbin and Adair to help them make sense of group work. As always when you consider these approaches to groups, ask yourself, 'How will knowing this make me a more successful student?' For, in the end you must work out if and how knowing those things will help you to succeed in your group activities.

Belbin's group roles

There are eight key roles that management experts like Belbin (1981) have described in group activities. We have listed these below indicating the possible strengths and weaknesses involved.

- *Company person*: dutiful and organised – possibly inflexible.
- *Chair*: calm and open minded – not necessarily creative.
- *Shaper*: dynamic – but impatient.
- *Creative thinker*: brilliant ideas – but may be unrealistic.
- *Resource investigator*: extrovert, responds well to the challenge – may lose interest.
- *Monitor*: sober, hard-headed, keeps everything on track – may lack inspiration.
- *Team worker*: mild, social person, plenty of team spirit – may be indecisive.
- *Completer/finisher*: conscientious, perfectionist – may be a worrier.

You can find online questionnaires that help you discover the role you might like to play in your group; but be flexible and be prepared to adopt different roles in different groups – do not just stay with a role with which you are already comfortable – this is your time to grow.

TIPS

- Even in a small group, make sure that you have a chairperson and a minute-taker so that everyone knows what their task is, what they are doing and by when it all has to be completed.
- Experiment with group work. Adopt different roles in different academic groups. Each time you vary your role in a group you will develop different aspects of your personality; this is a good thing.
- Use your group work experiences to develop your CV – and get you that job. So, as you move through team worker, leader, information gatherer, creative thinker, completer, etc., make notes on your experiences for your CV folder.

- Whilst eight roles are indicated here, research indicates that academic groups work best if they only contain about five people – any more and you start to get passengers. So, have a group leader, share the tasks, make sure someone keeps notes of group meetings – with action points. That is, at the end of every meeting there should be a list of all the things that the group has agreed to do – with a *name* by each activity. Everyone should leave a meeting knowing who is doing what – by when. Keep in contact – share email addresses and mobile numbers.

Adair's processes

Belbin describes the roles adopted in group situations, Adair describes the *processes* that groups go through. Adair argues that groups pass through distinct transformations, as they come together, complete a task and then dissolve. These have been described as forming, storming, norming and performing – some people also speak of a fifth stage, mourning. Read through these descriptions and see how they might help you work better in academic groups.

- *Forming* is where the group comes together and takes shape. It is a time of high anxiety as people work out:

  o who is in the group – and what they are like
  o what the assignment is – what it involves
  o what the 'rules' are – about their behaviour and about the task
  o what they will have to do to get the job done – and who will be doing 'all the work'.

---TIP---

Keep in contact, share phone numbers. Make dates to meet. Work out who is doing what by when.

- *Storming* is where conflict arises as people sort out all the confusions highlighted above. This is where people seek to assert their authority, and get challenged. Typically this is a 'black and white' phase – everything seems all good or all bad: compromise is not seen. At this stage people are reacting emotionally against everything as they challenge:

  o each other
  o the value of the task
  o the feasibility of the task (you cannot be serious!).

If you do not like group work, ask yourself, is it because you do not like conflict? Perhaps you just find this phase uncomfortable? If this is so, remind yourself that *this phase passes.*

- *Norming*, as the name suggests, is where the group begins to settle down. Here that sense of interdependence develops as:

  - plans are made
  - standards are set
  - co-operation begins
  - people are able to communicate their feelings more positively.

Be a team player. Be punctual for meetings. Apologise if you cannot attend. Pay attention. Keep in contact with the whole group. Do what you say you will do.

- *Performing* is where the group gets on and does what it was asked to do. Jobs get done – by everybody in the group. Success can be achieved as the research is completed, the presentation is delivered, the report written … Here it is useful if:

  - roles are accepted and understood
  - deadlines are set and kept to
  - communication is facilitated by good interpersonal skills.

Use those phone numbers and email addresses. If you are group leader, learn how to chivvy people politely; if chivvied – do what you said you would do.

- *Mourning*, the fifth stage, is supposed to follow a successful and intense group experience. As you work hard with people, you develop links and bonds. Typically you enjoy the sense of mutual support and commitment. The feeling of interdependence is very satisfying – and people can enjoy getting lost in the 'flow' of a really meaningful group task. When all this ends as the task ends, there can be a real sense of loss.

Be prepared for the sense of loss. Keep in contact with good team players, you may be able to work with them again.

Do you recognise any of these stages? Now that you have read about them, think how you might use this knowledge in your next assessed group activity.

A beginner's guide to group work

In your group, role-play the kind supportive person who wants everybody to contribute and succeed. Useful things to say include:

- That sounds interesting, could you say a bit more?
- This has worked for me before …
- I see what you mean …
- We are making good progress here – what does everybody else think?
- We seem to be stuck … does anybody have an idea about how we can move forward?
- You two seem to be seeing this differently, but what about …?
- Is there anything that we/you can find to agree on?
- To sum up, do you think this is what we have agreed so far …?

If you are required to write a reflective account of your group work as part of the formal assessment of your course or module:

- Do ask your tutor exactly what it is that they are assessing before you even start the group activity. In this way you can note the relevant things as they arise and have information there ready for when you perform your formal review of your group project.
- Do not just write things like, 'We all argued and did not agree on anything'. Or, 'I really like group work'. You need to comment on how you made your group function effectively. It helps if you note problems and how you overcame them.
- Do have a group observer who makes notes on how your meetings run – the issues you have – and how you tackled them.
- Do mention Belbin and Adair and how their theories helped you do better in your group task.
- Do use theory and practical examples from your weeks working as a group to justify your arguments and make your reflective account sufficiently academically rigorous.
- Do read Chapter 12.2 on the report to see one way to report back on your group experience.
- Do search online for LearnHigher's award winning 'Making Group Work'. This video resource follows students going through group work struggles. It runs like a mini-soap opera – with lots of advice and useful things to think about and do to make your group work.

Summary

We have used this section of the book to explore group work in the academic setting – from the study and friendship groups that will be personally valuable, to the more formal, assessed group work task that you may be set. We have stressed that group work can be a positive, supportive and interactive learning experience – especially if you tackle group activities with enthusiasm and commitment and with the co-operation of similarly committed group members. Finally, we suggested that where group activities require a formal reflective account, you will complete a better one if you make notes of all your ideas, problems and solutions as you go. Good luck with your group activities. Enjoy your group work – groups really can be supportive, exciting and productive.

Further reading

If you are interested in this topic you may wish to have a look at the following:

Adair, J. (1983) *Effective Leadership*, (1987a) *Effective Team Building*, (1987b) *Not Bosses but Leaders* (3rd edn, 2003). Explore Adair's publications – check out: www.johnadair.co.uk/published.html (accessed 15 October 2015).

Belbin, R. Meredith (1981) *Management Teams: Why They Succeed or Fail*. London: Heinemann.

LearnHigher resource 'Making Group Work'. Available at: http://archive.learnhigher.ac.uk/groupwork/ (accessed 15 October 2015).

Activity

Use the ten stage approach – with an observer

When undertaking a group task it still helps to use the ten step approach to assignments (Chapter 11.3) – and also to have one person who acts as a group observer or facilitator. The observer makes notes on how all the different people in the group are behaving – and how the task is getting done.

Your observer can feed back to the group at the end of each meeting – and everybody in the group should try to listen quietly to this feedback before responding. Try not to get defensive if it seems like you are being criticised. Try to work out – individually and collectively – what you can all do to make the group work better as a group. Use all these notes, reflections and discussions as the basis for your group work report:

1. Prepare to research *as a group*:
    i. understand the task – know what you have been asked to produce
    ii. analyse the question – all of it – know what you have to cover

    iii. have the overview – fit the task to the module learning outcomes

    iv. use creative brainstorming and notemaking strategies

    v. action plan – work out who is doing what, why, where and when.

2. Follow the action plan: do what you said you would do – when you said you would do it. Communicate: keep in contact with other members of the group. If a problem arises do not just disappear – talk to someone.

3. Review your findings: everybody should share their research – and share their ideas about how to finish the task.

4. Plan the final product – together. Know who will be doing which bits of the presentation or writing which bits of the report. Who will be preparing which sections of the newsletter – or who is responsible for which bits of the video or workshop that you are preparing together.

5. Prepare a first draft or first version or first 'cut' of whatever it is you have to produce as a group. If working independently, meet up and show each other what you have achieved so far.

6. Have a break from this task (and work on something else). Let the brain know that the task is not over – but put it on the back burner.

7. Review, revise and edit – agree on a final draft. The group has to come together to agree the final version of the presentation or report or other end product. This is another difficult time for a group – typically everybody thinks their version or opinion is the best – and it takes real skills to agree a version that everyone is happy with. Ride the storm.

8. If producing a written product, proof read. If preparing a group presentation, put all your ideas together into one poster, PowerPoint presentation – or one group website. And rehearse together as a group. *Make sure everybody knows the whole presentation in case someone does not or cannot turn up on the day.*

9. Hand in or deliver the final product on or before a deadline.

10. Review your progress – using your observer's comments – and the notes you made on how you developed your processes in the light of their feedback.

10

How to Harness a Digital You

The world is digital – and so is university. Make sure you leave university with more digital skills than you arrived with. Note: This chapter is supported by a PDF on Digital Literacy downloadable from the Sage website (https://study.sagepub.com/burnsandsinfield4e/).

- Introduction   128
- The 'e' guy says   128
- Become a digital student: work out loud   130
- E-learning and Virtual Learning Environments (VLEs)   134
- Using your PC for research   135
- Virtual assessments   141
- Summary   142
- Activity: get digital now   142

Introduction

> I took one look at the banks of PCs in the university laboratories – and all those very confident students sitting there working – and panicked.

Nowhere has university changed more dramatically in the years since we first started writing these books than in the use of technology for study. In the first edition we merely advised that it is useful to have a computer because it makes the writing easier. Now, it is impossible to imagine a world where the web is not a vital part of how we learn new things; how we communicate with our friends and family; and how we connect with colleagues, other students and with whole networks of people that we may never meet in person. This chapter seeks to explore how to gain confidence in using the virtual for successful study.

No matter what the level of your existing computer skills, you will be expected to leave university digitally proficient, for ICT (information and communications technology) skills will be expected in every job you apply for. We want to help you become digitally skilful whilst you're still at university – for you – to help you study successfully. This chapter is designed for everyone, from those who want to extend existing skills to those who are just starting to get digital.

---TIP---

Use your PDP to develop and demonstrate your development of ICT skills (see Chapter 13.1).

The 'e' guy says

> All employers have the first stage of their selection process online. You need IT skills just to apply for a job.

Being a student has changed. In truth it changes all the time and we adapt and engage in different ways. However, in recent years being a student has changed at an extraordinary rate and technology is the reason. We use technology for many purposes, in our social life and in our work, but more importantly we can use it when we study. Knowledge of the new technologies and how they can enhance our studies can give us a great advantage. Remember, being a student is like having a job; you need the correct tools to help you do your job more effectively.

Desktops, laptops, tablets and smart phones are available in abundance. Most students tend to use their own preferred device, but they all have their advantages and disadvantages. Working on an assignment with complicated diagrams can be difficult on a tablet or smart phone. However, using your tablet or smartphone to view or listen to yesterday's lecture on a commute or in the library can be brilliant. As an individual you need to understand what works best for you – and get the balance right.

Hardware, however, can only be as good as the software you choose to download onto it. Many of us know about Facebook and WhatsApp, but how many of us are aware of the free software that may be hugely beneficial to us as students? Check out Technology for Education, below – there is an abundance of resources waiting there. Understanding what software best suits you and what it can do will help you be a more efficient student.

A basic understanding of cloud-based systems is a good starting point. Do any of us still use memory sticks? As we can now write and save our work using Google Docs or Evernote, for example, it's easy to share our work and save it instantly to be viewed anywhere on any device later, wherever we are.

Dropbox has been around a while and is certainly one of the simplest ways to upload your files to a cloud-based storage system. But would you trust any of these software products with your final essay or dissertation? Always be aware of saving your work or backing it up. So the answer to the question, 'Do any of us still use memory sticks?', is not as straightforward as you might have thought.

One of the most helpful apps available to students at present is 'Reference Me'. A simple app for your smartphone with online back-up that automatically gives you the reference you need for your bibliography and the citation you require to be inserted into your essay. Your smart phone scans in the bar code at the back of the book and then gives you the referencing information that you can email to yourself. It even allows you to change the style of referencing depending on your course or tutor's requirements. As good as this software is, it is always best to consult your tutor before submitting your final work based on the references obtained electronically.

A great way to obtain information online is Twitter, voted again for the sixth year running as the best app for learning (http://c4lpt.co.uk/top100tools/). Would you have guessed that? Twitter is more than a communication app, it allows you to follow professional people in your field and help find new research papers on the relevant articles of your choice.

So do your research and find out what the best devices and software are that will enable you to be a better student.

- For a quick guide to useful educational software, check out, Technology for Education: http://chrisoreilly.weebly.com/technology-for-education.html.
- For a crash course on digital literacies, check out our website: http://learning. londonmet.ac.uk/epacks/digital-literacies/index.html.
- Big thing to remember: future employers *will* check out your social media sites. Get rid of those pictures of you dancing on the table.

Become a digital student: work out loud

Entering the age of digital teaching and learning can be unsettling for students and staff alike – we know all this technology is there, we even play with it – but we need some help to harness it effectively in our studies. In this section we are going to recommend a few things to do to help you 'get digital' and 'work out loud'.

Working out loud is when we blog and tweet about our learning, about the different projects we're interested in, about the reading and writing that we are doing. Many academics are doing this to build their own Communities of Practice and Personal Learning Networks (CoP and PLN). These are informal online communities of people that you may never meet in real life – but who may read and comment on your blogs and tweets – who discuss your ideas with you – and for whom you do the same. This makes the learning and thinking dialogic (it takes place in discussion with many voices) and productive. It is a great thing to do when still a student. We want you to initiate this by blogging and tweeting your learning – and by possibly undertaking a free MOOC (Massive Open Online Course).

Blog to learn

Blog about your learning on your course (see Chapters 1 and 8). This is working out loud: it helps us to understand and learn our materials. We may find ourselves in meaningful online conversations about our studies which deepens our understanding and it prepares us for elegant and confident assignment writing.

- Blog posts need only be 300–500 words long – the point is to be reflective and useful rather than descriptive.
- Your audience will be other students just like you – so write your posts for them: why will they be interested in what you have done or learned? What will you want them to think or do after reading your blog post?

- Blogs are less formal than essays – so find a writing style that works in a blog.
- Customise your blog – make it look good, add pictures – make your blog user-friendly and readable.
- Enjoy writing friendly, readable blogs.
- Read and comment on other student blogs.
- Each time you read someone else's blog, 'like' it – leave a comment. The point with the blogs is to create a friendly dialogue about what we are doing.
- To set up your own blog – try:
  - https://wordpress.com/
  - www.weebly.com/
  - www.blogger.com/
- If you blog about this book, use the hashtag #ESS4 – and then tweet out your posts … Other readers will find you in the Twitter hashtag link.
- Read and comment on as many blogs from other #ESS4 readers as possible. Boom: we become a community.

Twitter for learning

Twitter is *not* about what you had for breakfast or who that celebrity has married or divorced this time. Twitter is the site to join to keep up with the latest research in every academic subject you could possibly imagine. If you want to be a successful student in the twenty-first century, it is essential to join Twitter and 'follow' academic leaders in the field in which you wish to excel.

—TWITTER TIPS—

- No matter how sceptical you may be of Twitter – please open a Twitter account to use at least for this book: www.twitter.com.
- 'Follow' your tutors and other academics – 'follow' the people who write the books you read on your course.
- Check out the Education Twitter chats captured on this list: https://sites.google.com/site/twittereducationchats/education-chat-official-list.
- Tweet your blogposts and put alerts in Facebook when you write a new post – that way people will know about, read and hopefully comment on your post.
- If you're blogging and tweeting about using this book – use the hashtag #ESS4.

Do a free MOOC (Massive Open Online Course)

I can see that you can feel lost in an open online course … you need that little extra bit of self-confidence to throw yourself into a MOOC and hope that you connect to a

A key aspect of learning, teaching and assessment (LTA) in the twenty-first-century university is the ubiquity of the digital. Some parts of your course may be delivered online, for example, you may be expected to listen to online podcasts rather than attend lectures or you may have to access an online video or article – and familiarise yourself with that before you attend a seminar. You may be set an assessment where instead of writing an essay or a report – you are asked to produce a digital artefact. All this can feel pretty intimidating – but it is all do-able if you approach it positively.

One of the best ways to become informed about LTA in a digital and multi-modal world is to immerse yourself in a completely digital teaching and learning experience – and reflect on how it worked for you. Our advice is that you do undertake a free MOOC and reflect on it. There are MOOCs on everything from quantum physics to song writing and they are usually quite short, only a few weeks long, so they provide an intensive experience of what it means to be a student in a digital environment. From there you can move on to becoming a skilled student in the more 'blended' context of your university course.

Typically learning in MOOCs involves watching videos, reading online materials and engaging in online discussions – sometimes with thousands of people. The first MOOC that we did had 44,000 students participating from around the world. We found that the best way to get the most from our MOOCs was to blog and tweet. Yes, you may be invited to join in the online forums (or *fora*) – but most MOOCs seem to spin off multiple discussion groups via blogs, in Google+, in Facebook, in Twitter, and in all the other spaces you can imagine. Do not think about all the thousands of people or all the different places in which discussions take place – this can be overwhelming. Learn to use a couple of spaces, to dip in occasionally – and to enjoy those experiences.

In a MOOC, we all have responsibility for the learning – and for making other people feel good in the online groups. We all have to say hello. We all have to like and comment. If we all do this, no one feels left out. Now that I've realised this about MOOCs, I'm going to try it in my real life classes, too.

TIP

If you have just been set a digital assignment and are now screaming – *I've just got to grips with the university essay – and now they're asking me to produce something digital!!* – make the most of the opportunity it offers you – there is much more scope for your creativity and ingenuity in a digital assignment than there is in an academic essay. So embrace these changes when they happen. See the section on virtual assessments, below, and also Chapter 6 – being visually creative will help you produce engaging digital artefacts.

Creative MOOCs include:

#ccourses: http://connectedcourses.net/ – which explores the nature of co-creating knowledge in a connected world. Even when courses end, the resources are all cached on the website – with many videos to watch – and a blog roll of course participants which you can explore.

#ds106: http://ds106.us/about/ – that's Digital Storytelling 106. DS106 started as a synchronous MOOC in 2010. This MOOC was so popular that the community created refused to die. On this site the resources and activities are cached – and new synchronous courses spring up from time to time. If you have always wanted to 'get digital' but have been afraid to try, this site will take you on a friendly journey to digital storytelling – it will definitely help you to make those assessed digital artefacts.

For more traditional courses, try Coursera: www.coursera.org/courses. Search Coursera and see if they have anything on offer that you would like to undertake.

MOOC TIPS

Even if you feel that you have no time to do a MOOC right now – find a course that is running – join it – and just 'lurk'. See what other people are doing and read some of their blogposts. See how people teach and learn in the online space. Find the various *fora* (online communication spaces) in which people communicate their thoughts on the course – and follow some of the posts. Just enjoy it … and blog about it.

In all my MOOCs I have loved the FB groups best. Most people posted their blog links on FB as well as in Twitter – so the FB allowed access to many different strands of conversation. The FB page felt like the conversational space where you were all invited to join in … I felt that FB operated on many levels simultaneously: formal, informal, insider, outsider, long term tenant – barely passing through transient. Everybody is welcome there. What I also like about the FB – is that you can 'like', you can comment, without having to sign in, log on – without having to remember *all* your passwords. FB is words and visuals and friends at play!

E-learning and Virtual Learning Environments (VLEs)

> When I did my Globalisation course, we were required to do a group blog. I also had to access all the handouts from my tutor's website. My presentations were put online and I was expected to discuss the merits of my peers' work online as well. Some students also have to make videos/podcasts as part of their assessments. We were all directed to learning resources and external websites through the tutor's Blackboard site.

E-learning, blended learning and virtual learning are all terms used to describe learning activities supported by or accessed through electronic channels. If you are a full-time, 'face-to-face' student, you may well be a little surprised to find sessions on e-learning being discussed in your Welcome Week or induction activities. These are for you. As well as attending lectures and classes, you are expected to use any online materials or resources that your tutors provide.

E-resources for students are often gathered together in one place in a university VLE; here you may find some combination of lecture notes, seminar materials, course information, discussions, blogs, online assessment, a calendar, revision tasks, announcements, links to other resources, assessment information, and lots more.

Once you have access to your VLE, check that all your modules are there – and that you can access them. Also check if you have access to any more general resources. Some librarians put information up on the VLE, and many learning development or study skills units put material up in the VLE for all students to use. Then for each module check:

- Is my lecturer using the VLE for this module mainly to store lecture notes?
- Does this lecturer use a bulletin board to communicate changes?
- Is there a facility where I can add my questions?
- Is there a frequently asked questions (FAQ) section?
- Is there an area where I can get in touch with my fellow students?
- Is there any assessed work on the site – and by when do I have to do it?
- Do I use the site to submit my coursework?
- Are there any quizzes or other tools available to help me check my knowledge?
- Which areas will be useful when it comes to revision?
- Is my lecturer tracking my 'attendance' in the VLE?

You should definitely use your VLE. For one thing, VLEs help lecturers track your progress, so if you forget to login for a few days you may well get an email asking if you are having any difficulties. If you complain that you cannot do the assignment, they may just check to see if you have accessed their support materials in the VLE – if you have not, they may not help you.

Using your PC for research

Then there is using the internet for researching. We were always told not to use Wikipedia, but we were rarely told good ways in which to research online, other than to use Google Scholar. This is where Delicious enters the conversation as being one tool we use, but that site, although good, is now just one of 100s of similar sites/gadgets/applications. One of the problems I have now online is determining authenticity of information. It gets harder and harder the more advanced the internet gets. There is also the problem of plagiarism …

University study involves being in the university and being with your fellow students – never forget that – but it also involves using the world wide web for successful study. Here's how.

Using your library e-resources

Libraries are so much more than a collection of books. Your lecturer will expect you to show that you are reading broadly as well as deeply across your subject; so you need to show that you have used a mix of traditional (paper-based) and peer-reviewed e-learning resources to show you have effectively researched your subject.

Meet your librarian

Your subject librarian is a really important person. He or she will usually do a presentation at Welcome Week or in one of your first lectures. Find out his/her email address, because, like your lecturing staff, there will be specific days and

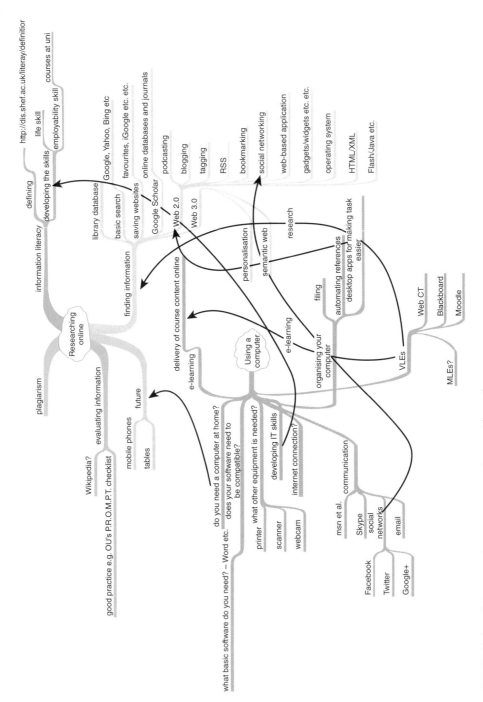

FIGURE 10.1 Mindmap – using a computer and researching online

times when they are available for consultation. Subject librarians can give you advice and assistance with all kinds of research, helping you to find a book or explaining the best key words to enter for successful searching of a particular online database.

Adding tools to help you with your research

As a successful student, you need to demonstrate that you are skilled in researching not just paper-based books, journals and newspapers, but are equally skilled at extracting *relevant information* from online resources. With so much information available on the world wide web, you can make the most of the web by using a few simple tools to manage and store your information. There are numerous gadgets and applications available free for students, or that can be downloaded for a small charge.

Google Scholar (http://scholar.google.com) provides a simple way to broadly search for scholarly literature. From one place, you can search across many subjects and sources: peer-reviewed papers, theses, books, abstracts and articles, from academic publishers, professional societies, preprint repositories, universities and other scholarly organisations. Google Scholar helps you identify the most relevant material across the world of scholarly research. It can be very useful for mapping out the key writers on your chosen area of research, and will assist you to identify the relevant 'key words' for using when you refine your research later. This site is great because it flags up where free copies of the documents can be accessed online.

TIP

Using too few key words will bring up thousands (or even millions) of websites. You will need to refine your research to get a more manageable number.

Try Google Books (http://books.google.com), and see how the site finds a book whose content contains a match for your search terms, and automatically links to it in your search results. By clicking on a book result, you will be able to see a few short excerpts to the entire book. Each book includes an 'About this book' page with basic bibliographic data like title, author, publication date, length and subject. For some books you may also see additional information like key terms and phrases, references to the book from scholarly publications or other books, chapter titles and a list of related books. For every book, you will see links directing you to bookstores where you can buy the book and (non-academic) libraries where you can borrow it.

Bookmarking

Having refined the key words and identified key authors using the Google tools successfully, you can source textbooks from your university library; check the electronic peer-reviewed journals for your area; and search for your lecturer by name in case they have published on the topic! You will find that you can gather quite a number of resources. It is useful to collate these resources, to keep them together in one place, and, if you choose, share them with others.

Bookmarking is an essential academic skill to develop, and it will save you hours of time trying to remember where you read or saw a piece of information later. Many universities have systems available via their catalogue to do this (Endnote and REFworks are the most common) but you may wish to use some of the free tools available like Mendeley or Zotero: www.mendeley.com/ or www.zotero.org/.

Zotero can collect all your research in a single, searchable interface. You can add PDFs, images, audio and video files, snapshots of web pages, and really anything else. It will automatically index the full-text content of your library, enabling you to find exactly what you're looking for with just a few keystrokes. The icons illustrate the different uses this tool can offer, so it can act as a personal research assistant as, once installed, one click will save and store your references, ready for exporting in the style you require.

Whatever your area of study, you will find that over time the same authors and themes keep re-emerging, and each time you locate a new source you can bookmark it. Over time, you will create a whole database of your reading. By the time you are writing your final year projects or extended essays you will have a whole

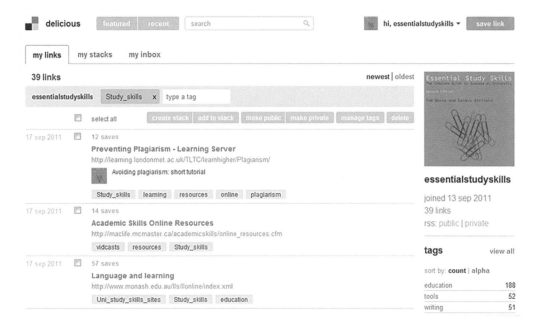

FIGURE 10.2   Delicious – an example of social bookmarking

collection of bookmarks in one place, covering various aspects of your subject. Even better, you can view the bookmarks of others on the same topics, which makes this a very effective tool to learn about. Delicious is an example of a free bookmarking tool (see Figure 10.2). Go to www.delicious.com and create your own account.

YouTube if you want to

Another favourite study application is, of course, YouTube (www.youtube.co.uk). YouTube can be customised and personalised by you – simply *create your own YouTube Channel* and save all the video clips you find useful for your studies. These can be 'tagged' and sorted – for example into themes, including sites you want to keep as part of your social life for your own hobbies and interests. There are tips and tutorials on all kinds of subjects and areas – they may not be peer-reviewed so you will need to make an academic judgement as to their quality – but if you're having problems with one of your subjects, you may find a YouTube tutorial that helps you understand it.

---TIP---

See Lee Lefever and his 'Commoncraft' YouTube clips. These are great, simple, illustrated tutorials on all the different social media tools (www.youtube.com/watch?v=6a_KF7TYKVc).

Wikipedia

Wikipedia (http://en.wikipedia.org/wiki/Wikipedia) is a useful tool for research. However, like all sources, not everything in Wikipedia is accurate, comprehensive or unbiased. Many of the general rules of thumb for conducting research apply to Wikipedia, including:

- Always be wary of any one single source, or of multiple works that derive from a single source.
- Where articles have references to external sources, read the references and check whether they really do support what the article says. Use *these* references in your bibliography – not Wikipedia itself.
- In all academic institutions, Wikipedia, along with most encyclopaedias are unacceptable as a major source for a research paper. Once you have read a Wikipedia entry, read at least one of the sources in the bibliography – and cite that instead.
- Check out: http://en.wikipedia.org/wiki/Wikipedia:Researching_with_Wikipedia.

---TIP---

Start your research in Wikipedia, but use other sources to support your arguments. Be careful – some lecturers will penalise you for citing Wikipedia as a source of information as it is not an academically peer-reviewed resource.

Evaluate your sources

Having located and collated a range of materials from different sources, materials that have been accessed via open access (i.e. not university provided) need to be carefully evaluated before inclusion in your work. There is an invaluable free resource to assist with the process, an online resource called 'The Internet Detective' (www.vtstutorials.ac.uk/detective/) – work through this early in your studies. The tutorial looks at the critical thinking required when using the internet for research and offers practical advice on evaluating the quality of websites. It is really important to develop your critical skills and learn how to judge how reliable a website is for your studies.

Virtual assessments

Some tutors are now setting digital assignments as well as the more traditional essays or exams. As always with any assignment, the trick for you is to work out why they have set that particular task: what aspects of the course do they want you to showcase? What digital skills or creativity do they want you to demonstrate? Once you know this – you are on your way to being successful.

On our courses we set our students the challenge of 'Develop a Digital Me'. We want our students to set their own digital challenge – and then to use simple online tools to tell their own story. Typically our students will want to tell their classmates a little bit about themselves – or a little bit about their learning journey. Both these

FIGURE 10.3 Evaluate your sources

are valid – especially as it helps the students to get to know each other and to bond as a class – as a CoP. We ask our students to reflect on their experiences by making a poster – and then we have a wonderful morning with a poster exhibition and digital showcase. If you would like to see some of what this year's students achieved, search for londonmet + posters-digital – or try this link: http://learning. londonmet.ac.uk/epacks/posters-digital/.

TIPS

- If making a video resource – it should be one minute long – definitely no longer than two minutes. After that you lose your audience.
- Check out the Upside Down Academy – www.upsidedownacademy.org/ – here you are encouraged to make a teaching resource – helping someone else understand something that you found difficult. This is a great way to think about making a useful digital artefact.

Summary

The aim of this chapter was to give some suggestions of how to be a successful student in a digital age. We have tried to show how to use the digital and the virtual in your studies – with an emphasis on 'working out loud' to create your own CoP and PLN – and on the tools that may be useful for you in organising your own learning: blogging, Twitter, MOOCs, Zotero, Wikipedia and YouTube. We concluded with a brief introduction to using the digital in assessments. We suspect this will be a growing part of university life in the future. If asked to produce a digital artefact – don't panic – you can always search YouTube for a tutorial on making animations … Good luck.

Activity

Get digital now

- Start and customise your learning blog.
- Check out Technology for Education: http://chrisoreilly.weebly.com/technology-for-education. html.
- Join Twitter – use a sensible name! Follow cool academics – tweet out your blogposts: #ESS4.
- Download and use the Digital Literacy PDF from the Sage website for more advice and tips (https://study.sagepub.com/burnsandsinfield4e).

- Make an artefact: create a short 'story' about any aspect of #ESS4 that has particularly intrigued or engaged you using at least words and pictures – though you can add animation and music if you want. Post the link to your artefact in your blog – and say what you did, why and how you think it turned out. Explore the following artefacts and blogs:
  - Terry Elliot's Zeega: http://zeega.com/162387.
  - #ccourses collaborative poem: https://titanpad.com/sXgaTJMniP.
  - These are some reflective artefacts from NTU students: http://thevirtualleader.blogspot.co.uk/2015/05/digital-storytelling-as-assesment-tool.html.
  - Use the Upside Down Academy: www.upsidedownacademy.org/.
  - This is what our students produced this year when teaching themselves technology with the tools of their choice: http://learning.londonmet.ac.uk/epacks/posters-digital/. Have a look – explore the posters and artefacts: think about whether and how you can use this in your own learning.

Access the companion website to this book and find helpful resources for this chapter topic:
https://study.sagepub.com/burnsandsinfield4e

PART III
THE BIG ASSESSMENT TOOLKIT
CRACKING ASSESSMENT

11.1
How to Make Sense of Your Course

 Not knowing what to expect from university was my problem. I had no idea what to expect, which made me anxious.

You cannot answer an assignment question unless you know what you have to *do* and *learn* to pass your course. Here's how to unpack your *module handbook* to take control of your learning.

- Introduction   148
- A beginner's guide to understanding and passing your course   148
- Summary   150
- Activity: use our exams checklist   151

Introduction

> I never enjoyed school, not at all. I never understood what we were doing or why. It was all so frustrating and I felt so powerless. Now I'm at university because I want to be, studying what I want to study, and everything is so different. It's great!

It is much easier to be a successful student if we know exactly what we have to learn and do to pass a course. No matter how engaged and excited you are about studying, you cannot show that you have learned your course material if you do not know what you were supposed to have learned in the first place. In this small chapter we reveal how to unpack course information – with a focus on the module or course handbook. Understanding how to get the most from your course will make a difference to your satisfaction – and to your grades.

A beginner's guide to understanding and passing your course

> I didn't care who had designed or validated the course! To me, learning outcomes came to my notice through module booklets. What was important to me was knowing what my course assessments were going to be, plus what the course would lead to in terms of future career and education.

Once you join your course there are several useful things to do immediately to gain your overview and take control of the course:

- *Read the module handbook.* Make sure you have a copy of the handbook for each course or module that you are taking. Usually this means downloading them from your VLE. Once you have a copy – read it! If you can access this information before you even get to university – do it.
- *Aims and outcomes.* Most handbooks spell out overall aims and the learning outcomes. These are the things you have to do and learn to pass that course. Read these – make lists – pin them up in your study space. Highlight key words. Make a list of everything that you will have to do or learn to pass each module. Pin this list up in your study space to help keep you focused on the goals of each module.

Prepare for a class or for your reading by re-reading your aims and learning outcomes – these tell you what you are listening and looking for.

- *Assessment.* Once you have analysed the aims and outcomes, look at how the course is going to be assessed. The course may be 100% coursework, 100% exam-based or a mixture of the two. Coursework tends to involve the production of one or more of the following: essay, report, write-up of a practical, presentation, etc. Exams can be just as varied, comprising seen or unseen papers (where you do or don't receive the exam in advance). Exams can be one, two or three hours in length. They might involve you writing essay answers, short answers or responding to multiple choice questions. They may be 'open book', where you can take certain books into the examination room, or 'closed book', where you can't.
- *Read the questions.* Often coursework questions or assignments are given at the beginning of the course, in the module handbook. Read them. You are not expected to know the answers yet – but if you read the questions you will know what the course is designed to get you to be able to answer. You will benefit from lectures; you will know what to look for when reading.
- *Look at the reading list.* Note essential reading – you should read some or all of these. Note the recommended reading – you should read some of these. When reading, keep a word from the question in your mind. These act like hooks and help you catch the information you need. Make notes that help you answer that part of the question.
- *Look at past papers.* If there is an exam on your course, find past exam papers and read them. These tell you what you should be able to answer by the end of the course. They help you to set your learning goals for the course.
- *Examine the syllabus.* If you have a timetable, syllabus or scheme of work, read it. Notice how the course has been put together. When attending lectures or seminars, have a word or phrase from the question in your mind, this should help you make relevant notes.

- **Know how you are going to be assessed for every module. In assessments you must answer the questions set – but you must also meet the learning outcomes. Think about the assignment before a lecture – before you read.**
- **Write out the question. Underline the key words. Pin questions on your wall. Free write a response to each question in your first week on the course (Chapter 11.2).**

Read around one word from a question at a time using your active reading strategy (Chapter 4). Listen for information on the key words in lectures and classes. Make memorable notes (see Chapter 5).

- Share the reading with your friends – talk about it – compare notes.
- Draw up weekly and termly timetables – put all your assessment dates on them. Put exam dates in every calendar you own (see Chapters 2 and 12.6).
- Colour-code your learning outcomes. Colour-code your syllabus. See which parts of the assignment are being covered in which weeks of the course.

- *Work on your PDP, CV and career options from the beginning* (Chapters 13.1 and 13.2):

  - Make an appointment with the careers service to see what jobs are open to you.
  - Decide to engage in volunteering or peer mentoring.
  - Think what extra-curricular activities you will do – for interest and pleasure, but also to develop your CV.
  - Check out your university's PDP process and decide to treat it as an opportunity not a problem.
  - Start a PDP/CV file – even if you just start with an old A4 envelope and start collecting information about jobs, you are beginning to take control of your learning.

---TIPS FOR SUCCESS--

Handbooks are designed to make sense – they are designed to tell you what you need to do and learn to pass each course. University lecturers want students to succeed. But if your handbook is confusing:

- work through the learning outcomes and assessment criteria with a friend or study partner
- ask the course tutor to help you make sense of the outcomes and criteria
- ask the learning or writing development people for help.

Summary

In this section we have explored how to take control of your course – with a focus on using module handbooks to shape your strategies ... Good luck!

Activity

Use our exams checklist

Photocopy the exams checklist from Chapter 12.6, or download a copy from our website, and use with every module or course that you do.

Access the companion website to this book and find helpful resources for this chapter topic:

https://study.sagepub.com/burnsandsinfield4e

11.2

Probably the Most Important Thing on Writing You'll Ever Read

There is nothing more normal or more frustrating than having problems with writing. Here are practical strategies and activities to help you develop a writing habit.

- Introduction   154
- How's your writing?   154
- Some writing strategies   156
- A beginner's guide to free writing for assignments   158
- Overcoming writing blocks   160
- Image prompted writing   163
- Summary   165
- Activity: rich writing   165

Introduction

' When I was helping in the students' union, I used to get students talking about their council tax – or TV licence ... Once we'd got that out of the way – they'd want to talk about their essays, asking for help. Sometimes overcoming writing blocks means getting all the everyday non-academic stuff out of the way first. '

Writing for assessment can occasionally zip along, ideas flowing with a sense of creativity and wellbeing. More normally, writing is fraught with tension, stress and fear of failure. The stress of writing means that we tend to approach academic writing in strange and unhelpful ways. Rather than practise – a lot – as we would if cooking, driving or playing a musical instrument – we hardly write at all – and then always 'at the last minute' with little preparation and no practice. So academic writing is done under the most stressful of conditions and, strangely enough, academic writing continues to be stressful. In this chapter we explore practical activities designed to help us write, to overcome our writing blocks and to develop confidence in writing – but first, we ask you to reflect on your own approach to writing.

TIPS

- Visual and creative approaches to assignment success are covered in Chapter 6.
- Successful study strategies are tackled in Chapter 2.
- Using the course overview is in Chapter 11.1 and ten steps to better assignments follows this in 11.3.

How's your writing?

We have said that assessment can be daunting, take a few minutes to answer the following questions on your own writing:

1. What writing do you do at the moment (notes, poetry, short stories, essays, articles, texts, tweets, blogs, websites ...)?
2. What do you like about your approach to writing at the moment?
3. What do you dislike about your current writing strategies?
4. Are there any aspects of academic writing that make you uneasy?
5. What do you think would help you to become a successful academic writer?

Once you have completed your own questionnaire, please compare your points with these from a graduate looking back at how she experienced writing on her course:

> I actually do a lot of writing because I am working as a secretary to get me through university. I enjoy the challenge of writing – it does not mean that I feel any good at it though – and most students are terrified of writing. It is the worst bit about being a student for them.
>
> I dislike nearly everything about the way I write! Having been out of education for over ten years, I felt very anxious about undertaking my first piece of assessed work – I didn't want to be judged negatively, because it might overwhelm me and make me want to give up the course.
>
> What makes me uneasy is not knowing the level of learning required – what an A-paper or a B-paper looks like. I could have used some general pointers on the level and detail of work at degree level. My last studying had been ten years earlier at GCSE level and it was impossible to know how high I had to jump from that to succeed at degree level.
>
> A lot of my writing skills were self-learned and self-developed so inevitably I made a lot of mistakes. My early writing was not good quality and certainly not good enough for the high standards set by my university. It was very much a matter of personal perseverance and motivation that enabled me to go on and succeed with some of my later writing.
>
> Referencing is also something I've struggled with.
>
> What would help me to be successful is more knowledge of what is expected of us and strategies of how we could reasonably achieve this. Small, manageable targets are better than masses of work with daunting deadlines. Some idea of the amount of time that should be spent on reading and making notes – this might have encouraged those with massive time pressures to get started, rather than leaving them to their own devices when they could easily become overwhelmed.

Does this make sense to you? Can you see anything in this that might help you with your own writing?

Writing involves drafting and re-drafting your work. You struggle to understand and use a whole range of differing arguments and opinions that you have found when reading. You struggle to shape your ideas and your evidence to answer a specific question. This may feel painful – but these are the academic practices of a successful student.

It is in the 'struggle to write' that learning happens. And we do mean struggle. As the typical writer says, 'Writing is easy – you just sit and stare at a blank piece of paper until your eyeballs bleed!' Writing is hard for everyone. Not just you. Once you accept that, you realise that writing is difficult because it is difficult. There does not have to be anything wrong with you if you are finding it difficult also.

- Read journal articles – try to find the *rhythm* of your subject – how the writing looks, feels and sounds.
- Build your self-confidence. Having confidence helps you succeed – low self-confidence can mean that you get defeated by problems rather than overcoming them – see Chapter 3.
- Use the writing packs on the Sage website (https://study.sagepub.com/burns andsinfield4e/) and the other resources on our Study Hub website: http://learning. londonmet.ac.uk/epacks/studyhub/writing.html.

Some writing strategies

> A few students I knew created 'headings' from different parts of the assignment question. They would make notes, add a reference or a quote under each heading ... Eventually everything under one heading became a paragraph. When that was done they wrote a conclusion. After lots of correction the headings would be deleted and they'd print it off. Read it again and make changes. Finally they would write the introduction to finish off their work. It was a slow process but seemed to work for them.

There are many different ways to start to write assignments – there are whole books on the subject – here are a few strategies that have been proven to work with other people – try them out and see which ones work for you.

- *Practise brainstorming*: sit down with a list of questions. Give yourselves ten minutes to brainstorm and plan each answer. Choose the question whose brainstorm you like the most – but use ideas from the other brainstorms in your answer.

Remember – brainstorming and planning get quicker with practice.

- *Speed write paragraphs*: once you have an assignment plan, sit down and use the paragraph questions (see below and Chapter 12.1) to prompt your paragraph writing. Write quickly – put in lots of blah blah or 'I need to find a source here'... Use the first rough drafts to help you choose more material to read. Plug those gaps.
- *Do not aim for perfection*: write something, anything ... then change it.
- *Practise writing*: do not just write for assessment – get into the habit of writing something every week, every day.

- *Group writing*: form a group with some friends that you trust. At least: brainstorm and plan 'perfect' answers to your assignments together, especially useful when preparing for exams. At best: meet once a week as a writing group – just get writing.

TIP

At the beginning of a writing session everyone says what they are working on – at the end everyone says what they accomplished.

- *Talk yourself through an assignment question*: imagine the question: 'Evaluate the usefulness of pattern notes to a student' – how would you talk your way through that? What about:

> So – I am supposed to evaluate the usefulness of pattern notes to a student! Okay – so first I might have to find out what it means to be a student – what do they do – what do they need? Are all students the same? Would the same things be useful to all students? Perhaps I'll need to define 'useful' or offer several definitions: useful could be – saves time, makes you happier, helps you understand the material, helps you learn the material, helps you get better grades: all these things could be useful. I might sketch them all in – then choose one and say which one I'm writing about and why – and find some evidence!! Pattern notes: I'll have to say what they are. I wonder if I'll have to compare them with other notemaking systems? It's not in the question – but that often helps to make good points. How many words have I got? Hmmmm 1,500 words. Not enough – perhaps just sketch in that there are active and less active notemaking strategies (saying why active is good) – pattern notes are good non-linear notes – and Cornell are good linear notes? Then I'll have to argue why pattern notes offer something useful to students …

Can you see how this 'talking through' of all the different parts of the question is helping this student to take control of the whole question? This process is making sure that nothing will be left out. Moreover – it is a really active way of engaging with the question … and, as you know, the more active we are in our learning, the more we will learn.

- *Blog to learn*: write happy, interesting and informative blogs about your learning … You will find that you are developing a point of view and an authorial voice: you have something to say that you want people to read. You are also learning your subject as you write it. Students of ours who have blogged their learning find that their assignment writing and their grades improve. (We also mention blogging in Chapters 1, 8 and 10).

> I didn't understand why we were blogging at first – and I found it really difficult … Then I 'got it'. I write about what I've done in class, I write about the reading. Suddenly my writing is getting better – and I actually enjoy it.

A beginner's guide to free writing for assignments

I've tried loads of things to get me writing. Wheel diagrams when I was a first year. You can make lists, you can do free association ... You can talk out loud. You can make pattern notes. There is also specialist software (Inspiration) and the old fashioned scribbling down of ideas.

Free writing is a bit like brainstorming; however, rather than looking at and responding to a title word-by-word in notes, in free writing you read the title and then write briefly in a 'stream of consciousness'. Free writing can really surprise you, often revealing that you know more about a topic than you previously thought. Practising free writing can help you develop a writing habit – and when you write more – your writing improves.

- Free write on your assignment questions as soon as you get them: just sit down and write something when you see the question. Do not try to get it right, just write. Use free writing to help you understand your course – and your reading.
- Free write after every lecture: sum up the main points. Write about how the ideas in the lecture will help with your assignment. Put the main arguments in your own words.
- Use writing prompts: collect postcards – or make your own index card collages (Chapter 6) – use these to prompt your free writing on assignments.
- Search YouTube for Peter Elbow videos on writing, free writing, spelling, punctuation and grammar. Blog about Peter Elbow, recommend free writing to other students.
- Search online for 'An Essay Evolves' to see how the writer of the online Freud essay used free writing to approach the assignment. Have a look at the free write that this student did on the Freud essay question and consider the *editing strategies* she used to start her Freud essay journey.
- Use our online free writing tool: http://learning.londonmet.ac.uk/TLTC/freewrite/FWT.html. We have built a free online free writing resource that anyone can use. When you go there, you set a time limit for your writing – you may paste in your assignment question, and then you just type without stopping and capture your first thoughts on the question. Once you have finished, you can use the second box that opens up to capture your thoughts on your free write. Copy the writing and save to a Word document if you want to keep a record of all your free writes.

The free write tool in action

Free write session 1: Topic – free writing

So free writng is all about writing without censoring – without pausing to correct your writing – to think of better ides – or even to be correct – to get it write. this

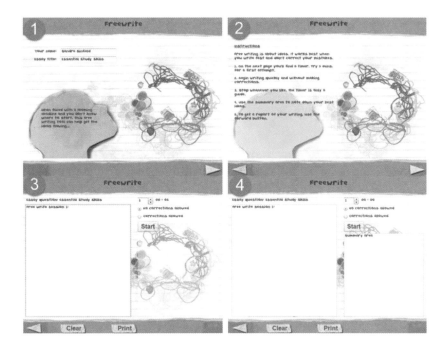

is about writing to unblock and get all your ideas out – to not block yourself with the dseire for perfection – but to celebrate that your ideas can flow – that you can produce words especially if you do not try too hard to be on top of it all. If you are prepared to have a go and get it wrong – and then to look through your owrds an see what good ideas lurk in there somehwehrer for good ideas are always in ther esomewhere even if fgood spelling elideas me mostly. I don't know how long I have been writing now – but it feeols liek quiet a long time – and I am aware that my spelling is even worse than normal – but you know what – it is cool not to keep going bakc to check. It is cool to fgeel that words oare actually pouring out – and that I will share them – no matter how bad they are.

What does that look like to you?

We know people who look at brainstorms and pattern notes and free writing – and all they can see is a *mess*! To them it all looks uncontrolled and uncontrollable. It makes them feel uncomfortable. They hate it. They want everything to be more ordered and orderly.

The trouble is, the need for order – for everything to be smooth and shiny and right and absolutely correct, first go and all the time – gets in the way of how we engage with ideas and learn. Learning can be messy – it involves making mistakes and getting things wrong …

Giving yourself the permission to be a bit messy – to get things wrong – to make mistakes and learn from them – frees you up to learn. Needing to be in control and perfect all the time, actually stops you from learning – it definitely stops us from writing. Free writing can be messy – but it can generate loads of good ideas for you to follow up and develop. Give it a go.

Use free writing to get yourself started on your assignments. Sit down with an assignment question in front of you – and allow yourself to write for 10 to 15 minutes without pause. Then go and collect some information. Once you have collected some information for your assignment – and maybe sketched out a quick essay plan – then free write the paragraphs. Once you have a rough draft free write your introduction and conclusion. Then work out what you have to read and write to finish the assignment.

What other students have said:

When we first started free writing I didn't get it at all. What's the point? Then I realised that I could just let myself go. Things started to happen. I do it with all my assignments now.

When we did that free writing every week, I got the best mark I've ever got for an essay.

All the free writing helped me to take control of the module. I think it helped me be more creative.

When I did the weekly writing, I finally understood why I was reading!

Overcoming writing blocks

Try this overcoming writing blocks activity to help you identify what might be blocking your writing. Try it on your own – or with other people.

Each person will need two pieces of paper plus pens or pencils.

- **Find a space in which you think that you would be able to write.**
- **Settle down with two pieces of paper in front of you – and all the pens and pencils that you could want. Label one piece of paper – *writing*. Label the other piece of paper – *commentary*.**
- **Give yourself a set time to write – at least 15 minutes and up to 30 minutes.**

- Write about anything that you can hear, see, feel or smell at the time of writing – or – write on your assignment question. Write continuously. *Do not stop.*
- *But every time you do stop writing*, put the reason for stopping on the commentary sheet of paper. No matter what the reason is – how silly, or small or trivial – make a note of it.
- After your set writing time, stop writing.
- Review all the different reasons you gave for stopping. Notice what your reasons for stopping are.
- If you have been working with other people, discuss all the different reasons given for stopping writing.
- Work out what to 'do' about some of your different reasons for stopping.

Here are some are reasons that other students have given for stopping:

Stopping to search for the right word.

Checking my spelling.

Wondering whether I've got the sentence right.

Checking my grammar and tenses.

I kept checking the time.

Thinking of a new idea.

I was trying to think of a better idea.

It was too hot.

I was uncomfortable; I kept wriggling in my chair.

I was thirsty.

I heard a noise.

Someone left the room and I wondered what they were doing.

I could not see the point of this activity – I felt stupid and wanted to stop.

Are these anything like your reasons for stopping? There appear to be certain key reasons for stopping work:

- *Getting it right:* searching for words and spellings, tweaking the structure, checking that the work is correct.
- *Searching for ideas:* thinking of new or better ideas.
- *Feelings of discomfort:* feeling uncomfortable physically – hungry or thirsty or too hot or cold or uncomfortable; or mentally – hating the task, wondering what other people are doing.

All these things are perfectly reasonable – but they do not help us to write and stay writing. Here are some useful things to do instead.

Getting it right

Most students we know have *no time*!! They are busy at home, they have jobs and they are working hard on their course. When they start their assignments they want to do them as quickly as possible. They want to save time. So they read and read – and then sit down ready to write that perfect answer – in one go – just the once. They aim for *one draft writing*. The problem is that this means they want to *produce* ideas and *edit* them at the same time. This rarely works.

It may seem counter-intuitive – but in the end it is much quicker if you write first – letting the ideas flow – and then you edit later. Look at the question – free write, brainstorm and use the question matrix. Write – read – write again. Read some more. Write some more … Then – review, revise and edit your work to make those ideas better.

When we write in this more fluid way, we start to really understand what we are writing. We suddenly see the point of the question. We understand the course more. We understand that article we were reading. We start to 'get it'. This is *writing to learn* – and it is a rich approach to writing that works with the way that our brains actually work.

TIP
_____

Use the Free Write Tool. If you like using online tools to help you study, practise using our free write tool with your assignments: http://learning.londonmet.ac.uk/TLTC/ freewrite/FWT.html. (If the link breaks, search online for Londonmet + freewrite tool.)

Searching for ideas

Another reason people stop writing is that they start to worry about the question – have they understood it? Are they answering it? Have they got enough ideas? Obviously – thinking is good. But not when it stops you writing.

Get into the two-stage habit: plan/write – edit later. That is, see an assignment and start free writing; or brainstorm a question and then write; or talk yourself through an assignment question – and then write. But once you start writing – go with it – don't stop. Revise it later. Write first – improve later. Trying to do both at the same time writes you into a block.

The trick is to write before you think you know it all – and to use the writing to help you find the answer to the question. The idea is not to be perfect – but to 'go with the flow'. Do not interrupt the flow of ideas, for in doing that we will lose the thread of our thinking. Always remember to review, revise and improve those initial drafts.

Feelings of discomfort

Sometimes we cannot write because we feel uncomfortable either with *where* we are writing, with *why* we are writing or with *what* we are writing. This could mean that you have not yet sorted out 'where' to study: your 'place to write'. Perhaps you have not sorted out 'why' you are writing. Perhaps you hate 'what' you are writing – either literally, you hate your own writing – or you hate the assignment.

- *Where*: have a place to study that works for you. When you are in your study place, develop the habit of writing. See Chapter 2 for advice on when, where and how to study.
- *Why*: are you resentful about all that writing or all the time university is costing? Being a student is full on and full time – you will not want to give that much time to something you hate. If you have chosen the wrong course, make an appointment to see your personal academic tutor or careers service. If you are on the right course and still struggling; perhaps you need to see the student counsellors – or the learning development people?
- *What*: if you feel frustrated with your writing or a particular assignment – write on two pieces of paper. Use one to write the answer to the question – use the other one to write about all the reasons you hate the assignment or to write about all the things that you would like to write in the answer but feel that you cannot. This often unblocks us – and frees us to write that essay or report.

Image prompted writing

As with the overcoming writing blocks activity, above, this is an activity you can try on your own – or with other people.

Each person will need paper plus pens and pencils. Before you start to write you need to collect together photographs from magazines or newspapers or old postcards or use your own index card collages (see Chapter 6); you can write quotes from philosophers or people you are studying on large index cards and use those.

(Continued)

(Continued)

The pictures and cards need to be mixed up and then there are two different ways forward – one where you randomly choose a card without seeing it – and one where you do look at the cards – and choose one that 'answers' the question for you. So do one of the following:

- Place cards face down on a table so that no one can see what is on them. Here you are using this exercise as a loosening up activity.
- Place cards face up on the table. Here you are using this exercise to answer an assignment question – so have a question ready before you choose your card.

The activity

- Find a space in which you think that you would be able to write.
- Settle down with your paper in front of you – and all the pens and pencils that you could want. Everybody chooses one 'prompt' picture or card – either at random or with an assignment question in mind.
- Give yourself a set time to write – at least 15 minutes and up to 30 minutes.
- Write about anything that pops into your head when viewing the prompt card. Write continuously. Do not stop.
- After your set writing time, stop writing.
- Review this writing process – how similar to or different from your academic writing process was it? Notice what was good about writing in this way. Notice if there was anything that you did not like about writing in this way.
- If using this to help you start an assignment, review your writing – is there anything there that you could use in your essay? Is there anything there that you can follow up in your reading?
- If you have been working with other people, discuss what you liked and disliked about writing in this way.
- Work out how you can learn about what encourages you to write from this activity – and build what you learn into ways of approaching your academic writing.

What other people have said

 I just loved having other people in the room working at the same time as me. I did not know that about myself. I will work in the library more often now, that will encourage me.

I started to write, then thought that everybody else had chosen a better card than me. I was convinced I'd chosen a bad card ... This *is* the way I am on a course. I keep thinking I've made a bad choice and this gets in the way of me getting anything done at all. *I have to believe I've made a good choice and then just get on with it.*

I found that I wanted to write about two different things at once. I do get like this with my essays too – I feel blocked because I really want to say something, but I know it's not really what the question wants. I think next time that happens I will have two pieces of paper and just write out what I want to get off my chest – and then dump it.

TIP

Are these comments anything like your own? What advice would you give to other people who are having problems with their writing? Tip: Why don't you write a blog in which you give someone else some good advice about how to get writing?

Summary

This chapter has explored writing through a range of writing activities. We have focused on free writing and overcoming blocks to writing because we want you to get into a writing habit. Our fear of writing is often our worst enemy – but getting into a writing habit helps us overcome this fear … we write … and our writing improves. We hope that you now feel less apprehensive and more confident about writing generally. Yes, writing is a struggle – but that is because it is meant to be an active learning process – so it takes effort. At the same time, this process gets easier if we can overcome our fears and get into a writing habit. Your academic writing will get easier with practice – so practise it. Look out for more free writing resources on the Sage website (https://study.sagepub.com/burnsandsinfield4e/).

Activity

Rich writing

Choose an object or a picture or a photograph in your home or in an art gallery. Sit with it for one hour – just focusing on it and being with it. Do not let anything outside of this activity interrupt your hour. You can make notes, doodles or draw pictures in your hour – but no conversations, no phones, no checking your accounts … After one hour, write just 300 words on your object – using your notes. Be strict and only write 300 words. Once you have edited your writing down to just 300 words, blog about the experience – sharing a picture of your artefact and sharing your writing. Reflect on how to use this experience to improve your academic writing. (For more on rich or thick writing – and other creative strategies, check out Paper Monument (ed.) (2012) *Draw It with Your Eyes Closed: The Art of the Art Assignment.* New York: Paper Monument.)

11.3

The Ten Step Approach to Better Assignments

Assessment can seem mysterious and daunting – we look at the why, what and how of assessment with a ten step approach to taking control of all your assignments.

- Introduction   168
- University assessments   168
- A beginner's guide to better assignments: ten steps ...   170
- It's a struggle – and then there's the feedback   175
- Dealing with feedback   177
- Summary: becoming a successful writer   178
- Activity: use the paragraph questions to prompt your writing   178

Introduction

Nobody really enjoys being assessed, being judged, it means that we can fail; we can make mistakes – mistakes that reveal us to be foolish or inadequate. Funnily enough, that is not really the point of assessment. Assessment is designed to be *of*, *for* and *about* learning. That is, a good assessment is designed to provoke active learning as we produce an assignment that 'shows what we know'. University assignments contribute to our final qualification – the final tally of your grades is used to award the level of your degree. Essays, reports, presentations, seminars … are some of the major forms of assessment used in universities; they each have their own structure and function. We look at these common assessment forms – and then offer a ten step approach to succeeding in any assignment that you are set. We conclude by discussing feedback and how to use it.

University assessments

As you read these, work out how knowing the information might help you to be a more successful student.

The essay

An essay (Chapter 12.1) is a discursive tool – you are supposed to argue for and against a topic and come to a reasoned conclusion using mainly theoretical evidence (what you have read). The essay demonstrates your analytical and critical thinking. One of the most formal academic forms, essays are typically written in the third person, past tense with extensive accurate references to supporting arguments and evidence taken from the key players in your discipline.

The report

A report (Chapter 12.2) is a practical document where you write up the findings of your investigation into real-world problems – think scientific experiment or business report. Reports are written for specific readers, in the third person, past tense and are signposted with headings and sub-headings.

The dissertation

A dissertation (Chapter 12.5) is an extended piece of writing associated with Honours level projects or postgraduate study – Masters or PhD. The dissertation records the findings and conclusions of independent research into specific phenomena. The typical dissertation structure is like that of a formal report, but it has an extended literature review and is written discursively like the essay.

The literature review

The literature review (Chapter 12.5) can be part of a dissertation – though some courses set a literature review as an assignment in its own right. The literature review demonstrates your exploration and understanding of the most up-to-date literature and research in the area that you are studying. The process of reading for and writing a literature review is designed to enable you to gain deep knowledge of the key issues and debates. Your literature review becomes your analysis of the most up-to-date and relevant knowledge-claims in your area and becomes a measuring stick against which you can compare your research findings.

The presentation

A presentation (Chapter 12.3) is a talk of a set length, on a set topic – to a known audience. It is similar in structure to the essay – but is supported by audiovisual aids. The purpose of the presentation is usually to demonstrate the student's subject knowledge and their oral communication skills.

The seminar

The seminar combines written and oral elements. The seminar giver has to present their research, normally to a group of fellow students. The research is discussed and new ideas generated. The workshop is becoming more popular than the seminar – here you teach something to a group of your peers and in a very inter-active and creative way. (For both see Chapter 12.4.)

The exam

The exam (Chapter 12.6) is designed to test learning. Students use information learned on a course in new situations. Exams can be open or closed book, time or word length limited, or other variations. Always know what sort of exam you are preparing for.

The reading record

A reading record is not an essay or a literature review. It is designed to be an annotated account of the reading a student has undertaken on a particular course. The annotations are not supposed to be descriptive: 'This book was about …' but analytical: 'This text is key for this topic outlining the major theoretical perspectives of …' or 'This text could be used to support the arguments of …' or 'However, Y and Z would take issue with the following aspects of the major arguments …'. A tutor might set a reading record to test that students are reading in an active and analytical way (Chapters 4 and 7) – thus your annotations should demonstrate your understanding of the text and its relationship to the key debates in your subject.

The annotated bibliography

An annotated bibliography is a condensed version of the reading record. A conventional bibliography records author (date) *title*, place of publication: publisher, in alphabetical order, by author's surname. In an annotated bibliography, you also note down information on a text's strengths or weaknesses; on how useful it was and why – in relation to the aims and learning outcomes of the module and the key theoretical debates of the discipline.

The digital artefact

A digital artefact (Chapter 10): as universities enter the digital age, some tutors are setting digital rather than written assignments. The most typical one that we have encountered is where students are asked to produce an artefact that could be used to teach or revise some part of the course. If set a task such as this, discover whether there are certain tools that you have to use – investigate just how creative you are allowed to be.

A beginner's guide to better assignments: ten steps …

We have looked at the *why* and the *what* of assessment, so let's now move on to *how* to prepare and write your assignments. We have broken this down into ten key stages.

1 Preparation

> The Americans talk about the five paragraph essay. This is where a typical 1,500 word essay has an introduction; three paragraphs and a conclusion. You are looking for one big idea per paragraph.

Start to work on an assignment as soon as possible: week one or two of your course would be good. Open a folder or an A4 envelope for every module that you do – and every question that you have to answer. Open the folder early and put information in there. Start collecting information from week one. Allow several weeks for reading and writing – and several more weeks to re-draft and refine your work. Work on it for half an hour a day and your academic life will be turned around.

PLANNING TIPS

- Write the whole question out exactly as it is.
- Put the question in your own words and say it back to another student or a tutor.
- Free write before you read.
- Underline every important word in the question – each is a research opportunity.
- Be creative: brainstorm and question matrix the key words (Chapters 6 and 7).
- Make sure that you do something about every word – don't leave any out.
- Add key words from the aims and learning outcomes module – research these as well (Chapter 11.1).
- Action plan: what will you now read? If working with a study partner or group – who will read what, when?

2 Targeted research and active reading

Once you understand the question and know what you are doing, read actively and interactively, using your active reading technique (Chapter 4) and asking questions as you go. Remember to get physical with the texts – mark them up, annotate, make comments and cross-reference. You will get much more from your reading when you do this.

Don't look for the whole answer to the question in any one piece of reading. When reading, look for references to plug the gaps in your free writing – or the answers to the questions generated by your brainstorm or question matrix (Chapters 6 and 7). Be generally alert and make notes of useful things you see, read and hear, and put the notes in your research folder. Record the source on the outside of the envelope – write: author (date) *title*, place of publication: publisher … and you will build up your bibliography as you go.

3 Make paragraph patterns

Gather information by topic – rather than by source. That is, as you read, do keep an index card record of everything that you read (Chapter 4) – but also put ideas and information straight into paragraph patterns. Paragraph patterns save time. Use the flowing steps to make paragraph patterns:

- Use really large sheets of paper – A1 rather than A4.
- Write on one side of the paper only – this way you can see all of your notes.
- Remember to put author (date) *title*, place of publication: publisher, and page numbers for quotes.
- Put a key word or phrase from the question in the centre of each sheet: your *paragraph pages*.
- Collect notes from different sources onto each paragraph page – once you have a few ideas or references – you can turn each paragraph pattern into a paragraph.

4 Write – read – write

As you are reading and making notes (and building your paragraph patterns) – take the time to draft possible paragraphs for your assignment. Do not wait until you have finished reading to start the writing.

─TIPS─

- You are not looking for the one right answer that already exists – there are usually several ways of tackling a question.
- Write your 'favourite' paragraph first to get you started.
- Free write a conclusion to get an idea of where you want your answer to go – change the conclusion later.
- Write ideas on separate pieces of paper. Move these around to discover the best structure for the answer.
- Remember a reader who keeps saying, 'What if …?' Your reader will be thinking of the opposite arguments and evidence: do not just ignore inconvenient or contradictory evidence – know what it is and argue against it.
- Remember a reader who keeps saying, 'So what?' Make points – remember the question (see Chapter 12.1).

5 Settle on a first draft

After you have struggled to write, read and write – settle on a first draft. Then and only then write a draft introduction and a draft conclusion to this first draft.

An introduction should acknowledge what an interesting or useful question it was – and should give the agenda of your essay – you should indicate how you are going to answer the question.

A conclusion has to prove that you have answered the whole question. Use the words from the question in your conclusion. Remember – do re-state main points; do not introduce new evidence.

6 Leave it!

Once you have achieved a first draft you feel great, your answer is great, your friends are great and life is great. Do not believe this! Put the work to one side and leave it for a while. This will give you some distance and objectivity, but more than this: your unconscious mind will seek to close the gaps that you left. The brain likes closure and will not be happy with all the gaps in your assignment. Thus your brain will struggle to close the gaps that you have left. If you allow a break in your writing process you are allowing the brain to close the gaps – you are working with your brain.

7 Review, revise and edit: struggle to write

This is the stage where you go back over your work and struggle to make it the very best it can be. Here you have to re-read what you have written – and change it. Sometimes we have to change everything – and nothing of our first draft gets left. This does not matter. We are writing to learn, so our thoughts *should* change as we write. Also, we would never get to a good version if we did not go through our rough versions.

Be prepared to draft and re-draft your work. Don't even try for perfection on a first draft – it is bad technique and it can actually stop you writing anything. On your first review, you might read from the beginning of your essay and improve, polish, as you go. After that, try to concentrate on one paragraph at a time – and not always in the order it is written but in any order.

TIPS

- Allow plenty of time for revising.
- Revising is where you go back and put in the 'best' word. This is where you put in the verbs. This is where you shorten long sentences so that you make clear, effective points.

- Index surf to brush up your paragraphs. That is, once you have completed your major research, and you are happy with it, you can index surf to get little extra bits and pieces to take your work that little bit further.
- When you have finished polishing paragraphs, check the 'links' between paragraphs – make sure that they still connect with each other.

8 Proof read

Once you are happy with your assignment, you are ready to stop revising it and to say: 'This is the best I can do'. Sometimes we are never really 'happy' with our work, but there still comes a time to stop and move on to the next task. At this point you have to proof read the final version.

Proof reading is not editing: you are not looking to make huge changes to what you have written, you are going through looking for mistakes, grammatical errors, tense problems, spelling mistakes or typographical errors.

You know that the brain likes closure – it will work to fill the gaps. This works against us when we are proof reading, it can mean that our eyes will 'see' what *should* be there rather than *what is there*. To get over this we have to make our proof reading 'strange'.

TIPS

- Read your assignment aloud (if it is a presentation, rehearse before a critical friend).
- Swap assignments with a friend – proof read each other's work.
- Cover the assignment with paper and proof read one sentence at a time.
- Proof read from back to front.
- Proof read from the bottom of the page to the top.
- Proof read for one of 'your' mistakes at a time.
- Like everything else we do, proof reading gets better with practice.

9 Hand it in – celebrate

You should now be ready to hand your work in on or before the deadline. And remember that deadline. On most university programmes a late submission is awarded an automatic fail – at best many marks are deducted. This is serious.

So once your assignment is done – congratulations! But before you rush off and celebrate remember to always keep copies of your work. Never hand in the only copy.

Obviously if you are writing on a computer, save your work to the hard drive and to a memory stick and email it to yourself and save in a 'cloud' – you can't be too careful!

If writing or producing something by hand – photocopy. And if the assessment unit loses your assignment, do not hand in your last copy – photocopy that. A student of ours came back and told us that the assessment unit lost her essay – the same one – three times!

10 Getting it back

When we get work back, we look at the grade, feel really happy or really unhappy, throw the work to one side and forget all about it. This is not a good idea.

What is a good idea is to review what you have written, and see if you still think it is good. As an active learner, you should try to take control of your own work and you have to learn how to judge it for yourself and not just rely on the tutor's opinions.

At the same time, you should also utilise the feedback that you get from the tutor. Be prepared to use that feedback to write a better essay next time. So a good thing to do is to perform a SWOT analysis of our own work, that is, look for the:

- Strengths
- Weaknesses
- Opportunities
- Threats.

When you SWOT your work look for the things that you think you did well or not so well. Then look for the things that the tutor appears to be telling you that you did well or not so well. Resolve to do something about your strengths and your weaknesses.

It's a struggle – and then there's the feedback

So assignments provide evidence of your achievement, but most importantly, the *process* of preparing an assignment is heuristic – it brings about powerful active learning. That is, as you wrestle with a question and struggle to read and write about it, you learn your subject. The learning cycle is completed when we receive and act upon feedback on our assignments.

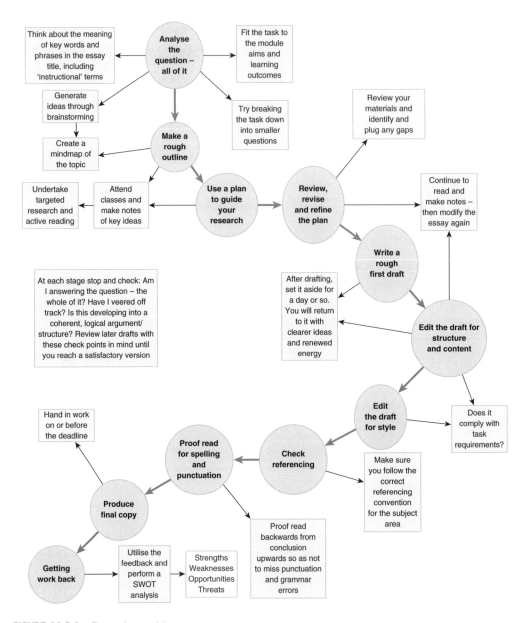

Think about the meaning of key words and phrases in the essay title, including 'instructional' terms

Analyse the question – all of it

Fit the task to the module aims and learning outcomes

Generate ideas through brainstorming

Make a rough outline

Try breaking the task down into smaller questions

Create a mindmap of the topic

Review your materials and identify and plug any gaps

Undertake targeted research and active reading

Attend classes and make notes of key ideas

Use a plan to guide your research

Review, revise and refine the plan

Continue to read and make notes – then modify the essay again

At each stage stop and check: Am I answering the question – the whole of it? Have I veered off track? Is this developing into a coherent, logical argument/ structure? Review later drafts with these check points in mind until you reach a satisfactory version

Write a rough first draft

After drafting, set it aside for a day or so. You will return to it with clearer ideas and renewed energy

Edit the draft for structure and content

Hand in work on or before the deadline

Proof read for spelling and punctuation

Check referencing

Edit the draft for style

Does it comply with task requirements?

Produce final copy

Make sure you follow the correct referencing convention for the subject area

Getting work back

Utilise the feedback and perform a SWOT analysis

Strengths Weaknesses Opportunities Threats

Proof read backwards from conclusion upwards so as not to miss punctuation and grammar errors

FIGURE 11.3.1 The assignment journey

Assessment and feedback

- Formative assessment is developmental. Designed to measure a student's progress at a particular moment in a subject, there should be an emphasis on tutor feedback where that feedback is designed to help you do better in the summative assessment.

- Summative assessment is final. Usually at the end of a programme of study, it is designed to measure the student's overall achievement in the unit, course or programme.
- Feedback. The best forms of assessment bring about learning in the student – especially when you can use the feedback that your tutors provide. Whether the assessment itself is formative or summative, most tutors will give you feedback on what you have written. This is a critical commentary designed to show you what you have done well (look for the ticks) – and what not so well (look for the advice about what you should have read – or referenced ...). Most students look at the grade – but forget to look at or use the feedback.

Always try to find three things that you did well in an assignment – and three things that you could have done better.

It helps if you view assessment in a positive light. Try to see assessment as a chance to:

- **be dynamic and creative and show what you know**
- **write to learn your material**
- **write often – for 30 minutes a day**
- **use the feedback (see below).**

Dealing with feedback

It's hard to take feedback – it can feel like a personal attack or rejection. We have to learn how to use the feedback that we get. Here is how one student responded to some short sharp feedback. (Examples taken with permission from 'An Essay Evolves': http://evolvingessay.pbworks.com/w/page/19387227/FrontPage.)

The assessor's feedback on the assignment:

... could be improved by having a clearer focus and a stronger take-home message, which could perhaps be achieved by interpreting the title in a narrower way.

The student's response:

I feel that in this case (and in some others!) I slipped away from my main task which is usually identified by a thorough question analysis. Looking back, instead of presenting the strengths and weaknesses of Freud's theory of personality as measured against the yardstick of evidential science I decided at too early a point to become an advocate for it. I tried also to question the appropriateness of the paradigm often used to assess Freud when it might have profited me (in terms of more marks) to stick with it. It may have helped me achieve the stronger take-home message counselled by the assessor. And interestingly, in this case I carried out my question analysis belatedly.

,

That's a brilliant way to respond to what must have felt like really negative feedback. She had worked long and hard on that task – and then it must have felt like it was being attacked. Would you have been able to do that? It is something we all have to learn – how to listen to feedback whilst not taking offence – not taking it personally – but thinking of what to do differently next time.

For more of this student's essay, search online for 'An Essay Evolves' – and read the essay as it developed – and the student's blog about her thoughts and feelings when writing the essay.

Summary: becoming a successful writer

We have considered the what, why and how of assessment – arguing that the assessment *process* is part of becoming a graduate whilst the *products* provide tangible evidence of your work. We stressed the active learning aspects of assessment: all the reading, thinking, discussing and struggling that you do to produce an assignment. We divided the assignment process into ten manageable stages – and considered how to approach feedback. You should now feel in a better position to approach your assignments.

Activity

Use the paragraph questions to prompt your writing

For each paragraph that you write – answer the following questions:

- What is this paragraph about?
    - introduce topic (and claim)
- What exactly is that?
    - define/clarify/explain
- What is your argument?
    - give argument in relation to question

- What is the evidence? What does it mean?

  ○ offer evidence and discuss it

- What is the opposing evidence? What does that mean?

  ○ Therefore …?

- What is your final point (in relation to the question)?

  ○ tie what you have written to the question. It is not down to your reader to guess what you are try-ing to say – or to think 'I wonder how this relates to the question?' If your reader has to do that then something is missing from your answer.

Access the companion website to this book and find helpful resources for this chapter topic:
https://study.sagepub.com/burnsandsinfield4e

11.4
How to Reference and Avoid Plagiarism

'Many students I met did not understand referencing straight away. They wanted to write something that showed what *they* thought, not what someone else had said. We didn't understand that using someone else's argument is a tool to support our own. Students are very keen for you to "see" them, to hear their voice. In many ways we are puppies wanting to please. We need to know why referencing does not detract from our own voice being heard.'

- Introduction   182
- Should I reference?   182
- Some reasons for plagiarising   183
- Summary   185
- Activity: use your index cards   186

Introduction

> To my mind there is a solution. We need to chill out. First year students should be given time and freedom to learn. During this time plagiarism should not result in punishment for the student, but should be seen as a weakness of the teaching. Students should be free to make mistakes, and every university should be teaching referencing positively with the same rigour you would expect for any subject. After all, if it is that important, then we should be willing to give students time to learn how to reference correctly.

The English university system is based on research and independent learning: you are not *taught* your degree, but are expected *to read for it*: in the process you are acquiring ideas, arguments and evidence from other people. This may feel frustrating – you want to tell us what you think; but it is the academic way – you are expected to learn from and use the ideas of others. The reading that you do to prepare for your assignments helps you to engage with the thinkers in your subject – and it provides you with more ideas, knowledge-claims, arguments and evidence to develop your thinking and your writing. Yes, you are not 'empty', you do already have ideas and thoughts of your own, but you are supposed to do this reading to deepen your understanding and engage with the key people, ideas, concepts and theories that make up the subject you are studying.

Much is made in university of plagiarism and plagiarism offences – even first year students may be punished for not correctly showing their sources even if they stumble into plagiarism by accident. The aim of this chapter is to briefly discuss the what, why and how of referencing – and to explore some common reasons for accidental plagiarism – and how to avoid them. Meanwhile, keep this image in your mind: if studying is exploration, your *references are your maps* – recording your footsteps through the subject as it already exists.

—TIP—

When you read, record your sources immediately. Use online apps or index cards to keep a record of everything that you read – as you read it. Read Chapter 4 on how to survive academic reading.

Should I reference?

> Soon after the end of my first semester at university I heard about a course friend who had been accused of plagiarising. I never saw him again as he left soon after,

his confidence having been taken away by the experience. His 'crime' was simply that he had been educated in a different country that looks upon these things in a different way, and he had not fully understood the consequences of not properly referencing. To me though, the real crime was that education had lost a bright and inquisitive mind.

When you write, when you deliver a presentation, you must reference every time you 'refer to' or quote other people. This includes when you paraphrase their ideas – it even includes when you agree with them. For example, if you believe that we learn best when we learn actively, you might write:

Burns and Sinfield (2012) argue that we learn best when we learn actively and interactively.

Acknowledging a source does not weaken your own opinion – it demonstrates that you have ideas – and that you are prepared to do the reading to support your ideas. Your references show what a good student you are. Check out the flow chart in Figure 11.4.1.

TIPS

- Use Manchester University's Academic Phrasebank for examples of *how to write about your sources*. This link takes you straight to that section: www.phrase bank.manchester.ac.uk/referring-to-sources/.
- This easy to use resource from Nottingham shows how to reference: www.notting ham.ac.uk/nmp/sonet/rlos/studyskills/harvard/.
- If you want to follow this further, feel free to use both our Preventing Plagiarism and our Heroes & Villains websites:
  - http://learning.londonmet.ac.uk/TLTC/learnhigher/Plagiarism/ – if the link breaks, search online for LearnHigher + preventing plagiarism.
  - http://learning.londonmet.ac.uk/epacks/heroes-&-villains/ – if the link breaks, do an online search for Londonmet + Heroes and Villains.

Some reasons for plagiarising

Here are some reasons other students have given for plagiarising. As you read, think about how you could avoid making the mistakes that they made:

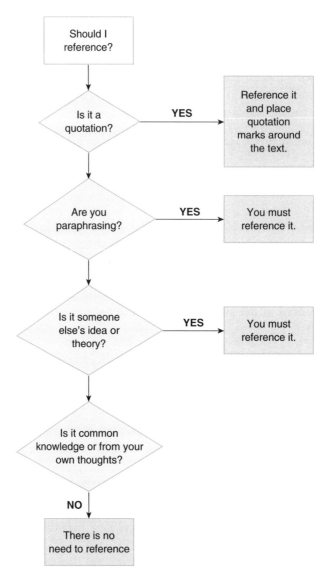

FIGURE 11.4.1 Should I reference?

 We were working on the assignment together. It was a group project – but we were supposed to write individual reports. Somehow, I couldn't write a different report to my mate – so I copied her version and handed it in as my own. I was punished for plagiarism and got zero for that module.

I had done the reading for that assignment ages ago. When I finally wrote it up, I couldn't remember what was my work and what I'd read. I really didn't know that this was plagiarism ...

I found an essay on the web that was exactly on my topic. I did write my own introduction and conclusion – but it was still plagiarism. I'm lucky I didn't get suspended.

Well I did read that stuff – but it was what I was thinking anyway – so I didn't think I had to give any sources. Turns out I was wrong …

I just thought I had to write a bibliography at the end. No! You have to mention your reading as you write. You have to give the name and date of the source *where* you refer to it – and you have to give the page number as well if you actually quote it. Then you have to give the full author, date, title, town, publisher in the bibliography as well.

I thought I was doing well. I put all the good quotes down on the page – and just wrote little bits of essay around them. But that didn't work. You have to put it in your own words – still giving a reference – and discuss it. The tutor said I'd just handed in my notes rather than an essay. She said I was lucky not to be accused of plagiarism – and to digest my reading first next time. It's quite hard getting this bit right – harder than I thought it would be.

What advice would you have given these people? What advice would you give yourself if you find yourself doing these things? One big piece of advice would be to give yourself *time* to read, write and understand.

Further, these students did the reading but obviously did not record enough *source* information. Develop the habit of recording your sources every time you make notes. You save time – and you have your index cards to use again in future assignments. Remember to record the page numbers too in case you want to quote. Read Chapter 4 on how to survive academic reading.

A third issue seems to be about not understanding the referencing tradition in academic life. You are supposed to note where ideas come from. Even when you agree with what you are reading – or where the author agrees with you – you still have to acknowledge that those ideas also emerged from somebody in your subject. Your subject has not just been born – the ideas are out there – they exist in the history and practice of your subject. You are showing off what a good student you are when you reference these ideas – when you acknowledge those debates – especially when you do so correctly.

Summary

 So, what do I think? Well, I feel all this stuff on plagiarism comes from the wrong angle and I would turn this topic on its head. It isn't about plagiarism and in many ways it isn't about referencing, it's about being honest and having integrity. It is also about community. I reference every single day through sharing on Facebook, re-blogging and re-tweeting on Twitter. I want to acknowledge (and associate myself) when someone has said something I agree with or with something that supports my argument or beliefs. It is positive – and in social media it is inclusive and empowering for the person you're sharing.

We hope that you can see that giving references reveals that you are an engaged, thinking, focused student – yes, you have opinions of your own – but you have also done the reading. When you write with reference to your reading, you are showing that you have understood your subject, you can use sources well and you are joining your academic community – you are joining the conversation.

In our experience, many students plagiarise because they do not understand the convention of referencing – or because they agree with what they are reading … Do not plagiarise by mistake! Give yourself time to read and digest information. Keep good records of your sources and make sure you understand how to reference correctly – both in your writing and in your bibliographies. Plagiarism is treated as a serious academic offence – even when you do it in ignorance or by mistake. If in doubt, explore our Heroes & Villains website – or use the Preventing Plagiarism tutorial (search online). In the learning resources section of that resource, there are small animations that show you how to reference correctly – from a range of sources. Look at these animations and make sure you see and understand what is going on.

Activity

Use your index cards

Every time you read, keep a record – author (date) *title*, place of publication: publisher:

Author(s):

Date:

Title:

Place published:

Publisher:

Key quotes (and page numbers):

Always note these essential details so you can cite them correctly in assignments – and in your bibliographies:

- Record details of your reading on your index cards. Note the information above on one side of the card.
- Experiment: you could note what essay you used the book for; you could note the chapter or paragraph headings – so that you have an outline of the book; you can note a couple of good quotes … The trick is to make this process as useful to you as possible.
- There is software, extensions to browsers and apps for phones, tablets and computers which can also be used.

PART IV
THE BIG ASSESSMENT
TOOLKIT
ASSESSMENTS – HOW TO EXCEL

12.1

How to Write Great Essays

The essay is the most persistent and the most popular academic assessment – with tutors. We explore the what, why and how of the essay. The trick is to have a point of view and use the essay to argue for it. Note: this chapter is supported by an Essay Writing Pack downloadable from the Sage website (https://study.sagepub.com/burnsandsinfield4e/).

- Introduction 192
- What is an essay? 192
- The essay – legal precedent 192
- The essay explained 193
- Why write essays? 196
- How to prepare and write an essay 197
- How to use the question 199
- A beginner's guide to essay writing 201
- How to write paragraphs: it's a conversation 202
- SWOT it: using feedback 204
- Summary 204
- Activity: use the essay checklist 205

Introduction

The essay is the most common form of assessment – it requires you to struggle with a question – and then to struggle to answer it. You are supposed to write using evidence you have found in your reading … and shape the essay in a way that answers the question set. Some resent the essay as it feels a bit boring to just give back to the tutor everything that they have just given you on the course. You can change this if you are engaged and interested: so, find your course interesting and be creative with your thinking. Learn to enjoy writing persuasive essays that convince your reader of your point of view in relation to the question and your stance in relation to the reading. Make your essays enjoyable to read. If you do this – you may actually get to enjoy the essay writing process. In this chapter we are going to look at the what, why and how of essays.

What is an essay?

The essay is the great analytical and critical thinking form. It is where we write about our research (our reading) in a way that is designed to answer a set question: it is *discursive* writing. Discursive means coming to a conclusion not based on intuition (I believe or feel that this is right) or assertion (I say that it is right) – but by reasoning: by the use of argument and evidence. Good essay writing involves learning to communicate effectively in concise, targeted writing – that answers the question. If we can communicate our ideas effectively we will get better marks.

The word 'essay' comes from the Latin word *exagium*, which means the presentation of a case. When building an essay, think like a lawyer prosecuting or defending a client. When defending a client, it is not enough for the defence to say, 'He didn't do it, your honour!' The defence has to look for evidence to prove their client's innocence. They also have to predict what the other side will say – and look for evidence to counter it. They have to make a case. That is what the academic essay is all about.

The essay – legal precedent

The defence might open with an introduction that lays out the whole case in brief:

> The defence will prove that the case against our client is utterly mistaken. In particular we will prove that he could not have been identified as being at the scene of the crime for it was too dark to make a definite identification. We will tell you

that the so-called witness suffers from poor vision and therefore could not identify our client. Finally, we will conclusively prove that our client was somewhere else at the time.

The defence then elaborates upon those three key points:

1. The alley was too dark blah blah …
2. The witness was not wearing his glasses blah blah …
3. My client has an alibi for the time blah blah …

The defence might conclude by reiterating all those points:

In conclusion, we argue that despite everything that the prosecution has said, you must find our client innocent because we have conclusively proven his innocence. He definitely could not have been identified as being at the scene of the crime. Firstly, it was too dark to positively identify anyone, further the witness was too short sighted to have any value placed upon his testimony and finally we proved beyond a shadow of a doubt that our client was somewhere else at the time of the incident.

TIPS

When it comes to searching for the answer to academic essay questions, use the legal model and:

- **break the whole question down into mini-points that can be covered one at a time**
- **think of a case that you want to make**
- **think of the separate arguments that would go to making your case**
- **search for evidence for and against your arguments – from your reading**
- **write your introduction/conclusion last**
- **see the essay plans/structures shown in Figures 12.1.1 and 12.1.2, below.**

The essay explained

An essay has a formal convention – a set style to which it must conform or it is not an essay. The convention is as follows:

The body

This is the section of the essay where you answer the question that you have been set. It can be 80% of the total word length. You answer the question in a

Body/Main argument = 80% length

Answer the question in a chain of paragraphs that build and present a *case*.

Each paragraph should contain:

One big idea
Introduce
Define
Offer argument
Offer evidence and discuss
Make final point

The reader is asking you – and your writing should answer – the following questions:

- What is this paragraph about?
- What exactly is that?
- What is your argument on this (in relation to the question)?
- What is your evidence? What does it mean?
- What is the final point (in relation to the question)?

Remember to include a title and any other information asked for in your module booklet

Introduction = 5% length

Tells the reader how you will answer the question. Your introduction should:

- Comment on the title or topic of the essay
- Define or explain any difficult or ambiguous terms in the title
- Direct the reader by stating which aspects of the topic you intend to cover and *why*

Write last, once you know where the essay is going

Conclusion = 15% length

- Re-state your arguments
- Re-state the main points
- **Do not introduce** new evidence
- You could make recommendations
- Proves that you have answered the whole question

Plan, Draft, Review, Revise & Edit

Bibliography
Author (date) *Title*, Place of publication: Publisher, Page numbers. In alphabetical order by author's surname

FIGURE 12.1.1 Developing a plan or structure for your essay

chain of paragraphs that you have organised to build a well-argued case. Note: Typically written in the third person, past tense. That is: It can be argued that … *not* I think this …

Paragraph structure

Each paragraph also has a set convention: introduction; definition; argument; evidence plus discussion; final point. This is where it is useful to remember that you are communicating with a *reader*. When writing, imagine your reader asking you questions and make sure that your writing answers them.

Paragraph as dialogue

- What is this paragraph about?
  - Introduce your topic.
- What exactly is that?
  - Define, explain or clarify.
- What is the argument – in relation to the question?
  - Say something about your topic.
- What is the evidence? What does it mean?
  - Say who or what supports your argument. Give evidence. Say what the evidence means.
- What is your final point? (How does this paragraph relate to the question as a whole?)
  - Take the paragraph back to the question.

---TIP---

Write these questions out on an index card and stick them on your computer screen. Look at them when you write.

The introduction

This is the first part of the essay. It can be between 5% and 10% of the total length – written as one long paragraph. In the introduction you write some remarks that acknowledge the importance of the topic and tell the reader how you are going to answer the question. You then give the agenda of the essay.

---TIP---

Write the introduction *after* you have written the essay paragraphs – when you know where the essay is going. Writing it too soon will give you a writing block.

The conclusion

This is the last, often long, paragraph of the essay. It can be 10 to 15% of the length. In the conclusion you restate your main arguments and points in a way that proves that you have answered the whole question. You do not include new information or evidence, but you may make recommendations if appropriate.

─TIP─

Use the words from the question in your conclusion to prove that you have answered all of it. Obviously write your real conclusion last – but some people like to draft a conclusion first to see where they want the essay to go.

Bibliography

Literally a book list, it is a record of all the sources you have used to construct your essay.

─TIP─

The most popular form of bibliography entry at the moment is the Harvard system: author (date) *title*, place of publication: publisher:

Burns, T. and Sinfield, S. (2016) *Essential Study Skills: The Complete Guide to Success at University*, London: Sage.

Why write essays?

All assignments are designed to be heuristic, to bring about active learning; the essay is the form that is designed to get you to undertake *deep* learning of your subject. There are many who say that we cannot be said to really understand what we are learning until we can write an essay on it. Make the most of your essay writing opportunities. Read the key books and journal articles. Make notes that you can use to answer *this* question – but that you might also use again and again at university. The trick is for you to find a way to say what you want to say on the assignment, whilst using the rules of the essay correctly. Don't let worrying about the essay stop you from thinking your own thoughts. You just need to argue your case using the evidence that is right for your subject – and for *that* question.

─TIP─

Enjoy your course. Be clever and original and yourself.

How to prepare and write an essay

 So I learned how to write and I learned how to structure from my reading. Sometimes I used to copy from the book to see the way they just write it down ... then through that experience I started knowing how to structure my phrases and my writing. It just ... I don't know, it just got better through practising. That's the main thing.

We cover the ten steps to assignment success in Chapter 11.3 – and that is the general rule when approaching your essays: break down the question – write/read/write – settle on a first draft – leave a time lag – review/revise/edit – proof read.

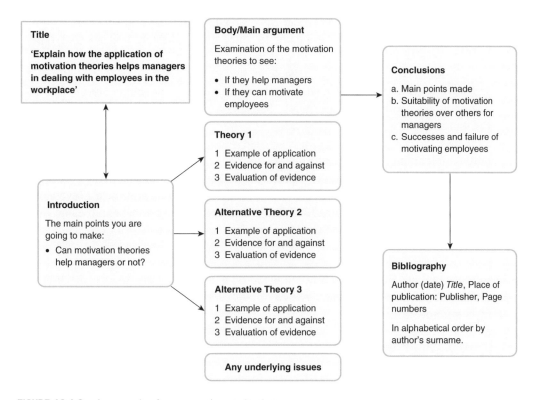

FIGURE 12.1.2   An example of an essay plan or structure

ESSAY WRITING TIPS

- *Blog it*: don't just write for an assignment, write little and often and you will see that your writing really does improve with practice. It is very similar to learning to play a musical instrument; you only get better if you practise. So write a daily or weekly blog of your learning – enjoy this writing – and all your writing will also improve.

- *Free write* (see Chapter 11.2): when you get your module handbook go straight to the assignments. Give yourself ten minutes to start writing an answer to any of the questions that look interesting. Do not worry about getting the answer 'right', just write and see what comes out. When you have finished you should be able to see what you already know about the subject – and what you need to find out. This will help you make more sense of the course – and it will help you to make more sense of the reading you have to do.

- *Learn how to concentrate on one thing at a time*: typically, you will be studying several courses or modules at the same time. Each course will have several assignments and often hand-in dates will be the same or very nearly so. In any one assessment week you may have to hand in two or more different assignments. So, if you are writing essay A, you need to be able to *not worry* about essays B, C and D; you need to be able to put the other essays on a mental shelf and only take them down one at a time when you are going to concentrate on them. This is a trick that gets easier with practice.

- *Get a receipt*: when handing your work in always get and keep a receipt so that you have proof that you handed work in on or before a deadline. Never miss a deadline, even to improve your work, because a missed deadline tends to mean the work will be awarded a fail grade.

- *Read 'An Essay Evolves'*: if you are worried about writing essays – or if you are really not looking forward to writing essays – check out the *An Essay Evolves* wiki and blog – see how an essay on Freud evolved. See what that psychology student writing the essay thought about the *process*. Find it here: http://evolving essay.pbworks.com/w/page/19387227/FrontPage (or do a web search using the key words: Evolving essay + Freud).

Use proof reading symbols: Proof reading can be easier if you use the proof reading symbols that publishers use when you go through various drafts of your work. So try using the following:

⊔⊓ TRS, transpose words

≡ UC, upper case

≢ LC, lower case

⋋ Insert word or letter

⌒ Delete word/section

⌢ Close gap

⋎ Insert gap

.... Stet – Leave as it is

How to use the question

Essay questions never ask you to write all you know on a topic – they always tell you *how* you are supposed to go about answering the question. It just takes a little practice to understand what the question is asking you to do. Some argue that it helps to break the question down into the following components:

- *Instruction*: what is the question telling you to do? Assess, discuss, evaluate? It is important to interpret these words properly.
- *Topic*: what is the essay about?
- *Focus*: once you know the topic you need to know which aspect of it to focus on.
- *Limitations*: a question is never: 'Write all you know about …'. The restrictions will limit your discussion and help you shape your essay.

Here is an example to demonstrate what we mean:

- *Essay question*: 'Assess the importance of free writing for a student's academic success'
  - *Instruction:* assess the importance
  - *Topic*: free writing
  - *Focus*: academic success
  - *Limit*: student

In this example you are not asked to write all you know about free writing, but you are expected to assess its usefulness in promoting academic success for students. You would need to understand something about being a student – and about what constitutes academic success. You would have to define *free writing* – and say what it can do – but you have to show how a *student* might benefit from using that to enhance their *academic success*.

Knowing what the essay is asking you to do moves you on from *describing* a situation to *using* information analytically and critically to answer the question. It diverts you from seeing one key word in a question and writing about that (big mistake!) to seeing the whole question. There are several instruction words used in essay questions – sometimes thinking about these words helps you think about the essay as a whole. The list below gives advice on how to approach them in your thinking.

Common instruction words

Account for	**Give reasons for; explain why something happens.**
Analyse	**Break up into parts; investigate.**

(Continued)

(Continued)

Assess	Decide the importance of and give reasons for.
Comment on	Identify and write about the main issues; give your reactions based on what you've read/heard in lectures. Avoid just personal opinion.
Compare	Look for the similarities between two things. Show the relevance or consequences of these similarities. Perhaps conclude which is preferable.
Contrast	Bring out the differences between two items or arguments. Show whether the differences are significant. Perhaps give reasons why one is preferable.
Critically evaluate	Weigh arguments for and against something, assessing the strength of the evidence on both sides. Use criteria to guide your assessment of which opinions, theories, models or items are preferable.
Criticise	Requires an answer that points out mistakes or weaknesses, and which also indicates any favourable aspects of the subject of the question. It requires a balanced answer.
Define	Give the exact meaning of. Where relevant, show you understand how the definition may be problematic.
Describe	Give a detailed account of.
Discuss	Investigate or examine by argument; sift and debate; give reasons for and against; examine the implications of.
Distinguish between	Bring out the differences between.
Evaluate	Assess and give your judgement about the merit, importance or usefulness of something. Back your judgement with evidence.
Examine	Look closely into something.
Explain	Make clear why something happens, or is the way it is; interpret and account for; give reasons for.
Explore	Examine thoroughly; consider from a variety of viewpoints.
Illustrate	Make something clear and explicit, giving examples of evidence.
Interpret	Show the meaning and relevance of data or other material presented.

Justify	Give evidence which supports an argument or idea; show why a decision or conclusions were made; answer the main objections which might be made.
Narrate	Outline what happened.
Outline	Give the main points/features/general principles; show the main structure and interrelations; omit details and examples.
Prove/disprove	Both of these require answers which demonstrate the logical arguments and/or evidence connected with a proposition: prove requires the 'pro' points, and disprove requires the 'contra' points.
Relate	(a) Narrate (b) Show similarities and connections between.
State	Give the main features briefly and clearly.
Summarise/ outline	Draw out the main points only; omit details and examples.
To what extent ...	Consider how far something is true, or contributes to a final outcome. Consider also ways in which it is not true.
Trace	Follow the development or history of an event or process.

—TIP—

Make some notes about key words and how they will help you write your essays.

A beginner's guide to essay writing

If you are writing an essay right now, smile, try to enjoy it, and put the ten step process into operation – but first – really, really focus on the question. *Write down the whole question – underline key or task words.* Then:

1. Write down in your own words what you think the assignment is asking you to do.
2. What do you already know about the subject matter of the essay?
3. What background information do you need to help you to complete this essay?
4. How do you think this essay differs from or is similar to other assignments that you are working on at the moment?
5. What are you going to read – and why?
6. As you begin to read for your assignment, make notes with the essay in mind.

Is this how you would normally approach an assignment question? If not – have a go at using this with your next assignment. Afterwards – reflect on how well it works for you.

Now – apply in practice the ten stages of the assignment journey.

┤TIPS├

For a quick reminder of the ten stages – check out our Prezi: https://prezi.com/lpabb3d2fohv/ten-stages-of-assignment-success/.

1. *Prepare*: analyse the question (as above) and devise an action plan – note what you are going to do and read to get the essay ready. When will you do these things?
2. *Targeted research and active reading*: photocopy chapters from books and print journal articles. Read actively and interactively, marking the texts as you go and always keeping the question in mind. Make active notes focusing on one key word or phrase at a time.
3. *Paragraph patterns*: construct notes as paragraph patterns. Collect together all the information for each potential paragraph (see Chapter 5).
4. *Write – read – write*: follow the rough structure you have found. Write quickly and without correcting yourself. Go with the flow. Use the paragraph questions. Make sure you leave gaps – and write blah blah rather than struggling for a perfect draft first go. Read some more.
5. *Settle on a first draft*: your rough draft should have gaps and prompts so your brain knows your writing is incomplete.
6. *Leave a time lag*: put the work to one side, think about something else. Let your unconscious continue working on the essay.
7. *Review, revise and edit*: struggle to draft and re-draft your essay. Make sure each paragraph does answer all the paragraph questions. Make sure the essay is in the best 'shape'.
8. *Proof read*: at some point you have to stop writing and decide that the essay is finished. Proof read the final draft. Correct your mistakes. Keep copies on different devices.
9. *Submit*: hand in on or before the deadline – and get and keep your receipt. Go and celebrate – be happy – be proud.
10. *SWOT your progress*: get your essay back and do not just look at the grade – look at the feedback you received and work out how to build on your strengths, correct your weaknesses and write a better essay next time.

How to write paragraphs: it's a conversation

One way of writing a paragraph is to imagine a conversation between you and your reader. Imagine your reader's questions and write to answer them.

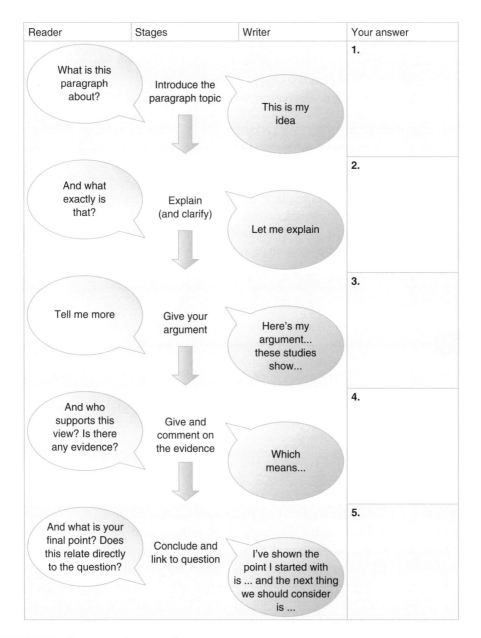

Reader	Stages	Writer	Your answer
What is this paragraph about?	Introduce the paragraph topic	This is my idea	1.
And what exactly is that?	Explain (and clarify)	Let me explain	2.
Tell me more	Give your argument	Here's my argument... these studies show...	3.
And who supports this view? Is there any evidence?	Give and comment on the evidence	Which means...	4.
And what is your final point? Does this relate directly to the question?	Conclude and link to question	I've shown the point I started with is ... and the next thing we should consider is ...	5.

FIGURE 12.1.3   The paragraph conversation

TIPS

- Photocopy the paragraph conversation diagram and use it when writing your real essays. This works!
- Print your essay. Cut up the paragraphs. Mix them up. Put them in the best order.

SWOT it: using feedback

Always make the effort to go and get your work back – yes, you only care about your grade, but there is so much to learn from the thing itself, especially if you have a tutor who likes to scribble all over your assignments. SWOT your essay:

- *Strengths*: go through the essay very carefully; look at all the ticks and positive comments. These indicate that you have done something well. Check out the good things you have done – make a note to do them again.
- *Weaknesses*: look at all the passages without ticks or with comments suggesting that something is missing or incorrect. Note these: make a note to do something about them. Go and find the missing information – correct errors.
- *Opportunities*: think what you can do now to learn the subject better or improve your grades. Think how to write a better essay in your next module.
- *Threats*: ask yourself if anything is stopping you from doing better work. Find out what it is and do something about it. Sometimes we can be frightened of success just as much as of failure – is this you? What are you going to do about it?

TIPS

- **If you can answer an exam question on a topic previously covered in an assignment: improve it – reduce it to key points – put it in your revision folder.**
- **Share it. Read each other's work, discover different writing styles and other ways to answer a question – this stretches our thinking.**

Summary

The essay is the big elephant in the room in education. Most people do not like writing them – it feels artificial to just pour back all the 'stuff' that you have been taught in this way. The big trick is to find something enjoyable or interesting or quirky in your course – and use that to get you interested or engaged in your own thinking/writing. Discover something that your tutor obviously cares passionately about – and work that into your essay – whilst still remembering to answer the question that you were set. In this way you add additional challenge to the task and that makes it more interesting.

Remember the structure of the essay and use that to build a logical case using argument and evidence from your reading. Enjoy the 'struggle to write' – it is the learning process: we write to learn rather than learn to write. Finally don't forget the ten stages to preparing your assignments – this process gets you through the struggle in the most straightforward way possible. We hope that you now feel in a better position to approach your assignment essays. Good luck.

Activity

Use the essay checklist

For every essay check:

- ☐ Have you answered the whole question?
- ☐ Have you addressed the aims and learning outcomes?
- ☐ Is there an introduction that acknowledges the significance of the question and gives the agenda of the essay?
- ☐ Would that agenda actually answer the question set?
- ☐ Are the paragraphs in the best possible order?
- ☐ Does each paragraph have its own introduction, definition, argument, evidence and final point?
- ☐ Have you referenced your evidence?
- ☐ Have you discussed your evidence?
- ☐ Is there a conclusion re-stating the main arguments and points?
- ☐ Do you use all the words from the question to prove that you have answered the whole question?
- ☐ Is there a comprehensive bibliography (referring to every source you have mentioned in the essay)?
- ☐ Is the bibliography in alphabetical order by author's surname?
- ☐ Have you proof read and made corrections?

Access the companion website to this book and find helpful resources for this chapter topic:
https://study.sagepub.com/burnsandsinfield4e

12.2

How to Produce Excellent Reports

Whilst the essay is theoretical, discursive, the report is more practical, investigating a real world issue or problem in order to find practical solutions. This chapter is designed to help you to plan, prepare and produce excellent reports. Supported by a Report Writing Pack downloadable from the Sage website (https://study.sagepub.com/burnsandsinfield4e/).

- Introduction   208
- What is a report?   208
- The ideal report   210
- Why write reports?   215
- A beginner's guide to writing a report   216
- Reports our students have written   218
- Summary   223
- Activity: answer the reader questions   223

Introduction

Report writing has always been part of science and business courses and it is becoming an increasingly popular academic assessment in other subjects too. The big difference between the report and the essay is that whilst the essay is theoretical and discursive, the report is practical and analytical. In this chapter we will be looking at the what, why and how of reports. As always – the trick is to try and enjoy this form of assessment as much as possible. Where you are given some choice in what to investigate for your report, choose something in which you are really interested and you will be more successful. We think that our students demonstrate this in their work – see the excerpts from their reports that we have included at the end of this chapter.

What is a report?

The essence of the report is that it is a document designed to deal with the real world. Specifically, a report is a practical document that details or analyses a situation in the real world such that the reader can make decisions or take specific actions about that situation.

In a business report a company's recruitment policy might be analysed to see if it is attracting the 'right' people. Here there may be an active drive to recruit more diverse employees, for example. The report writers would know that they were investigating only a specific aspect of recruitment – whether they were diverse enough – and they would know who they were writing the report for – usually senior managers. Thus they might use a SWOT analysis to investigate how their recruitment did and did not attract diverse applicants – and then write the report for those managers – using the right language, tone, style and evidence.

A typical science report might detail a laboratory experiment – at its simplest this would be a third person past tense account of what you actually did: the aims of the experiment; the method that was adopted (20 mm of XX was pipetted into 30 mm of YY …); the results obtained; the conclusions drawn. This detail allows a neutral reader to judge the usefulness of the way that the experiment was carried out – to judge the validity of results obtained and the conclusions drawn.

It could be argued that what these reports have in common are:

- Each report is designed to investigate a real issue and give information to specific readers.
- Each writer of a report knows what sort of reader they are writing for: this affects the research they do – and how they present their information.

	Literature Review	General Scientific Report	Chemistry Report	Laboratory Report	Non-scientific Report	Standard Business Report	Research Report
1	Title page	Title page	Title page	Title page	Title page	Title page	Title page
2	Abstract	Abstract	Abstract	Introduction	Introduction	Executive summary	Executive summary
3	Introduction	Abbreviations	Abbreviations	Materials and methods	Main body of text	Acknowledgements	Introduction
4	Main body of text	Introduction	Introduction	Discussion	Conclusion	Table of contents	Method/methodology
5	Conclusion	Materials and methods	Results	Conclusion		Main body of text	Results/findings
6	References	Results	Discussion			Conclusion	Discussion
7		Discussion	Materials and methods			Recommendation	Conclusion
8		Acknowledgements	Acknowledgements			Bibliography/References	Recommendation
9		References	References			Appendices	Appendices
10						Glossary	Bibliography

FIGURE 12.2.1 Types of report

- The writer will expect the reader to understand and perhaps act on the information in the report.
- The reader knows what to look for in the report – and will know how to use the report to make decisions.

—TIP—

Think about these aspects when writing your own reports. Always ask: why have I been asked to write this report? What am I supposed to investigate and why? Who is my reader? What should I read to get my evidence? What should I do?

The ideal report

In this section we discuss the different parts of a report in some detail – as always – as you read – think: how will knowing this help me write better reports? Make notes so that you do not forget the important points.

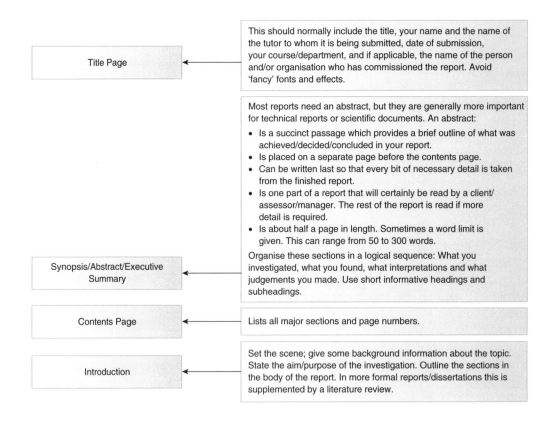

Title Page

This should normally include the title, your name and the name of the tutor to whom it is being submitted, date of submission, your course/department, and if applicable, the name of the person and/or organisation who has commissioned the report. Avoid 'fancy' fonts and effects.

Synopsis/Abstract/Executive Summary

Most reports need an abstract, but they are generally more important for technical reports or scientific documents. An abstract:

- Is a succinct passage which provides a brief outline of what was achieved/decided/concluded in your report.
- Is placed on a separate page before the contents page.
- Can be written last so that every bit of necessary detail is taken from the finished report.
- Is one part of a report that will certainly be read by a client/assessor/manager. The rest of the report is read if more detail is required.
- Is about half a page in length. Sometimes a word limit is given. This can range from 50 to 300 words.

Organise these sections in a logical sequence: What you investigated, what you found, what interpretations and what judgements you made. Use short informative headings and subheadings.

Contents Page

Lists all major sections and page numbers.

Introduction

Set the scene; give some background information about the topic. State the aim/purpose of the investigation. Outline the sections in the body of the report. In more formal reports/dissertations this is supplemented by a literature review.

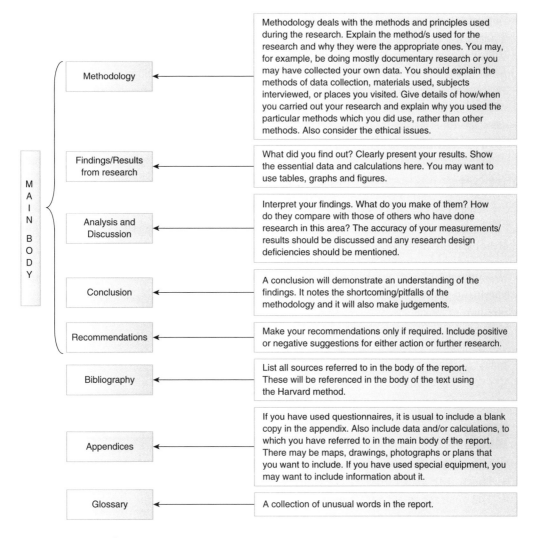

FIGURE 12.2.2 The ideal report

Title page

This is the front sheet of the report. This should include: title, sub-title; date; author's name and position; distribution list (reader(s) name(s) and positions(s)); reference number/course details/statements of confidentiality:

- *Title and sub-title*: usually divided by a colon. The title gives the big picture of the report – the sub-title narrows this down. Thus the title gives a focus of the report and the sub-title indicates the scope of the report – the 'terms of reference' of the report.
- *Date*: places the report in real time.

- *Author's name and position*: when you write a university report you are often told to assume a position – public relations expert, tax consultant … You have to write the report as though you were that person. Revealing who you 'are' tells the reader where the report is 'coming from' – and thus it reveals what angle you might be expected to adopt on the topic.
- *Distribution list*: as your position as writer might be revealing with respect to the report, so might the list of readers and their positions. You would write a different report for the bank manager than for the trade union rep.

Abstract

(Not always necessary – check with your tutor.)

The abstract – synopsis or summary – is the essence or gist of your report. The abstract might include:

- overall aims
- specific objectives
- problem or task
- methodology or procedures
- key findings
- main conclusions
- key recommendations.

─TIPS─

- Journal articles typically begin with an abstract – see how they do it.
- Check with your tutors to see what they expect.
- The abstract refers to the whole report – write it last!

Contents page

The contents page lists all the major sections of the report, including subsections and appendices – with page numbers. The contents page allows the reader to navigate your report. Use detailed, clear headings in the report – and put them all in the contents.

─TIP─

Check out the contents pages of books. Do they help you as a reader? How? Make yours useful for your reader.

Introduction

The introduction should help the reader understand the what, why and how of your report. It needs:

- *Background to the report*: either why you were interested in the topic or why the report was necessary.
- *Terms of reference*: the focus, aims and scope of the investigation – its purpose or goal, any specific limitations.
- *The method*: the research methods you used to put the report together – literature review and something more practical – interviews, questionnaires … image mediated dialogue, collaborative writing.
- *Literature review*: this is your analytical review of the key literature that you have read to prepare for the research itself – not usually required in small reports. In larger research projects both the method and the literature review have their own sections.

Findings

The findings is where you *summarise* your key findings from your investigation or research. The different sections of this part of the report can have sub-headings. Reports, as with essays, require clear but formal English – there is no room for abbreviations or slang.

Discussion

Findings are followed by the discussion. This is where you discuss your findings referring back to your literature or to your literature review, connecting your findings to what other experts have already said on the topic.

Conclusion

Each finding should have a conclusion. Conclusions point out the implications of your findings, that is, you tell your reader what your findings mean. Your conclusions should relate to the evidence in your findings – you should not just be writing about your own good ideas!

Recommendations

Each conclusion should lead to a recommendation. Whilst the conclusions tell us what the findings mean, the recommendations tell the reader what to do about them. As your concluding remarks should relate to your evidence – your recommendations should relate to your conclusion.

Bibliography

As with the essay, you should list in alphabetical order by author surname the sources that you have referred to in your report, for the Harvard system: author (date) *title*, place of publication: publisher.

Appendices

An appendix is something added on or attached to something. 'Appendices' is the plural of this. In this section you can show your reader some of the things that you have used to compile your report. For example, if you used interviews or a questionnaire, you would place examples there. If you used images to prompt responses, you may include the pictures your participants chose or made in answer to your questions.

Appendices do not count in the word limit for your report – but this does not mean that you can just put everything in there. You must mention appendix items in the main parts of your report, otherwise they should not be there.

Glossary

A glossary is literally a list of unusual words. This is especially useful in a report accessible to more than one reader: for example, a technical report that will also have to be read by a layperson (member of the public).

PRESENTATION AND STYLE TIPS

Make sure your report is:

- Neat and easy to read.
- Consistent in style: a simple basic layout used consistently throughout your whole report. Decide where you will number, underline, embolden, italicise.
- Save a report template (pattern) and use it every time you start work; check for a department style – use that.

Why write reports?

Whilst essays are theoretical and discursive, reports are designed to be practical, evaluative and analytical. You are supposed to 'see' and analyse a real world issue. Reports are academically challenging and prepare us for reflective practice and for conducting and publishing our own research. Preparing a report as a student gives you practice at developing different ways of seeing and writing about the world. More importantly perhaps, there are two characteristics to reports that make them significant for you:

- University reports model the reflective way that we will be asked to work after university. That is, in the professions you are supposed to work thoughtfully – and engage in continuous reflection on your own practice in order to improve it (see Kolb's cycle in Chapter 13.1). Preparing reports at university prepares us for the work we will do and the way that we will write about it.
- Reports also model academic research – the results of which are written up in journal articles. That is, academic research often involves the investigation of real world issues, so that we 'see' and understand them differently, and discover more about them. The goal is deeper understanding – and ways of doing things differently. Research projects at university are the same – they require us to investigate, analyse and report upon a real issue.

The reader

Each report that we write at university is designed to investigate a particular topic – to be read by a particular reader – and to achieve a particular purpose. In the process we need to make a case to persuade our readers to take a certain course of action. Two useful questions to keep in mind when we write:

- Why am I writing this report – what issue am I investigating? How do I gather relevant information?
- Why am I writing this report – how do I address my reader?

Key questions to consider here might be:

- Who is my reader? Yes – it is your tutor who is a knowledgeable expert in your subject. Are you also writing as if for a senior manager or an account executive?
- What can I expect my reader to already *know* and *believe* about this topic?
- What does my reader *want* from this report?
- What will I want my reader to *think* and *do* after reading my report?
- What language, tone and style will my reader respond to?

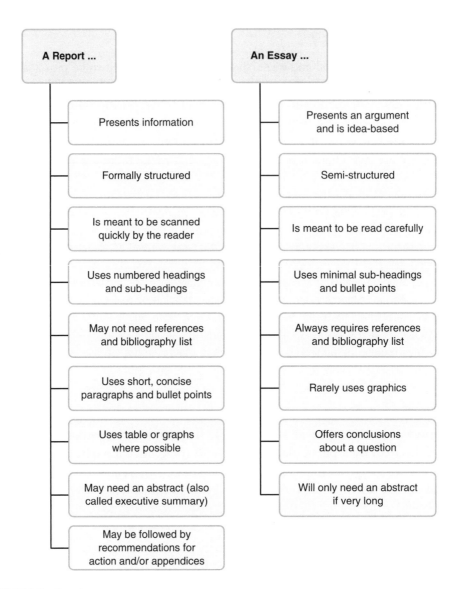

A Report ...	An Essay ...
Presents information	Presents an argument and is idea-based
Formally structured	Semi-structured
Is meant to be scanned quickly by the reader	Is meant to be read carefully
Uses numbered headings and sub-headings	Uses minimal sub-headings and bullet points
May not need references and bibliography list	Always requires references and bibliography list
Uses short, concise paragraphs and bullet points	Rarely uses graphics
Uses table or graphs where possible	Offers conclusions about a question
May need an abstract (also called executive summary)	Will only need an abstract if very long
May be followed by recommendations for action and/or appendices	

FIGURE 12.2.3 Reports vs essays

A beginner's guide to writing a report

When writing reports, don't forget the ten steps to assignment success – they work with reports as well:

1. Prepare
2. Targeted research and active reading
3. Gather data – theoretical and empirical: background reading on key concepts plus a practical investigation

4. Write – read – write
5. Arrive at a rough draft
6. Leave a time lag
7. Review, revise and edit: struggle to write
8. Proof read
9. Hand in
10. SWOT feedback.

If this is the first chapter in the book that you are reading, you might like to read through Chapter 11.3 before proceeding.

Questions to ask yourself

When preparing any assignment – it is always useful to wonder why a particular task has been set. Knowing the *why* can help you know *how* to do the work. Useful report questions might be:

- Why has my tutor asked for this report?
- What am I supposed to 'see' and investigate?
- What will my tutor want me to read and do to prepare this report?
- Why is this report necessary? What is the background, situation or problem that needs to be tackled?
- What am I trying to achieve with this report?
- What might I want my reader to do differently after reading my report?
- What reading will I have to do before I start my practical investigation?
- Who is my reader? Is it just the tutor – or am I presenting the report as if to someone in a company?

  - What might they know on the topic?
  - What might be their beliefs/attitudes?
  - What might they want from my report?
  - What will I want them to think and do after reading my report?
  - What language, tone, style – and what *evidence* – will convince them of that?

- What practical investigation will I have to do to gather useful information and *evidence*?
- What *method* will I use?
- How will I justify my method – what can I say about interviews/questionnaires/focus groups/ other?

Choosing your method

The *method* is the way that we gather data for our reports. Many of us have heard about interviews, questionnaires and focus groups – but think, *what other methods are out there that I could use?* Read relevant journal articles and see what methods the writers and researchers there have used – and how they *justify* their methods. That is, how they argue that the method they have chosen is the right one for the research that they are doing.

We encourage our students to use visual research methods or free writing as we believe these generate richer data. Image mediated dialogue (see Chapter 6), collaborative writing, free writing, collages, mindmaps or drawings are less under the control of the research subject or participant; it is argued that these emerge from people's unconscious and can be *interpreted*. This is different from when people fill in a questionnaire or participate in an interview, where it is argued that their minds take more control of their responses: where they can shape the response that they think you want – or the one that shows them off in the best light. These sorts of responses are often just *explained* – not interpreted. Richer data may be more difficult to use because it does have to be interpreted or analysed – but the findings are often more interesting because of that. Whatever your method – you will have to make sense of your data – so you will have to ask: *How will I critically analyse the data that I collect?*

TIPS

- See Chapter 6 – and think how to adapt the visual approaches to collect data. Think: *image mediated dialogue, mindmapping, collage-making.*
- Read Chapter 11.2: Think – *can I use free writing or collaborative writing as a way of gathering data?*
- Search the University of Brighton's visual learning site for information on visual research methods: http://about.brighton.ac.uk/visuallearning/visual-research-methods/.
- If you are using interviews, questionnaires or focus groups to gather information:
    - How will I design my questionnaire? How will I keep the questions open and useful? Who will I get to fill them in? How will I make this happen?
    - How will I design my interview questions? How will I conduct interviews and make sure I do not influence the outcomes – but get real information?
    - Should I try to run a focus group? Who would I get to take part? How can I get real opinions?

Reports our students have written

We thought that you might like to read about how we prepare our students for their first year research projects – and we also wanted to give you extracts from their reports to read to see what a report could look like in real life.

Getting students started: how we do it

Our students get their first taste of report writing for us when they undertake their first year research projects. We ask them to investigate something about teaching, learning or studying that is of interest to them. We hope that doing this research in their first year helps to prepare them for their final year dissertations (see Chapter 12.5); we also hope that because they are investigating something that does really engage them, they will enjoy the research process.

To seed their thinking, and in their first few weeks, we ask our students to rove around the buildings and rooms of the university as participant observers – seeing where and how learning is happening. We ask them to explore formal and informal learning spaces: to really *see* and then *analyse* what is happening. This is the essence of good research – to make the normal 'strange' so that you see it differently.

As our students are all learning – we hope that this real research will also help them to become more successful students.

TIP

If this intrigues you – why don't you have a go at doing this yourself in your own university?

We ask our students to give presentations on their preliminary findings – using posters to illustrate the points that they make. This helps them to reflect on what they have discovered; telling other people helps them to understand better.

TIP

So if you do undertake this project for yourself – blog about it.

Finally, we ask our students to choose their own research project, exploring an aspect of teaching or learning or assessment – and seeded by something they noticed perhaps for the first time when they were observing learning around the university. They then have to read what other people have written on the aspect they are investigating – this will become their literature review. How might you adapt this approach to help you get ready for your report investigation?

Preparing for a report investigation

So, if you want to succeed in your report writing, do not rush to conclusions – really 'see' the issue first. Make preliminary investigations to see what is happening – then focus in and investigate more deeply – drawing on the relevant literature:

- Observe the situation – really see it.
- Scope – what is happening? Who is doing what? How? What effects are there?
- Focus – what is interesting? What might you investigate further?
- Read – what have other people said about this?
- Prepare – what investigative method will you use and why?
- Collect data.
- Analyse data.
- Prepare findings – conclusion – recommendations …

Every year we are fascinated and impressed by the range of our students' interests – and by their findings. Even though these are first year projects – new information is always uncovered. Our students have been the first ones to write that students enjoy group work because they can get lost in the 'flow' of the task and that students will adopt more visual notemaking systems if they can adopt a 'can do' mindset.

Here are some extracts from our most recent first year student research reports. We have taken extracts from the introduction to the recommendations – but from different projects. See how the writing is doing its work – and doing it differently in the different parts of the report.

Real research reports

From a research project into *student attitudes to writing* (with permission from Jennifer Dixon)

Introduction

In this project I intend to investigate students' attitudes to academic writing. The issue of academic writing and gaining an academic voice that is a student's own is of central importance to this project. The focus of the study will be students at XXX University specifically second or third year students or recent graduates. In addition they will be over 18 years of age …

Method

To gain qualitative data for this study, I will use mindmapping, which is a visual form of notemaking (Kandiko Howson, 2010). Within the study, participants will be asked to create a mindmap of their attitude to academic writing. Mindmapping will allow the participants to show how they navigate themselves through academic practice as well as showing any concerns they may have during their studies and possibly how they overcome these concerns.

In my research I am hoping to explore and answer the following questions:

- What strategies do students use to achieve good academic writing skills?
- Does notemaking add value to academic practice?
- What strategies do students use to improve their academic writing skills?
- How do students find their academic identity through their writing?

From a research project exploring the *different forms of notemaking* – with a focus on visual notemaking and the benefits that drawing can have upon learning (with permission from Chloe Noble)

Findings

The participants trialled each method of notemaking for a week and after they had trialled all the methods their booklets were given back to me to analyse.

Skeleton prose was the method most commonly used, especially by my participants. Participants described it as an easy way to organise their notes because they structured them in a sequence of numbered points or paragraphs although they agreed that they were prone to copying what was written on the board, word for word. Since trialling the other methods my participants agreed that this [skeleton prose] did not present a challenge, they did not feel engaged with their notes and would not research ideas further once they got home.

The Cornell method was new to participants but once they mastered it they agreed that they felt the benefits, as they had been able to devise their own questions based on the information they were processing. Here the participants said that they had been able to engage with their notes and their lectures. With this method the participants felt that they *had* to do the extra reading provided by the lecturers. They agreed that by doing the extra reading they went to lectures prepared and engaged and with a better understanding of what was to be discussed in the lecture. Some had even prepared questions beforehand to ask the lecturer during the lecture. The project left the students with a better understanding of the Cornell method and how to use it.

Mindmapping was a particularly easy method to follow and my participants took to this method. It was nice to see the use of images instead of words for some and for the majority the use of bright colours. I noticed participants had used the colours to highlight key points of information, separate ideas, colour code branches or just to colour

(Continued)

(Continued)

the images they had drawn. Some participants took to drawing pictures alongside their mindmaps and when asked in interviews they were easily able to recall the pictures they had drawn, why they had drawn them and what they meant – as well as being able to recall more information within the lecture as compared to other notemaking methods. With these doodles they now associate their drawings to that particular subject which helps with memory retention on that subject but most of all they enjoyed creating them too. ...

Discussion

The participants enjoyed the Cornell method and mindmaps the most as a way of making notes; they felt that they had engaged with them more and got the most out of them ... They felt that these methods presented a challenge, made them question themselves and the topic and they also found themselves wanting to research the topic further. With these methods there was much less copying from the lecture slides word for word and more actually trying to understand the subject at hand with the possibility of going home and spending more time with their notes ... Visual notes were the least enjoyable method and most of them admitted to giving up before they had even started. It appeared that before they put pen to paper they had decided that they could not do it, they did not think their drawings would be 'good enough' or they thought that they 'cannot draw'. This accords with Dweck (2010) who argues that people with a fixed mindset believe their abilities are 'given' and fixed ...

From a research project into student use of *social media for study* (with permission from Perry Campbell)

Conclusion

Social media sites were created for and are primarily used for connecting people and socialising. Each participant in this research had active accounts on social media websites, Facebook and Twitter and had also experienced using micro-blogs and wikis in educational contexts. It would seem that although web tools and e-learning are in place in education, the best way of using the tools is not yet embedded in the educational framework and not used by students and faculty alike. Education has a long history and perhaps curricula have not adapted to using these tools. However, whilst it is evident that young people in particular are equipped with the knowledge to utilise the web tools on offer today, they perhaps feel that they do not yet know how to use them to enhance their educational work.

**From a research project into student *learning styles*
(with permission from Tanya Pinnock)**

Recommendations

The following recommendations are offered in relation to this research into students'
learning styles in higher education:

- lecturers incorporate different teaching methods into their lectures, which will
  address students' different styles of learning
- lecturers incorporate more group work and activities that will touch upon different
  learning styles
- lecturers, to enable students to explore their individual learning styles, use a
  variety of different modes of learning and should not be restricted to a formal
  style of teaching where they are always directing the learners.

What do you think of these different extracts? Make notes of what you have
learned – and how this might help you write your own reports in the future.

Summary

We have looked in some detail at the academic report, making links to the strategies
necessary for any successful academic assignment. We hope that describing the way
that we work on the report *process* with our students has given you something to think
about – and to adapt for your own studies. We also hope that you have been inspired
by the extracts that we have given, taken from our students' first year research projects.
Use these as models for your own writing where you can. As always, we recommend
that you reflect on everything that you have read and done, and what you have learned
about the report. Make brief pattern notes to remind yourself of all the things that you
will now follow up and do to plan for, research and write a really great report.

Activity

Answer the reader questions

When writing your report, think of your reader – and write to answer all the questions that a
typical interested reader would ask:

What are you going to investigate in this report?

= INTRODUCTION

Why was this report necessary?

= INTRODUCTION – BACKGROUND/CONTEXT

What are aims of your report and the limits on your research?

= INTRODUCTION – TERMS OF REFERENCE

How will you carry out your own research?

Why have you chosen to carry out the research in that way?

= INTRODUCTION – METHOD

What did you find out – what are the key highlights?

= FINDINGS

What overall conclusions do you draw from your findings?

= CONCLUSION

What should be done differently in the light of your findings?

= RECOMMENDATIONS

What did you read to support your report?

= BIBLIOGRAPHY

Access the companion website to this book and find helpful resources for this chapter topic:
https://study.sagepub.com/burnsandsinfield4e

12.3

How to Deliver Excellent Presentations

Okay – we're all terrified of public speaking! This chapter is designed to crack the code of the academic presentation. This chapter is supported by a Presentations Pack download-able from the Sage website (https://study.sagepub.com/burnsandsinfield4e/).

- Introduction   226
- What is a presentation?   226
- A beginner's guide to presentations   229
- Why do we set presentations?   231
- How to succeed in presentations: the four Ps   232
- Get creative   238
- Presentations: essential things to do   238
- Summary   239
- Activity: use the presentation checklist   239

Introduction

> I really hated the thought of presentations, but once they were over I felt so good about myself. In the end I wanted more of them.

Presentations are meant to exploit the fact that most of us are much better at speaking than we are at writing. Of course, what this glosses over is that students, like every other normal human being on the planet, tend to be terrified of public speaking, of presentations. In this chapter we are going to explore the what, why and how of presentations. We cannot make all the fear go away, but we can help you to realise that you can get really good at presentations – you might even get to enjoy them.

What is a presentation?

There are several 'whats' to a presentation that we are going to cover here – they are all true. The trick for you, as always, is to think, 'How will knowing this help me to give better presentations?'

It's a talk

> I remember this presentation, it was on breast cancer, a really frightening topic, and the students had left all the funny noises on their PowerPoint. So there they were giving life and death statistics and scaring everyone silly, and all the while there are explosions, whistles, flying noises and breaking glass!

A presentation is a formal talk of a set length on a set topic given to a set audience. When preparing your presentation you have to think about all these factors: time, topic, audience. That is, you have to fit the topic into the time you have been given – and no longer. Check with the tutor if there are penalties for going over time.

You also have to pitch the topic at your actual audience. Again, as with the report, think about real people with real knowledge, thoughts and feelings. You have to make sure that your language, style and tone are just right for the real people that you are going to address. Finally, you have to make sure that any audiovisual aids (AVA) – your supporting material, handouts, PowerPoint, websites, photographs, posters – are appropriate and will connect with your actual audience. There are two main purposes of using AVAs:

- to help the audience follow and make sense of your presentation, e.g. an outline of the whole presentation, a poster or pattern note of the whole presentation
- to illustrate, emphasise or underline key points, e.g. a quote, a picture, an example, a physical object.

TIP

Use posters to support your presentation – even if not asked to – they help your audience follow and understand your talk. Prepare a creative visual collage – or go for the more formal academic poster: www.fobit.biz/?p=1605.

It's an act

No matter what anyone else tells you, remember that a presentation is a *performance*. You are standing in front of people and talking to them: they are looking at and listening to you – this is a performance. Therefore you are a performer. Use this knowledge – and *act*. To make presentations work for you, act happy, confident and interested – even if you are bored silly or scared witless. If you are happy, your audience can be happy, if you are not, they cannot. If you are bored – your audience will be too … So act your socks off.

TIPS

Positive body language

- Do face the audience.
- Do not only look at the wall or whiteboard behind you.
- Do stand or sit straight.
- Do not hold anything in front of your face.
- Do smile.
- Do not tap your foot or make chopping motions with your hands.
- Do draw people calmly into your presentation with brief welcoming gestures.
- Do not hold your arms defensively in front of your body.
- Do stand in a relaxed manner.
- Do not stand there with clenched fists or looking as if you want to be somewhere else.
- Do dress for success.
- (In a group presentation) do not act as if you hate everybody else on the team.
- Do *act* calm, confident and in control.

It's interactive

As a performer, you will have to build a rapport with your audience and create a relationship with them: you *interact* with them. This means that you will need to *look at them*. You will have to make eye contact with your audience.

So ignore those who advise you to look at the ceiling at the back of the room. That may be okay if you have an audience of 1,000 or more people, but in a small group it looks weird, and not in a good way. You will need to look at people to draw them into your talk and take them with you. You will need to check that they are following and understanding what you say – to check if you need to repeat or explain something. You will never discover this if you do not look at your audience.

Finally, for it to be a successful interactive performance, just like an actor on the stage, *you must never, ever speak from a script*. You must not read a presentation. You must learn your presentation and then deliver it fresh, as though for the first time. Reading a presentation is the quickest way to lose your audience and lose marks.

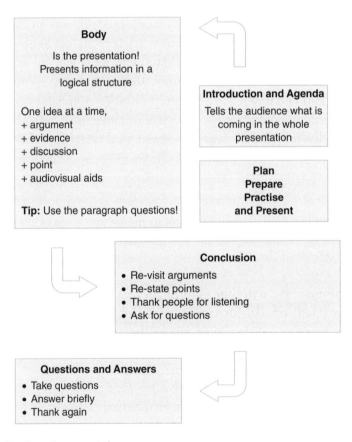

FIGURE 12.3.1 Structure of a presentation

It's a formal convention

The presentation has the same shape as the essay – and it has the same need to address real audiences as the report. Therefore, you should have a sense of the presentation already from what you now know about essays and reports.

A beginner's guide to presentations

Introduction

The introduction should include a clear agenda:

- Introduce yourself.
- Give the topic title.
- Hook your audience.
- Give the agenda.

The introduction is where you acknowledge the question and help the audience understand how you are going to tackle it. Think hook and agenda: the *hook* tells them *why* they should be listening to you: are you going to be interesting, useful or funny? Will it help them pass an exam or get better grades? Will it save them time or effort? Think of something. The *agenda* is where you tell the audience exactly *what* is coming in your presentation. Without an agenda the audience does not know where the talk is going. This is unsettling – and confusing. A confused audience is not a happy audience. Tell them what is coming … and this simple technique will dramatically improve the presentation itself – and your marks.

Presentation body

This is the presentation. This is where you answer the question that you were set, making a logical case. As with the five paragraph essay, think: three big ideas – introduction – conclusion. For each idea, think: argument – evidence – AVA.

TIPS

Use the paragraph questions to structure *each section* of your presentation:

- **What is this section about?**
- **What exactly is that?**

- Tell me more?
- What is your evidence? What does it mean?
- How does this relate back to the question as a whole?

Conclusion

As with the essay conclusion, this is where you draw the whole presentation together. Re-visit your main arguments, re-emphasise your main points – and use all the words from the question to prove that you have answered the whole question.

TIPS

- Write introductions and conclusions last.
- Accept this is a repetitive structure: tell them what is coming; tell them; tell them what you told them. This can feel silly, obvious or uncomfortable, especially in a short presentation. But this is what is required, so bite the bullet and do it!

The question and answer session

It's over – you want to rush out screaming! Don't. You now have to thank the audience for listening and ask them for questions.

TIPS

- Do re-phrase difficult questions – check that you have understood.
- Do keep answers short.
- Do keep answers good-natured.
- Do notice when people put their hands up – take questions in order.
- Do not fight with your audience.
- Do not try to make everyone agree with you.
- Do not think that you have to know everything (unless it is a job interview or an oral exam).
- If you cannot answer why not try: 'That is a very good question – what does everyone else think?' If no one else knows, 'Well, that has given us all something to think about. Thank you again for listening!'
- Do bring the question and answer session to a firm end. The audience likes to know when it is all over safely.

Why do we set presentations?

As with planning and preparing any assignment, the process of preparing a presentation is designed to be an active learning process. As you plan, prepare, practise and perform your presentation you are really getting to grips with and learning the material. As you think about how to *communicate* a topic effectively to your audience you are synthesising and using information.

It's an opportunity

> I did everything you said and practised again and again. The tutor said I was a natural – if only she knew.

And, yes, presentations really are an opportunity to shine. Before you have successfully delivered and survived your first presentation you may find this hard to believe, but once you have done this, you may find that given the choice between an essay and a presentation, you would choose the presentation every time. Once you have cracked how to do presentations well, you will realise that it is easier to get good grades for a presentation than for a piece of writing.

It's a job skill

Further, good oral communication skills are definitely required by employers – some even require a formal presentation as part of the interview. Developing good presentation skills whilst at university can make the difference between getting that job you want – or not.

TIP

Make notes on what you did well in all your presentations and put these in your CV folder (see Chapter 13.1).

It's self-confidence

Finally, once you can do presentations, your self-esteem really improves. From the very first one that you plan, prepare, practise and present, you start to feel better about yourself as a student and this enhances all your studies. This is not just something that we are telling you here to make you feel better – this is something that all our students have told us: succeeding in presentations is the best confidence booster they have ever had.

┤TIP├

Think positive thoughts to drown out your negative ones: *I can do this; This is a great presentation.* Check out Chapter 3.

How to succeed in presentations: the four Ps

Here we will be looking at the four presentation Ps: plan, prepare, practise and present.

Plan

Think about your time limit, your topic and your audience:

- *Time limit*: how can you fit the topic in the time you have been allowed? What will you have to put in – what will you have to leave out?

┤TIP├

Be interesting!

- *Topic and audience*: remember – an audience is made up of real people with real knowledge and expectations of their own. They will not want to be patronised – they will want to learn something.

┤PLANNING TIPS├

 I knew a postgraduate student who went all the way to Japan to deliver a presentation based on a video. The technologies were incompatible, they couldn't show the video. The whole thing was a huge and expensive disaster!

When you start planning your presentation, consider the following:

- What can I expect my audience to know about this topic before I start?
- What will I want them to know when I have finished (= the aim of your presentation)?

- How will I get them from where they are to where I want them to be (= a logical structure to your presentation)?
- What language, tone and style will be right for this audience?
- What arguments and evidence will they understand – and relate to?
- What audiovisual aids will help – and will work with this audience?

  - think of visual aids to *illustrate the topic* – photographs, charts, diagrams, key quotes, posters
  - think of visual aids that will help people *follow your presentation* – have the agenda on a handout or write it on the board, make a large pattern note of your presentation, and display it, make a poster.

- How will my audience react to this topic? Will they be resistant, happy, frightened, interested? What will I have to do to get them to respond positively?
- What questions might they ask me? What answers will I give?

Action plan: now that you have considered all these things: what will you do, read, find and make to get your presentation ready?

Prepare

 I must stress the research and preparation!! When I've participated in presentations, either on my own or in groups, confidence came from how well we had worked together and how much research we had done.

Preparing a presentation requires the same research and hard work that an essay does, and then you have to make audiovisual aids as well.

Some preparation guidelines
- *Remember the ten steps* (Chapter 11.3): brainstorm the topic, link to the learning outcomes …
- *Read actively and interactively*: gather all the information you need to answer the question.
- *Plan the presentation*: give it the shape that will take your audience from where they are to where you want them to be.
- *Be interesting!* Never tell the audience everything from A to B to C. This is boring. Choose an interesting aspect of the topic – focus on, elaborate and illustrate that.
- *Remember to make your AVA*: with backups (e.g. handouts of PowerPoint slides).
- *Convince yourself first*: if you can act as though you believe it, it will help the audience to believe you.
- *Prepare a script*: once you have collected all your data and understood and shaped it, you may wish to prepare a script for the presentation. A script can give you a sense that you have

taken control of your presentation and organised your material to your satisfaction. That is okay – if you remember that you must not read from your script. So at some point you *should destroy your script.*

- *Prepare your prompts*: make cue cards or prompt sheets to guide you through the presentation itself. This could include:

  - key words or pictures instead of words
  - key examples and quotes
  - key names and dates.

- *Number your cue cards and your points.*
- *You must destroy your script* – no really!

TIPS

- **You must not read from a script – you will be boring and dull and you will lose your audience.**
- **Re-create your presentation from the key words on your cue cards.**
- **It does not matter if you forget something – the audience won't know. Better to be lively and miss a bit – than say everything and be dull and boring.**

Practise, practise, practise

The success of the group presentation relied very heavily on how well we had got on before the day and the solo presentation relied very heavily on how much effort I had put into the preparation and research. There were very few students who could 'wing' it and often those that tried fell short when questions were put to them.

Once you have a shape to your presentation, with your prompts prepared, you are now ready to review, revise, edit and learn your presentation – and this comes through practising or rehearsing your presentation. You must not say the presentation for the first time in front of an audience – the words will sound extremely strange to you. You will confuse and upset yourself. This is not a good thing. You must learn and be comfortable with your presentation.

There are several key stages to your rehearsal:

- *Tidy it*: your first rehearsal allows you to review, refine and finish your presentation – and turn it from a written thing to an oral thing. When speaking we have to get to the point – quickly.
- *Learn it*: rehearse your actual presentation – in front of a critical friend. Keep making it shorter – more direct – more effective. Walk around your home delivering the presentation to your cat or a chair. Make yourself feel comfortable speaking those words out loud.

Do not rehearse in front of your children. Our mature students always say that their children tend to say 'it's boring, it's silly'.

- *Refresh it*: once you are comfortable with speaking out loud and you know your presentation by heart, then you need to practise until you can say it every time as though you are saying it for the first time. This will keep your presentation fresh and alive and it will appeal to and grip your audience.

Perform: tips and tricks

> I think one of the pitfalls of doing the presentation is not approaching it in the same way as any other assessment ... and forgetting the extra element of practising beforehand.

Okay – you are going to be nervous. Do not focus on that. Think positive thoughts and get on with it. Here are some positive things to do.

Before your presentation

- *Be positive*: read 'Believe in yourself' in Chapter 3. Practise your positive thinking. Keep saying: 'I am prepared', 'This is a great presentation'.
- *Be mindful*: when travelling to your presentation, run through your main points with and without your cue cards. Reassure yourself that you do know it.
- *Be early*: get to the room early so you will be as cool, calm and collected as you can be. Rushing in late will increase your stress levels.
- *Be organised*: take control of the environment. Organise the seating. Where will you want people to sit so that you feel good and they can all hear you? Do you want them in rows, in a semi-circle, sitting on the floor?

Arrange to stand behind a desk or a lectern. This small barrier between you and your audience will help you feel safe and in control.

- *Be in control*: check that the equipment is working.

Have a back-up system in place – have print-outs of your PowerPoint slides to circulate as handouts if the computer does not work.

- *Be alert*: use your adrenalin – it will help you think on your feet.
- *Be positive again*: say, 'I am prepared' and, 'I can handle this'.
- *Be physiological*: stress has a biofeedback effect where the things our bodies do when we are stressed actually increases our stress. We have to learn to de-stress our bodies. If too stressed before or during your presentation:

  - stop
  - sigh
  - drop your shoulders (we hold our shoulders up when tense and this increases tension)
  - wriggle your toes (we clench our feet when stressed and this increases our blood pressure and hence our stress levels)
  - unclench your fists – this is a typical anger/fear reaction – let it go
  - take a few deep, slow breaths (deep quick ones and you will pass out)
  - start again more slowly (stopping and refocusing never counts against you, it can even impress your tutor).

- *Be on the ball*: write your agenda on the board, on a handout, on an overhead transparency (OHT) or on the flip chart.

During your presentation

- Introduce yourself and your topic.
- Give a brief introduction and say your agenda even if it is written up.
- Speak slowly and clearly. Let people hear and follow you.
- If you get lost – don't panic! Pause, look at your prompts, and carry on.
- Remember to use linguistic markers: 'We have looked at …', 'Now we are going to cover …', 'Moving on to …'
- Make good eye contact – look at everyone in the room.
- Do stand so that you can see everyone and everyone can see you. Don't stare fixedly at one person so that they want to get up and leave.
- Use your AVA with confidence. Make sure everyone can see your AVA. Allow people to notice what is there – then take it away.

Do not write an essay on your slides: key words or pictures only.

- Remember your conclusion – re-visit and re-state your main points … no matter how silly it seems. Your audience does not know the topic as well as you do – they will need to be reminded of what you have talked about and what it means.
- Thank people for listening – ask for questions.
- Chair the Q&A session fairly – keep those answers short and sweet. Bring the Q&A to a firm conclusion. Thank people again.
- After your presentation, review your performance.

After your presentation – be a SWOT

As with the essay and the report, it is useful for you to be able to review and evaluate your own presentations. However, because of the especially emotional dimension of presentations, we recommend that you undertake this in two stages:

1. Immediately after your presentation, tell yourself what a wonderful presentation it was and how brave you were for giving it. Do not dwell on anything that went wrong; this just makes it harder to do a presentation next time. So make this first review a very positive one.
2. After some time has elapsed undertake a more detailed SWOT analysis of your presentation.

   - What were your strengths? What did you do very well? What sections of the presentation were you particularly pleased with? Why? Sometimes we are so busy correcting our faults that we forget to repeat our strengths. Make notes so that you remember.
   - What were your weaknesses? What did not go so well? Why was this? Was it *form* – perhaps it was not structured or presented properly? Was it *content* – was it a poor argument unsupported by evidence? Did you forget to discuss your evidence? Did you forget to refer back to the question? Make notes.
   - Opportunities: now, go on, try to think of just how good you can become at presentations and of all the opportunities this gives you, both as a student and in future employment. Make notes.
   - Threats: if you are still feeling threatened by presentations, what are you going to do next? Will you practise more? Do you need more support with your positive thinking? Do you need to find a study partner? Do you need to seek out Learning Development or Academic Support and get some more help? Make notes.

TIPS

- **Make notes of your strengths – repeat them.**
- **Make notes of your weaknesses – repair them.**
- **Use your tutor feedback.**
- **Use video play-back to refine your performance.**

Get creative

> One presentation that really impressed me was one on Fibonacci numbers in maths. The group used sunflowers and pineapples to illustrate the numbers in nature. One played the flute to illustrate the link between maths and music. There were wonderful drawings illustrating numbers and rabbits (don't ask!) ... I thought it was excellent.

The presentation can be more flexible than the essay. Whilst it is not usually a good idea to write a poem when you have been asked to write an essay, it can be a good idea to be creative with a presentation. If your tutor is the sort of person who will appreciate a little creativity, then play with how you will communicate with and involve your audience. We have seen tutors really impressed when students have performed a mini-play instead of giving a straight presentation. So when thinking about your presentation – do all the good planning and preparation discussed above – but also think whether a different sort of performance would actually get you a higher mark – and go for it.

Presentations: essential things to do

> I feel that you need to really emphasise group presentations, as they can differ greatly and rely heavily on the success or failure of the group. My group presentations worked because we got on – we worked together well – and we rehearsed together.

- *The three-minute presentation*: before delivering an assessed presentation for your coursework, practise by preparing and delivering a three-minute presentation to a friend, study partner or study group. Choose a simple topic like a hobby or a holiday – but something that really interests and engages you. Use your energy and enthusiasm for the topic. With this presentation get the form right: introduction, agenda; body = logical structure + AVA; conclusion; Q&A. This will build your confidence for your assignment.
- *Rehearse, rehearse, rehearse*: for an assessed presentation, practise with a critical friend. Use their feedback.

TIP

Use the presentation checklist to evaluate yourself and ask your friend to complete one for you, too.

- *Team work*: if asked to prepare and deliver a group presentation – plan together, get together, make the AVA together, rehearse together:

  - Have a *team leader* and a *note taker* – help people play to their strengths. Encourage everybody – hate no one!
  - Do *look like a group* – have badges, dress in similar colours.
  - Do *act* as though you were a good group that worked really well together – even if you all now dislike each other!
  - Do *listen to each other* when presenting – do not chat whilst someone is speaking – look fascinated.
  - Do *learn each other's sections* – be ready to carry on if someone disappears.

- *Role-play*: build some element of dramatic performance into your presentation, especially with a group. When students act out a scenario or role-play a point to illustrate it, tutors are usually really impressed and give higher marks.
- *Poster presentations*: even if not asked to prepare a poster for your presentation, make one anyway. Research indicates that audiences find it easier to follow, understand and enjoy a presentation that has been backed up by a well-designed and beautifully illustrated poster.

Summary

We have looked in some detail at the academic presentation, emphasising the opportunity for developing your communications skills, your self-confidence and your employability. As with all assignments, presentations are heuristic, they bring about active learning – and the presence of an audience is an excellent incentive to ensure that you communicate well what you have learned. Try to enjoy your presentations – and use the four Ps of the presentation: plan, prepare, practise and present – and the 'fifth P' – positive thinking.

Activity

Use the presentation checklist

Photocopy this checklist and use it to review your own presentations.

- ☐ My introduction: tells the audience what I am talking about and why.
- ☐ It has a 'hook' telling the audience why they should listen – it is …
- ☐ I have a clear agenda telling people the 'order' of my talk.
- ☐ I will write my agenda – and speak it.
- ☐ I have a logical structure – it does answer the question set.
- ☐ I have thought about my audience – in terms of language, tone, style and interesting AVA.
- ☐ I prepared a script – made my cue cards – then destroyed my script.

- [ ] I have illustrated my main points in my AVA.
- [ ] I have made a poster to support my presentation – and will display that as I speak.
- [ ] I have made a PowerPoint or Prezi presentation and embedded all my resources on that.
- [ ] I will not pass anything around because that disrupts a presentation.
- [ ] My slides and handouts are simple and clear – I have used mainly pictures – and few words.
- [ ] Each part of my presentation follows the paragraph questions.
- [ ] I discuss my evidence.
- [ ] When I want people to make notes, I will pause and let them do so.
- [ ] I have concluded each section by making a point that relates back to the overall question.
- [ ] I have remembered my signposts and my discourse markers.
- [ ] I have a conclusion that revisits my main arguments and re-states my main points.
- [ ] I am prepared for the question and answer session.
- [ ] I have checked my mannerisms or gestures (I won't fiddle with a pen or scratch my nose).
- [ ] I have practised my positive thinking.

Access the companion website to this book and find helpful resources for this chapter topic:
https://study.sagepub.com/burnsandsinfield4e

12.4

How to Run Your Own Seminars and Workshops

Seminars and workshops are more interactive than a typical presentation – this is how to do them well.

- Introduction   242
- What is a seminar?   242
- Why engage in seminars?   243
- Seminars: five top tips   244
- The advantages and disadvantages of seminars   246
- Workshops   247
- Summary   249
- Activity: get visual   249

Introduction

Typically students at university attend lectures and seminars – and the *seminar* is where you are encouraged to discuss and engage with the ideas in the lecture. You may have to prepare by reading or watching videos – and in the seminar you are supposed to be active, to take part. If you are asked to run a seminar or workshop, take these things into account for you will have to get your participants actively engaged with your information; and you may be assessed on how well you managed to get your audience to participate and do things – rather than just sit and listen to you.

You may be asked to run a seminar as a postgraduate or as part of a third year project or dissertation. You may be expected to share your research findings with your audience – in the hope that feedback from your audience will develop the ideas you already have so that your final project or dissertation is improved.

However, many university courses now want their students to be more active in their learning overall and students may be asked to run seminars or workshops as alternative assessments – for we learn best when we teach something to another. There are also projects like Students as Partners or Students as Producers where you may be expected to take much more of an active role in the life of your university and in the teaching and learning of your course (search online for more information on these projects).

TIP

Whatever the reason for your seminar or workshop, remember, you are usually being expected to teach your fellow students something, not by *presenting* information or by telling them something – but by getting your fellow students *doing* something to help them to learn. Organising this is a powerful learning opportunity for you.

What is a seminar?

'Giving seminars and workshops is also common when participating in extra-curricular academic and students' union activities. Our SU used to train people to give seminars and run workshops. They help to develop transferable skills and help make you employable ... Have a look at the SU packs on 'Key Skills' and their 'Training Games Guide'.'

Typically, a seminar is made up of four parts: paper, presentation, discussion, conclusion.

- *Paper*: prepared by you, the seminar leader, and circulated in advance to all participants. Check with the tutor as to what form the paper should take – essay, report, journal article. Can it be something creative – poem, animation ... other?
- *Presentation*: given by you on the seminar topic. Not just the paper read aloud, but a proper presentation that captures the key aspects of your research to date.
- *Discussion*: this is not just the question and answer session that normally follows a presentation. You must make sure that the audience engages with your ideas in some way. Give your audience questions to discuss. Divide them into groups and give each group a different question. Allow time for discussion – and hold a plenary where you collect all the feedback.
- *Overall conclusion*: you, the seminar leader, have to draw together everything that was covered in the paper, in the presentation and in the group discussion. If this is part of a research process, you should also say how the seminar will help to shape the next step of your research.

Why engage in seminars?

The seminar is highly interactive, engaging and productive; designed to enhance both individual and group learning processes. If you are giving a seminar you will have to work out how to manage each part of the seminar process: paper, presentation, discussion and conclusion. This develops your active learning and communication strategies. For those attending a seminar, it is a chance to participate in learning with their peers; it can be an interesting and intense active and interactive learning experience. It can model good practice for participants as they get to read other students' papers, hear other students' presentations or participate in their workshops and engage in lively discussion on a range of topics.

As a seminar leader, you will have to take control of your own seminar and then think how to manage the learning of your audience. You will have to make your discussion topics useful – to your audience and to your own thinking. If running a workshop you will have to plan a range of activities to get people involved and to help them to learn something from you. The audience has to commit to engaging generously and enthusiastically with the teaching and learning situation that you create.

You will have to develop interpersonal skills to manage the discussions and make sure that everyone participates positively. They have to learn how to act like enthusiastic and engaged participants. By the end of a seminar or workshop you should have enhanced your analytical and critical faculties and your communication, team work, interpersonal and leadership skills – and your participants should have had an interesting, engaging and intense learning experience.

Seminars: five top tips

1 Know what you want

> When I gave my seminar I put people into groups and got them discussing different subjects – I got some great ideas – and it meant I was able to work more closely with the people in those smaller groups whilst they were talking.

You can run a seminar early in your dissertation process – to get feedback on what you are doing, and how you are conducting your research. You can run a seminar later – and get feedback on your writing – your audience can comment on how you are presenting your information, or on how you are interpreting it. So, if you are weak on *process* – go early – if you feel you are weaker at the *writing* – go late.

2 Plan the whole seminar

- *Plan the paper*: if you are delivering early, your paper may consist of quite brief notes of what you are going to do in your research and why. You might note the context of your research (what makes it a valuable or interesting topic and what gaps there are already in this field) and the reading and other research activities (interviews, questionnaires, mindmaps, drawings, collage-production) that you have already undertaken. If you are going late, your paper may very well look like a nearly finished draft of what you would expect to hand in. Think about highlighting the areas of the paper upon which you would appreciate critical feedback.

TIPS

- **Do you have to present papers that look very similar to journal articles – or can you be more creative? We have papers presented as poetry or proclamations; whilst this was a very creative strategy it might not be appropriate for you.**
- **Write your 'discussion' questions on your paper. As the paper is typically circulated in advance, it means that your audience will have already read and thought about your questions before they attend your seminar.**

- *Plan the presentation*: whatever style of paper you have circulated in advance, you should expect your audience to have read it; thus there is no need to cover the whole paper again in your presentation. So, in your presentation you need to focus on the interesting bits. Outline the aims and purpose of your research, say why you were interested in that topic, why you took the approach that you did, highlight any problems that you encountered. You might describe how you overcame your problems – or invite solutions from your audience.

- Be interesting! Keep your voice lively, display enthusiasm for your subject and invite real collaboration from your audience.
- If you have managed to engage your audience they may well give you really good advice about how to extend, develop or refine your research or how to improve your paper.

- *Plan the discussion topics and discussion strategy*: it is very easy to waste the seminar opportunity by just seeing it as an ordeal to get through rather than the collaborative learning event that it can be. If you want to benefit from your seminar, think really hard about your discussion topics. Set real questions upon which you want your audience to think – and the answers to which could take your own research further forward.

- Do set questions that will help your own research.
- Do divide the audience into small groups and give each group a question to discuss.
- Do allow a set time for discussion. Hold a plenary to get feedback from the groups.

- *Plan the overall conclusion*: remember that you will have to sum up your whole seminar at the end. Prepare most of your summary in advance: key points from paper; key points from presentation; discussion questions. Then the only thing you have to capture in the seminar itself will be the discussion points raised by your audience.

- Give flip chart paper to your audience. Invite people to write key points on the flip chart pages and collect these at the end.
- Sum up these key points and keep the pages to make sure that you have the ideas to use in your research.

3 Practise, practise, practise

Refine your paper – rehearse your presentation – draft and re-draft your work.

Read or re-read Chapter 12.3 on presentations.

4 Have confidence and enthusiasm

The most important thing for you to do is to enjoy your seminar. Relish the opportunity of running an interactive learning event that will engage your fellow students – and hopefully take your own research or writing forward in the process.

TIPS

- If getting students to discuss your questions in groups, move amongst the groups to check that they are discussing your topics.
- Give flip chart markers out as well as the paper, so they make notes that can be seen.
- Allow a plenary session where everyone can briefly discuss each other's points.
- Think about how what you have learned really will help you with your research.

5 SWOT it

What were your strengths and weaknesses? What will you do next in your research project? Make notes.

The advantages and disadvantages of seminars

As with any group or collaborative learning experience there are advantages and disadvantages to the seminar.

Advantages

- Collaborative, collegiate experience.
- Active and interactive learning.
- Intense learning experience.
- Extends knowledge of a topic.
- Models good practice – rehearsing your writing, presentation and discussion techniques.
- Develops research angles.
- Improves grades in associated dissertation and essay work.
- Develops personal, interpersonal and communication skills.
- Develops organisation and time management skills.
- We learn best when we teach other people.

Disadvantages

- Lack of commitment in the seminar leader produces an uncomfortable event.
- Poor techniques – e.g. reading a paper instead of giving a presentation – switches audiences off.
- Ill-prepared discussions become embarrassing.
- Ill-managed discussions can become exclusive, alienating or confrontational.
- Lack of commitment in an audience can mean that little or no learning actually takes place.

Obviously all the disadvantages can be turned into advantages with the proper planning and commitment.

Workshops

 My favourite workshop was on witchcraft. The students divided the class into witches on trial, the judge and jury and witnesses for the prosecution and villagers. They read out a proclamation – and then ran the session like a proper witch trial. It was engaging, emotional and powerful. We remembered more from that workshop than from a hundred lectures.

These days students are more likely to be asked to run a workshop than deliver a formal academic seminar. The workshop is another mode of active and interactive learning. Typically, you will be asked to 'teach' a topic to your fellow students, but not by lecturing at them – rather you will be expected to develop an event with interactive elements designed to get your audience to think about, explore and understand a particular topic. All the advice about running a good seminar still applies – but overall you have to prepare a much more engaging and interactive event. The following suggest great things to do in workshops – and even in seminars.

Play learning games

Set up some form of role-play where participants have to adopt different roles and then act out a learning scenario. For example, if studying refugee education, you might ask some members of the group to be refugees, another to be a passport controller, another to be a member of the public. You could set the scene rolling – and the participants would learn something from the way they developed the scenario. Search online for role-plays or simulations that you might adapt for your own session.

In recent workshops on one of our courses, one group of our students taught us how to make stop-frame animations. Another group had us playing a whole range of 'trust' games. Yet another group had us taking part in quizzes – to earn points, to get boxes of recyclables, to make unbreakable carriers for water-filled balloons that we all tested in the courtyard. All these sessions were designed and run by the students themselves – and were some of the most engaging and powerful sessions on the whole course.

Get visual

We have outlined in Chapter 6 how we can draw to think and explore, to reflect and communicate. You could open a workshop session by asking your group to draw representations of key words, theories or concepts pertinent to your session. Discussion of the drawings would reveal underlying understanding or misconception and can lead to further discussions.

You could conclude a workshop by asking students to draw a representation of everything that they think they have learned. If they are going to write on the topic that you have been teaching, you could ask them to make a collage plan of their proposed writing.

In your workshop, ask the participants to read a brief article relevant to your topic – and to then turn that into a collage which each group presents back to the class as a whole. Alternatively, you could give out collage materials and ask participants to make collage notes as you give your presentation – or ask everybody to make small collages that highlight the key points from your session. Engaging in these creative activities will help your participants engage with your workshop.

Write to learn

As art can be creative and exploratory, so, too, can writing. At the beginning of your workshop ask your group to write for two minutes on what they already know on the topic or ask them to write for one minute on what they want to get from the session. At the end of a workshop ask them to write a letter to an auntie explaining the workshop to them – or to reframe the whole session for a ten-year-old child. Or open up a Word document on the class AV system, so that everybody can see it, and write a reflection on the workshop in a zig-zag. That is, point to one student to begin the summary – and someone types up their words – the first speaker points to another student who continues – who points to another student … This is a very interactive way to involve everyone in a reflection on the session.

Combine drawing and writing and ask your group to make comic strips that illustrate the main points of your session – either for themselves or for that ten-year-old child.

TIPS

- Ask your participants to use their phones or tablets to make short videos that sum up the key points of your session – and post them to your group Facebook page, or to your own reflective blog.
- In lectures and classes or when other students are giving presentations, delivering seminars or running workshops, make notes of the interesting and engaging things that they do. Think how you can adapt those interesting activities in your own sessions.

Summary

The academic seminar and the workshop draw together oral and written communication strategies to form powerful interactive learning experiences. Workshops and seminars are more effective if you make them interesting and engaging – and if you get your participants to think for themselves and do things – rather than just telling them what they should know.

The activities suggested here give a flavour of what works in seminars and workshops. We are sure that you will be able to think of many more of your own once you get started. We really want you to engage positively and enthusiastically in your seminars and workshops – to make the most of them.

Activity

Get visual

We have emphasised how learning is improved when you are engaging positively – and when you think creatively about how to get your audiences to interact and think for themselves. In that spirit – when you make notes on this chapter – why don't you try:

- using only pictures
- making a PowToon animation or a short movie.

12.5

How to Write a Brilliant Dissertation

A dissertation is where you finally follow your own research interests and capture your own voice. Enjoy the challenge!

- Introduction   252
- Why dissertations?   252
- What is a dissertation?   252
- The importance of time management   254
- A beginner's guide to the dissertation   254
- Answer the reader questions   260
- Summary   262
- Activity: review these resources – record in your journal 262

Introduction

A dissertation or major project is a requirement for all Honours degrees – and is part of the majority of postgraduate courses. This chapter focuses particularly on the undergraduate student and their dissertation – but all the material here has been trialled with Masters and PhD students – who have also found it useful.

A good dissertation can get you onto a higher degree programme or get you that job you want – it is worth taking seriously. Your dissertation is the opportunity to take real control of your learning – and of your degree. For examples of dissertation style writing, see the end of Chapter 12.2. If you have to give a seminar or run a workshop as part of your dissertation or project see also Chapter 12.4.

Why dissertations?

Your whole undergraduate course leads into your dissertation, it is the moment where you take ownership of your degree by engaging in focused work on a topic of your own choosing. Your whole degree is an introduction to the breadth and depth of your subject – in your project or dissertation you choose to focus on one key aspect in more depth. This allows you to deepen your understanding and knowledge of an area of your subject for yourself and by yourself. It is where you say as an academic: *This is what I am really interested in.*

To help our students prepare for their final year dissertations, we set them a research project in their very first year – so they understand what being an academic is all about, and they start to realise what it is about their subject that really interests them. See the end of Chapter 12.2 for extracts from our students' first year projects – they model the style of writing you can use for your dissertation.

Even if your university does not prepare you in the same way, keep a journal of all the aspects of your course that fascinate you – that prompt you to read more or think more deeply. These may be the threads that you bring together into your final dissertation topic.

What is a dissertation?

A dissertation is very like a report in structure (see also Chapter 12.2). In Figure 12.5.1 we outline the basic dissertation structure but do remember that your department will have their own guidelines – check those out as well. Write your own notes, comments and tips to self on the table – make this your own.

Section	Features	Comments and Tips
Title page	Title of dissertation Your name Organisation/Course Date	
Abstract	Summary of every part.	Write it last.
Contents page	The sections of the dissertation clearly labelled. Page numbers.	
Introduction	Acknowledges significance of the area under research. May give the background or context to this project (why it was undertaken). Gives the terms of reference, the aims and scope of the project.	See Chapter 12.2.
Literature review	A significant section critiquing the relevant literature on the topic being explored in the research project. Relate the literature to your research objectives. You may utilise similar methods to those used by the theorists that you cite – or give reasons why you are using different approaches. In the literature review you may critique both the findings and the methods used in the literature you discuss. Gaps in the literature may give you an idea for your research project.	For models search: online literature reviews. When we did we got this: www.lib.ucdavis.edu/dept/instruc/files/finding-literature-reviews.pdf.
Method	Justifies the approach that you took in your research – whether you used quantitative or qualitative data and why.	PhD theses in your subject area will typically have justified their methodological approaches – note how they did this. When choosing your method – be aware of how you will analyse the data the method will generate. See Chapter 12.2.
Results/Findings	Presentation of the data acquired during the research phase.	See Chapter 12.2. See www.socialresearch methods.net/kb/.
Discussion	Interprets and evaluates your findings and reveals the significance of your analysis.	See Chapter 12.2. Go to journal articles/PhD theses to see how academics in your field discuss their findings.
Conclusion	This lays out the conclusions that can be drawn from the research undertaken, the findings and your discussion.	See Chapter 12.2.
Recommendations	Lays out the recommendations that can be drawn from the conclusions if appropriate.	See Chapter 12.2.
Glossary	List of terms, e.g. acronyms used.	
Bibliography	List of all references in the correct format.	
Appendices	Attachments, e.g. questionnaires and surveys used.	

FIGURE 12.5.1   The classic dissertation structure

The importance of time management

You need to be especially strategic with your use of time when undertaking a long project like a dissertation. You will have several key time-consuming stages to work through – and you will be more successful if you do these over time, rather than trying to do them all at the last minute.

Things to do:

- Refine your focus and decide on a manageable research topic.
- Research the literature to discover the key theories and developments that you are going to explore.
- Draft your literature review.
- Decide on your methods – and your analytical approach – justify.
- Write methods.
- Put research methods into practice and gather data.
- Analyse data.
- Write findings – summarise key points.
- Discuss findings – with reference to the points identified in the literature review.
- Draw conclusions – with reference to the points identified in the literature review.
- Review, revise and edit …
- Proof read.
- Bind.
- Hand in.

This complex and lengthy process requires even more systematic and strategic organisation of your time than usual. We go through this in more detail in the beginner's guide, below.

A beginner's guide to the dissertation

 I did my dissertation on the value of new media to actors, directors, camera operators and everybody technical in the film industry. When I applied for work in the business, I really did have information that made me stand out!

A typical first stumbling block for most students is choosing their research focus: they want to change the world – but are not quite sure how to phrase the question. The trick is to choose something interesting but that is also manageable – that is do-able in the time allowed. The most important thing is to think first: 'What am I actually interested in?' and 'What topic might help me get that job … or that place on the postgraduate course that I'm interested in?'

Look back over the reading that you have already undertaken on your degree – especially in the modules that have introduced you to the key theoretical concepts in your subject and key research methods. Ask yourself:

- What are the key issues?
- What interests me?
- What is hot in the job market?
- What would I like to explore in some depth?

TIP

We have included a dissertation pattern note towards the end of the chapter – follow it and it will help you generate your dissertation proposal.

Research question

> I have always been interested in Maths – and I wanted to teach in Primary where they always want Maths teachers. It was a no-brainer – I did my under- and postgraduate dissertations on different aspects of Maths in diverse classrooms. I am now working in a primary school. Result.

To decide on your question, think about your course: which modules were the most interesting and which topics sparked the most debate in class? Which did you think about long after the class was over? If gaining some sort of work experience: what is interesting about the job in real life? What aspect would be worth investigating further? The trick is to find something that you are really interested in and try to get a question from that. What would you like to investigate and why?

Things to think about:

- Are you in a placement or getting work experience? Keep a notebook in your pocket every day on placement or at work. Make notes of interesting things that happen. Connect what you see to the theories covered on modules that you enjoyed. Analyse these notes to kick start your thinking: how can I use this to shape a project? Could you do a research project in your workplace? What are the ethical issues? Who would you have to speak with?
- Don't know what to do? Make a collage – see Chapter 6. Gather collage materials – paper, glue, magazines and newspapers – think about your course and everything that you have enjoyed about it – choose pictures and words that appeal to you – cut them out – arrange them onto the large piece of paper in front of you – sketch the rough arrangement – remove the pictures carefully – then select them again, gluing them to your large piece of paper. *Describe* in words the collage that you have created – then *analyse*: why does this collage give me my dissertation topic? Why would this topic be interesting?

- What about the theory: ask yourself a series of questions. What theory will I be drawing on? What have I already covered on the course that relates to my topic? What additional reading will I be doing? What aspect of my *practice* relates to the theories I am exploring? Am I already engaged in relevant activities at work — or will I have to set up some specific activity to allow me to investigate the theories in practice?
- What about the methods: see also Chapter 12.2 on methods. After rejecting the 'easy' methods — find an interesting method. Ask: what methods give the richest data? What methods appeal most to me and why? What reading will I have to do to justify my methods?

Doing the research

Have a timeline: make sure that you plan what has to happen — and when it will happen. Consider the following: What will you have to do? When will you do it? What will you need to do *before* you gather data? What resources will be necessary? How will you set up your data collection phase? How will you make sure people engage? How will you make sure you do not influence your participants? What will you have to do *after* you have gathered data? How will you evaluate your findings?

---TIP---

The presentation and analysis of data are awarded so many marks! Give this part of the process real thought and real time.

Have a location: where will you conduct your research? How will you put your participants at ease? Where would that be most likely to happen? In people's homes — neutral locations — the workplace — the university? If you cannot undertake your project or dissertation research in your own university or workplace, where are you going to do it — and how are you going to arrange it? What sort of permissions will you need? Are there any specific ethical considerations?

Have an action plan: what will you have to do to set your research in motion? What resources are necessary? How will you set it up? How will you make sure people engage? How will you get participants? What follow-up action might be necessary or ethical? How can you make the very most of the data that you collect?

Ethical and legal constraints

 So I've got this Education student and she wants to investigate childhood obesity. She thought it would be a good idea to weigh all the children in her class — and to photograph their lunch boxes every day. I tactfully pointed out that this was a bad idea!

It is a requirement of all dissertations that they have clear ethical statements indicating that the research was conducted without harm, that anonymity was maintained (anonymity is more than confidentiality – it must be impossible to work out the identity of your participants), that participants are over 18 and have given informed consent and retained the right to withdraw from your research at any time – and that the research was carried out within the frameworks of the institution and your future profession, and within the laws of the United Kingdom. You must find and use the appropriate statements for your subject, department and professional body or association.

Scary bit: your question can be the point where things go horribly wrong – especially if we forget the ethics. This is where academia intersects with the real world, real people and real professional bodies. Are you researching vulnerable people or people under 18 years of age? Here there are extra legal and professional constraints – and if we get this wrong, a career can be ended. Your institution will have guidelines – you must use them.

Literature review

Your literature review is where you locate your dissertation in your academic discipline, it's where you join in with the conversation that your subject is having with and about the world. It is where you conduct research into the current literature in the area that you are interested in.

A literature review is *not* an annotated bibliography where you just write notes on everything that you read. It is a critical engagement with relevant up-to-date literature. It should also help you to understand how the people before you covered your topic, how they researched it – and the conclusions they drew. Once you have chosen and read your literature, you have to write a long essay drawing the ideas together – in a way that launches your own research. A good literature review gives focus and shape to the dissertation that is to come.

─TIP─

Read upwards of 30 sources – of these you may focus on one, two or five or more key textbooks. You might review ten or more journal articles – perhaps articles written recently by the people who wrote the chapters in the textbooks. This keeps your theory up to date.

Methods and interpreting data

All dissertations require you to justify your methods. You have to make a case for how you researched the topic – and how you intend to gather and analyse your data.

You will also be expected to critique your research methods. Be aware that the methods that you choose will also signpost an ontological, epistemological, philosophical and ideological position (if in doubt – look all these words up – then draw them – that will help you understand them!). That is, they fall into different camps: positivist, postmodernist, interpretivist, ethnographic – and you may be expected to consciously place your work within those paradigms and justify your decision. For the most part, the main issue is not contradicting yourself – for example, a postmodernist is unlikely to rely on quantitative data. See below for more information on the different methods.

- *Quantitative research*: encompasses a group of methods focusing on quantities, on numbers. It is argued that the larger the scale, the greater the reliability. This method includes randomised controlled trials, cohort studies and controlled studies. Generally falling within the positivist, normative paradigms, it is seen as more scientific, objective and rational than qualitative research because it is not supposed to involve personal or subjective judgements but objective, accurate noting of facts – of realities. Critics argue that it tells us the what – but not the *why* – of phenomena.
- *Qualitative research*: located within the social sciences and the humanities – dealing with social phenomena – beliefs and experiences – that have reference to the wider contexts of lived lives. Researchers in this paradigm utilise interviews, focus groups, participant observation and perhaps more visual (psychological) methods of gathering data, arguing that it generates deeper and richer data. This approach is criticised for being non-factual, subjective and unreliable – whilst others say that it is its subjective nature that generates deeper truth.

TIP ───

Follow up the Wikipedia entries on quantitative and qualitative research methods. Whilst tutors often dislike Wikipedia as a source of information, the links will take you to peer-reviewed material that tutors will like:

- http://en.wikipedia.org/wiki/Qualitative_research.
- http://en.wikipedia.org/wiki/Quantitative.

- *Mixed methods*: although specific types of methods are associated with particular paradigms, they are not exclusive and it is argued that by mixing methods we increase the internal validity of the research project – not by reducing bias but by supplying more data and from another angle. To do this, we could be conducting a survey or a questionnaire to flag up particular issues – this would then feed into our design for the next stage of our research. Here we are gathering one form of data to capture a snapshot of issues of concern to follow up in our qualitative research or *vice versa*. This *triangulation* is said to give richer, deeper material to analyse rather than necessarily offering any statistical relevance.

- *Interpreting data*: once we have gathered our primary data – we have to make sense of it. We may have investigated one or two participants' experiences in depth and represent that as a case study. We may have gathered written or visual responses to seed questions – and seek to interpret that. Typically we look at responses and try to identify themes and issues. For example, in research into education the theme of barriers to learning might emerge. These could then be broken down – coded – into sub-themes: financial, childcare, family attitudes to education, experience of prejudice. In qualitative research, it is not the amount of times that these ideas came up that is important – but what is said about them. However, if we were conducting quantitative research – it would be the number of times particular issues were raised that was important.

- *Spend time with your data*: many marks are thrown away because students do not make the most of the data that they have collected. We see many dissertations and projects where lots of effort went into the literature review – and really good data was obviously collected – but the writers did nothing with it. You need to spend real time with your data – describe it – summarise it – code it – think about it – analyse it. Draw conclusions – make recommendations. All this takes time, yes, but since you have the data anyway – use it!!

- *Take a tutorial*: if you are not sure about how to interpret and analyse data – you may want to do an online tutorial. You can search for one on YouTube – but we have collected a few here:

  - For a tutorial on the principles of data collection: http://archive.learnhigher.ac.uk/collect-this/ (or Search for LearnHigher + Collect This).
  - For analysis of quantitative and qualitative data, survey design, getting started with SPSS: http://archive.learnhigher.ac.uk/analysethis/.
  - For interactive quantitative/qualitative research methods tutorials, with explanation, quizzes and resources: www.nottingham.ac.uk/nursing/sonet/rlos/ebp/qvq/index.html.
  - For probability associated with inferential statistics tutorial, with explanation, quizzes and resources: www.nottingham.ac.uk/nursing/sonet/rlos/statistics/probability/3.html.
  - For descriptive statistics for interval and ratio scale – includes mean, mode, median, measures of dispersion and standard deviation – with explanation, quizzes and resources: www.nottingham.ac.uk/nursing/sonet/rlos/statistics/descriptive_stats/index.html.

Findings

Findings is where you present the data you have gathered via your primary research which may be accompanied with tables or graphs. You *briefly* summarise everything – but show, emphasise and say what your significant findings are. This is where many students do not do justice to their research – they just present all the data without identifying the most significant aspect. You need to say what is the most important and why.

Discussions and conclusions

This is where you link your significant findings back to the literature review – point by point. It can feel like you have already said what needs to be said; but this is where we are pulling it all together, spelling out to the reader what is important and why. Linking this to the literature review and your research question can feel repetitive, but needs to be done. If you have to read new literature to help you understand and explain something you have discovered – think about whether you need to now include that source in your literature review.

Recommendations

Some dissertations invite you to end with a recommendations section. Each recommendation should flow from a conclusion. Each conclusion should flow from a finding/discussion point – and this should all be supported in the literature review.

Recommendations might indicate a need to revise policy or practice – or the necessity for further research that needs to be undertaken, especially where it will overcome any limitations or problems that you have identified with your own data collection.

What now?

How do you now feel about your own dissertation or project? Hopefully – you are now feeling that this is an interesting and do-able task – one that you are beginning to look forward to. Remember – choose an interesting topic – read the relevant literature – and try out a rich method … Keep yourself interested and engaged and you can really enjoy this process.

Answer the reader questions

When explaining research project and dissertation writing to our students, we suggest that they think of their readers – and then write to answer all the questions that a typical interested reader would ask:

So what are you going to investigate?
Why would that be relevant to this course/discipline?
= INTRODUCTION

Why are you interested in that topic?

Why is there a need for this research project at this time?

= INTRODUCTION – BACKGROUND/CONTEXT

What have other academics already written about that topic?

= LITERATURE REVIEW

How will you carry out your own research?

Why have you chosen to carry out the research in that way?

How are you planning to analyse the data?

= METHOD

How will you safeguard your participants?

How will you make sure they give informed consent and that their identities are protected?

= ETHICS STATEMENT

What happened when you conducted your research?

What did you find out – what are the key highlights?

= FINDINGS

What do your findings mean?

How do they connect with the ideas discussed in your literature review?

= DISCUSSION

What have you learned?

What overall conclusions do you draw about your research from your findings/discussion?

= CONCLUSION

What should be done differently in the light of your findings – and of the conclusions you drew about them?

= RECOMMENDATIONS

TIP

Read the extracts from the research projects at the end of Chapter 12.2. Each part of a dissertation, except the literature review, is included there. Read them – get the feel of the different writing styles involved. Find your dissertation writing voice.

Summary

In this chapter we have tried to encourage you to see your dissertation as an opportunity – not a problem. It is your chance to explore something that you are really interested in. To give yourself time to focus on something that you think is significant or relevant; time to conduct research using a method that is appropriate – but also of interest to you. We have given an introduction to key aspects to think about and to plan for as you undertake your dissertation – remember to read the examples of this sort of writing at the end of Chapter 12.2. Good luck!

Activity

Review these resources – record in your journal

We have gathered together some links to online resources designed to help you with your research and the whole dissertation process. Review these resources, analysing how useful they will be to you in your own research. Make notes in your *dissertation journal* that you have completed this preparation – it will impress your supervisor.

- Cornell University site: www.socialresearchmethods.net/kb/.
- CETL-AURS – interactive research site for science students – how to conduct literature reviews and improve scientific writing: www.engageinresearch.ac.uk/index.html.
- Publisher's forum on research methods: www.methodspace.com/.
- Postgraduate – managing your research project: www.unisa.edu.au/ltu/students/research/default.asp.

The horror! The horror! Exams are not a universally popular form of assessment. We consider a positive and successful approach to exams.

- Introduction   264
- It's learning, Jim – but not as we know it   264
- How to develop your memory   266
- A beginner's guide to passing exams: SQP4   270
- Examination day!   274
- Summary   277
- Activity: use the exams checklist   278

Introduction

> I hated the very idea of exams. They left my stomach in knots at the sheer thought of them. The fear of them paralysed me, which probably resulted in my getting a 2:1 instead of a first.

Many students have a fear of exams – so if this is you – relax – this is normal. However, once you get past the stress of having to perform under exam conditions – on a certain day – at a set time … What is the real problem? After all, most people who want to pass a driving test – can. So what's different about university exams? Perhaps the problem is not with exams at all, but in how we were taught at school: yes, we are taught *content* but we are not taught *how to learn* that content. Content is good – but we need to know how to learn the material for ourselves – and how to use it under exam conditions. Without this, many people admit defeat and give up on exams, thinking that they are not cut out for them, they are not clever enough … We are going to explore things that people say about exams – and move on to discuss how to develop your memory with a multi-sensory approach to revision … We conclude with a very focused and practical discussion of revision and exam techniques. Before you read on – have a quick brainstorm: *what do I want from this chapter?*

It's learning, Jim – but not as we know it

Here are some things that our students say about exams – and some advice that we give. See if any of these apply to you – and think about what you are going to do to make positive changes:

> How long should the answer be? I'm dyslexic and write slowly.

There is usually no set length to an exam answer; in the end there is only what you can write in the time you have. Everyone has to discover how much they can write in the time allowed – and then get better at writing a good answer in that many minutes – in that many words.

For the dyslexic student who writes more slowly perhaps, this can feel like a problem. However, there are many positive things to do. First, if you think that you are dyslexic, you must get a proper test done. Go to the Student Support Services at your college or university to find out how this happens. If you are dyslexic you will get extra time in exams. Typically another ten minutes per hour in an exam – but check. More importantly, lobby to take exams on a PC, as this can have a marked effect on your grades. We know students who moved from fail to first doing this – perhaps because: word-processed work looks so much neater, it overcomes any unconscious prejudice in the mind of the examiner towards untidy handwriting; the student feels much more confident on the computer and therefore produces better work; the student practised more.

If you are not dyslexic and still write quite slowly, or even if you just are not very experienced with writing under exam conditions, you will have to practise condensing 1,500 or 3,000 words essays into something you could write in an exam: this is much more focused and condensed writing and it will take practice!

 I've got a really bad memory: how can you learn a whole year's work in three weeks?

Many people feel that they have a bad memory, often because they have not actually learned how to use their memories; they have not learned how to learn. Contrary to popular opinion, revision is not something that you should be doing just before your exams. Revision is part of active learning. You should be testing yourself after every lesson and learning your material as you go through your course. So do self-test after every lesson – not just before the exams – this should sort out your worries about your memory. What you should do just before the exams is practise timed writing.

> I know I'm unusual but ... I really love exams and hate coursework. Coursework means everything counts – now *that* really worries me! With exams, I only have to psych myself up to perform really well for three hours or so. It's brilliant!

Exams are designed to test your surface learning, your memory of key facts and data – and, importantly, exams test your deep learning, your *understanding* of key facts and data. Exams are designed to see how you *use* the information that you have learned over a whole course – but in a new situation. Read or re-read Chapter 11.1 on how to make sense of your course and Chapter 2 on how to learn and how to study. If you adopt the strategies recommended in these chapters, you will understand what you have to do and learn to pass each course you take – and you will be able to take control of your learning.

TIPS

- After *every lesson* test yourself: what have you learned?
- Summarise key points onto revision cards. Test yourself often.
- Enjoy the exam as a way to show what you know.

How to develop your memory

Whenever we ask a group of students about their ability to remember, the majority say they have a bad memory ... and this is one of the reasons they fear exams. We can all develop a good memory – with practice. Tony Buzan, who has explored the psychology and dynamics of memory with respect to study and learning, argues that we need *active revision* if we want to remember, if we want to learn.

Short- and long-term memory

Buzan's research refines our notions of the short- and long-term memory. The short-term memory is a very small and immediate working memory. This allows us to function day to day. Our long-term memories are memories that we create and build and reinforce over time. Our memories allow us to function in our lives – they become who we are. In terms of studying, the short-term memory may pick up pieces of information, but we need to get that information into our long-term memories if it is to be of any use to us. Getting information into our long-term memories does not happen by accident or chance. It does not happen quickly. It does not happen unless we do something to make it happen. Basically, if we do want to learn something, then we have to:

- Choose what to remember.
- Decide how we are going to remember it – our memory triggers.
- Be prepared to self-test to check that we have learned the information. We need to reactivate the memory immediately, then a day, a week and a month later.

How we learned in primary school

Think back to how you learned things in your earliest days at school – then compare your list with points taken from other students:

I learned the alphabet by singing a little alphabet song. It is still the way I remember the alphabet.

I remember the colours of the rainbow, you know: Richard of York Gave Battle In Vain. If you take the first letters you can get back to Red, Orange, Yellow, Green, Blue, Indigo, Violet.

One that my little girl came home with the other day was the spelling of 'because' – big elephants can always understand small elephants.

And then there is that other one – Never Eat Shredded Wheat – which gives you the points of the compass … North, East, South, West.

We were taught our sums by reciting the times tables. But I don't actually remember them now. I don't think I wanted to learn my tables – so that didn't work so well.

I went to a Montessori school, we would see it, hear it, say it and do it.

How did your list compare to ours? What we can see is that in primary school or kindergarten the teacher is designing the mnemonics, the memory systems or triggers, for the students – and then the teacher will help them to revise (repetition of rhymes and tables) and will test them. Where the trigger involves rhythm and rhyme (the alphabet song) or where the trigger involves something unusual or bizarre (Richard of York – or the big elephants) the material is remembered. However, even with a good system – where the student does not want to remember, all the repetition in the world is not making it happen.

What seems to happen as we get older is that we forget these ways of learning. Instead of taking control of this process for ourselves, we stop using these successful memory strategies, strategies that work with the way that our brains actually work. We put aside these successful learning strategies as if we deliberately forget how to learn. What we need to do is to re-learn how to learn: *want* to learn, be *active*, decide *what* to remember – and *how* to learn it, *self-test* to check.

- Design your own mnemonic systems for all the things that you need to remember.
- Use rhythm and rhyme.
- Use the bizarre.
- Reduce key information onto index cards, carry them about and self-test in odd moments.

Learning does not happen by accident

Buzan states that, without active revision, we forget 98% of what we encounter after just three weeks. This means that if we do not *act* to remember, we forget, almost immediately. This is obviously a real problem for those students who revise only three weeks before an exam: this is not revision – it is learning it all from scratch. And no, you cannot do that in three weeks. Buzan recommends an active revision cycle when encountering new and important material:

1. The same day that you encounter the new material, spend ten minutes making a short, dynamic version of your notes. Build in mnemonics – triggers to jog your memory. These might be cartoons, illustrations or diagrams that are funny, bizarre or bawdy – these are what make the memory work.
2. A day later spend two minutes self-testing, recalling your memory triggers – and the notes attached. What have you remembered? What have you forgotten? Mentally recall the information or actually re-draw the notes. Take steps to remember what you forgot the first go round. The more active you are the better.
3. A week later spend another two minutes re-testing, reactivating the memory – plugging those gaps.
4. A month later spend another two minutes reactivating the memory.
5. Reactivate every six months for as long as you want to keep the memory alive.

The revision cycle is a 'use it or lose it' cycle. It is a system based on transferring information from our relatively ineffectual short-term memories into our infinitely more useful long-term memories. In the process of doing this, we are building neural pathways and neural connections: we are actually building memories into our brains.

---TIP---

Each week reduce your lecture and reading notes onto index cards. Test yourself and see how much you have remembered. This will develop your memory – and the cards will be the building blocks of your revision.

See it, hear it, say it, do it

> I saw this student in the library preparing for the exam by trying to learn the PowerPoint slides from my lectures – all of them and in the same order that I had delivered them! I tried to explain that it's not about learning my lectures – it's about understanding and extending them – and then using the data to answer the questions set in the exam.

When you actively choose what and how to learn – do not learn textbooks, your lecturer's PowerPoint slides or whole essays by heart. Word-for-word recall of whole lectures or seminars, of whole essays or whole passages from books is ineffective. You are remembering padding rather than key information – you are being passive rather than active – and it can trap you in the way that other people have used information and stop you from being able to use it yourself.

To be both active and effective in our learning we have to develop our ability to strip back what we need to learn to the bare essentials: to the skeleton – which we learn by heart – by seeing it, hearing it, saying it and doing something. We need to be able to use information ourselves: in discussion, in drawings, in presentations and in our writing – including our exam writing. If we simply remember how other people have used the information it will never be our own.

TIPS

- *See*: visual learning includes reading, lectures, television, film or video. Make revision notes as colourful as possible – drawing in cartoons and visual triggers to help you to remember.
- *Hear/say*: auditory learning also includes lectures – and listening to the radio or podcasts or audiotapes. Discuss material – explain something to someone. Make your own tapes of key points – produce an audioblog. Put your key word data into jingles or songs – use funny voices when revising.
- *Feel/do*: build a physical dimension into your learning – move about as you study – *make* your pattern notes – *make* collage notes. Make a revision game and play it.

To learn the most, you need to see it, hear it, say it *and* do it.

Make revision games

We have found that it helps students to take control of their learning if *they design and play their own revision games* – in fact on some of our courses rather than set an exam – we ask students to build a revision aid for the course. Typically, our students have designed:

- *Quizzes*: here the students researched a specific course, examining the aims and learning outcomes. Once they identified the key data (names, dates, information) that ought to be learned by the end of the course, they designed questions and answers for them. A competitive edge was set up for the quiz by having several teams competing against each other. Playing the game revealed to the players both the information they had learned – and that which they had forgotten. The quiz utilises 'see, hear and say' strategies, and the playing of the quiz can become an emotional and even a physical experience.
- *Board games*: again, the students researched a programme examining the aims and learning outcomes. They constructed questions and answers that covered all the learning outcomes: the key data – names, dates, and information. But here they designed a colourful board game that could be played as the questions were answered. The board game scenario is especially good, as to play the game you will be working with other people and using see, hear, say and do.

A beginner's guide to passing exams: SQP4

> I prepare for exams the way I prepared for my driving test. There, I sorted out the written test first. I got the book with the questions in and tested myself until I thought I'd got them right. Then I got my friends to test me until I was sure I'd got it right. I only lost two points in the test itself. With the driving part, I had lessons until my instructor thought I was ready. When I was confident that I knew how to do it, I booked the test. Then my instructor and I practised all the things that would definitely come up in the test – you know, emergency stop, three-point turn, and parallel parking. When I could drive a car in my sleep – I took the test and passed first time. I do that with uni exams as well.

Do you prepare for exams the same way as the student quoted here? What we can see is a determined effort to want to pass – this student did the research and then all the preparation, hard work and practice that was needed to do well. It is exactly the same with university exams – you need to survey, question, predict, plan, prepare and practise (SQP4).

EXAM TIPS

- *Want to do well*: be interested, know what you want from the course, know why you want to get a good grade.
- *Do the research*: know what you have to do and learn to pass the course.

- *Learn the bones*: only learn key word points, don't fill your memory with padding. You want the skeleton, not the whole body.
- *Memorise*: take time each week to memorise key facts and self-test.
- *Practise*: turning key words into essays.
- *Study partner*: make sure you do have a study partner. Plan and prepare perfect answers together.
- *Board games!* Get Trivial Pursuit or some other board game. Put the questions to one side. Devise question and answer cards for all your exam topics – play the game with your study partner.
- *Be multi-sensory*: see it, hear it, say it, do it!

Survey

 I have a website for all my students to use – and I put resources up there. I also have a counter to see which pages students look at the most. I suppose you've guessed it, they look at past exam papers and model answers the least!

As soon as you start on a course, make sense of it straight away – get the overview – the big picture (see also Chapter 11.1):

- If you have a course booklet or handbook, check the aims and learning outcomes. Make key word notes summarising all the things that you will have to do and learn to pass the course.
- If supplied with a syllabus, read it and cross reference with the aims and outcomes – what is being covered when? After each session – self-test: what have you learned? What have you forgotten?
- Read the assignment question and link parts of the question with specific weeks of the course. Each week you should know what you are learning and why – and which bit of the assignment or exam you are tackling.
- Find and read past exam papers: How many questions will you have to answer – in how much time? How difficult or complex are the questions? What topics always appear? Be prepared!

TIP

Write an 'exam' checklist for each course that you are taking, note:

- How long will the exam be?
- How many questions will you have to answer?
- Whether it is a seen or unseen exam (where you may get the paper in advance).
- Whether or not it is an open book exam (where you may be allowed to take textbooks into the exam).

- Where are my papers? Sometimes past papers are given to students, sometimes they are not. Sometimes they are kept in the library – sometimes they are kept in your VLE. The trick is to find them and read them.

Question

Once you have spent real time surveying the course to gain your overview, you need to sit down and ask yourself: *what exactly do I need to do and learn to pass this course?* Make a list – pin it up in your study space. Do this for every course, module or unit that you are taking.

TIPS

- Draw up your lists with your study partner.
- For each exam, make a list of the topics that will come up.
- Link to learning outcomes.
- Link to course weeks.
- Link to assignment question.
- Put the lists on your wall and in your coursework folders.

Predict

Once you have examined all the course information that you have been given and all the past papers that you can find, predict the questions that will come up on the exam paper. Then decide which questions you will answer. Follow your interests and you will learn more: it is very difficult to learn if we are totally uninterested.

TIPS

- An exam question usually combines two or more of the topics set in the course-work assignments.
- If possible, do assignment questions that lead to an exam topic.
- If you are prohibited from answering an assignment question and an exam question on the same topic, work out a strategy with your study partner. Write your coursework on A and your exam on B – your partner does the opposite and you share your research.
- Open a revision folder on each exam topic that you intend to answer.

Plan

Once you have chosen your exam topics, you must plan your learning and revision strategy for each topic, drawing on what you now know about effective learning, memory and learning style. Plan to:

- Have a revision folder for each topic – in each exam.
- Put relevant class, lecture and reading notes into each folder.
- Answer assignment questions linked to exam topics.
- Put assignment notes into the relevant folders.
- Put the assignments into the folders.
- Put any extra work that you do following your tutor's feedback on your assignment in the folders.
- Put in press cuttings.
- Start a revision cycle for each of the topics that you want to learn – self-test and revise from week one of each course!
- Build a big picture, pattern note for each topic (see Chapter 5).
- Add information to your own big picture every week.
- Spend a few minutes reviewing your big picture every week.
- Reduce key information – summarise as key words on index cards. Carry them with you – learn them in a supermarket checkout queue, learn them on the bus, learn them in the lift.
- *Self-test after every lesson!*

Prepare

It is not enough to *plan* to pass your exams – you must actually do everything that you have planned to do: you must *prepare* for your exams. So, to prepare properly you have to:

- Keep a revision cycle going for each exam topic.
- Keep your revision folders and your big picture revision pattern up to date.
- Go through each revision folder from time to time, throwing out excess material.
- Each week add key points and illustrations to your big picture.
- Keep your index cards up to date. As you learn the material, reduce your notes, make your index card notes shorter.
- Each time you make your notes shorter, you are revising the material.
- Illustrate your notes with memorable cartoons.
- Make key word tapes using rhyme and music. Play these as you go over your big picture notes.
- Self-test and design quizzes – test your friends.

Practise

At last, we have come to something that you can do three weeks before your exams! All the above strategies emphasise learning key data – names, dates, key points of information – from the beginning of each course. What you need to do just before the exam is to practise using the information that you are learning *under exam conditions*. Typically, this involves practising timed writing.

As you study, you use information in class discussion, in group-based learning activities, in presentations and other assignments. You have time to plan and research your answers. You have anything from 1,500 to 3,000 or more words in which to answer a question. Suddenly in an exam, you have just half an hour or an hour to plan and write a perfect answer.

You now have to work completely differently from the way you have worked before. As with a driving test, you will not be able to do this unless you have practised doing it. You will not be able to plan and write a good essay in a time limit unless you have practised both planning and writing under timed conditions. It is as simple as that.

BEGINNER TIPS

- Know what you have to do and learn.
- Prepare revision flash cards – in paper or online – note key points – test yourself.
- Make colourful key word notes – pin them on your walls. Revise your course as you walk past your notes.
- Make and play revision games with your friends.
- Practise brainstorming and planning – develop the ten-minute brainstorm technique.
- Go through all the questions in your course handbook and past exam papers – ten minutes per brainstorm – plan an answer for each one.
- See how much you can write in half an hour.
- Practise writing something good in half an hour.
- Practise turning a long assignment essay into a half-hour version of the same essay.
- Practise timed writing with notes.
- Practise timed writing without notes.
- Practise preparing and writing 'perfect' answers with your study partner.

Examination day!

No writing on revision and exam techniques is complete without a look at the actual exams themselves. Here we are going to give some practical advice for examination day. So whatever you normally do around exam time, next time you have an exam try to do some of the following.

Time in the exam

Each exam is different. For each you will have to know how long the whole exam is and how many questions you will have to answer: this tells you how long you will have for each question. Time per question needs to be divided between preparation time, writing time and reviewing time.

- *Read the paper:* always read the questions carefully – if you've looked at past papers the actual wording of the question will not intimidate or confuse you. Choose your questions with care – use information in the other questions to help you answer your questions.
- *Plan each answer* (allow five to ten minutes per plan): as with your assignment questions, analyse all the key words in the question: brainstorm each word in the question. Use the brainstorm to plan the answer: number the different points in your brainstorm to plan your essay. Always plan before you write. Time spent planning is never wasted. Time spent writing without planning can be very wasted indeed.

TIPS

- **Brainstorm and plan each answer before you write anything – as you brainstorm one question, you may recall additional information for another question.**
- **Brainstorm/plan and write your favourite question. Then brainstorm/plan all the others and then write in order of preference. The advantage of this is that you feel good once you have a whole question out of the way.**
- **Brainstorm/plan and then write one question at a time.**

- *Start each answer:* you must begin to answer every question that you are supposed to. It is more important to begin than to finish (law of diminishing returns). Maximum marks are picked up at the beginning of your answers.
- *Write to time:* do not run out of time and give the same amount of time to each question. Time yourself. If you do run out of time, write: 'Ran out of time – please see plan'. This allows you to pick up points for key facts.
- *Review what you have written:* a few minutes checking your answer can make a phenomenal difference to your marks! Always cross out material that you do not want the examiner to mark – but leave your plans if they are good – you may pick up extra marks for something in them.
- *Never answer more questions than you are asked:* extra questions are just not marked.
- *This all takes practice!*

Think smart – think positive

You need to mentally prepare for exams. You must want to do well – and you have to work at believing in yourself (see Chapter 3) – here are a few tips for examination time:

- Remember that fear is normal – it does not mean that you cannot do well.
- Enjoy your fear – it means you are facing a new challenge.
- Think positive thoughts – I can handle this! I'm looking forward to this exam! I'm so well prepared!
- Act positive. Find out what it would take to do well in your exam and then do it. Give 100%.
- Have a positive study partner – encourage and support each other – no moaning!

Relaxation

We recommend that as a student you build in stress relief activities from the beginning of your course and throughout your life. If you are in the habit of running or exercising, of meditating or doing yoga, then it will be easy for you to just do more of this around exam time.

If you are not in that habit, it is unlikely that you will suddenly develop good habits in the nick of time. So here we would just like to reiterate our advice – build exercise and stress relief into your life from the start. If you feel that you will become sleepless around exam time, practise using a sleep audiotape before the exams come up, then your body will know how to use the tape when you really need it.

---TIP---

Search online for exam + meditation to find resources to help you relax.

The night before

If you have been putting successful techniques into practice over your course, you should feel confident that you do know your material and that you can plan and write an answer in the time allowed. So the night before the exam, you should not be trying to cram in new information, neither should you be panicking.

You should be quietly confident. You may wish to go over your key word notes – whether you have them on a big pattern on the wall, index cards or summarised onto sheets of paper. You may wish to practise a few ten-minute brainstorms – but the emphasis is on quiet confidence and rest. Have an early night.

Judgement day

Get up early and have a light breakfast even if you do not feel like eating. Exams are hard work and you will need energy. But do not eat so much that all your blood goes to your stomach – you need a good supply getting to your brain.

Arrive at the examination room in good time. Do not cram in new information. Avoid people who are acting nervous or scared – they will only unsettle you and it is too late to help them now. Worse, we have heard of students who deliberately behave negatively in order to unsettle others to make them do badly in the exam. They feel that this increases their chances of doing well.

Make sure you have working pens and a watch. Take some chocolate with you or a glucose drink – for that extra energy boost mid-exam.

Think positive thoughts. Read through the paper carefully and choose your questions with confidence. Brainstorm and plan before you write. Recall your revision notes by sight, sound and feel. Time yourself through each question – and *start* every question. Leave time to quickly review what you have written.

What examiners like to see

- Correct use of key words, phrases, terms and concepts from your subject.
- Questions answered in the correct format – essays where they want essays and reports where they want reports.
- Not writing 'all you know' on the topic but identifying the key words in the question and addressing those in your answer.
- Focusing on the question set – appropriately drawing on course material.
- Discussing course material critically.
- Using the time well.
- Neat presentation.

After the exam

Avoid discussing the exam with other people, comparing answers with others can lead to panic – and you do not need that if you have other exams for which to prepare. If you do have another exam the following day, treat yourself to another relaxed evening and an early night.

Summary

How to revise for and pass exams links several of the active and effective learning strategies covered elsewhere in this text with exam success. Specifically we discussed a whole course strategy for success – emphasising active learning, self-testing and practising for the actual exams you will be taking. We finished with a detailed look at the examination day – things to do before, during and after the exam. You should now be ready to put these ideas into practice in your own learning. Do use the checklist that has been included at the end of this chapter to help you. Good luck with your exams!

Activity

Use the exams checklist

What have you learned from this chapter? What will you now do? Make notes – and complete the exams checklist for every exam that you are going to take.

	Exams checklist		
	Subject		
Survey	*I have:*		
☐	received the course outline		
☐	read the course aims and learning outcomes		
☐	read the schedule and thought about the course structure and design		
☐	found and analysed past exam papers		
☐	paper is … hours		
☐	I have to answer … questions		
☐	I know the typical language used in exam questions		
☐	I know the topics that come up every year		
Question	*I have thought about this programme*	*Predict*	*I have:*
I need to know …		☐	predicted the likely questions for this subject
I need to learn …		☐	chosen … topics to revise in depth
Plan	*I have:*		
	opened a revision folder on:		
☐	Topic 1:		
☐	Topic 2:		
☐	Topic 3:		
☐	Topic 4:		

☐	Topic 5:			
☐	Topic 6:			
☐	made links between learning outcomes, coursework, assignments and my revision topic			
☐	placed coursework notes, press cuttings, assignment notes and assignments into the topic folders; on a big pattern on the wall; and on my index cards			
	I use a multi-sensory approach:			*I have made:*
☐	by sight		☐	pattern notes of the key points
☐	by sound		☐	tapes of me reciting the key points
☐	by feel/movement		☐	condensed charts of the key points.
			☐	revision games: I will see it, hear it, say it, do it.
Prepare	*I have:*			
	gone through my exam folders and have prepared condensed notes of everything that I need to remember for the exam for:			
☐	Topic 1:			
☐	Topic 2:			
☐	Topic 3:			
☐	Topic 4:			
☐	Topic 5:			
☐	Topic 6:			
	I am learning this by:			
☐	memorising my key point patterns/charts			
☐	reciting my key points along with my tape			
☐	testing myself and friends			
☐	carrying index cards with the key points on them			
Practise	*I have drawn up a revision timetable for this exam subject. It includes the following:*			
☐	positive thinking		☐	writing with notes
☐	brainstorming and planning answers		☐	writing without notes
☐	planning and writing 'perfect' answers with friends		☐	timed writing without notes
I am ready and confident!				

FIGURE 12.6.1   Exams checklist

PART V
THE EMPLOYABILITY
KIT

13.1

PDP and HEAR

Knowing Who You Are, Becoming Who You Want to Be

Whether or not we bother to apply for the jobs that we could do, can boil down to how much we really know ourselves and what we are capable of. Self-awareness does not come naturally but it can be developed and the PDP process is all about developing self-awareness. Be active in your university to enjoy yourself more – develop yourself more – and in the process develop your self-awareness and your employability.

- Introduction   284
- What is PDP?   284
- Why PDP?   285
- A beginner's guide to PDP   287
- What are transferable skills?   287
- Reflection and reflective cycles: Kolb   289
- HEAR   291
- Summary   292
- Activity: get involved with how your university tackles PDP and HEAR   292

Introduction

> Panicky! Suddenly it hits you, what you have to do ... I saw this enormous building and I couldn't even find my room. How could I pass my degree if I couldn't even find the classroom? I was really scared ... It's frightening.

Personal Development Planning or PDP is a process with which many students are expected to engage. It may be embedded in specific modules – or it may be something that you are invited to do alongside your modules – but overall it is a reflective process where you are supposed to reflect on ALL that you have learned and developed in and about yourself whilst a student. The idea is that this sort of meta-reflection allows you to become more self-aware, more in control of how you are developing as a whole person whilst a student – and it is designed to make you more employable. The PDP process is designed to help you make conscious your skills and qualities so that you can 'pitch' them at potential employers through your job applications. This chapter is designed to make conscious the what, why and how of PDP so that it makes sense to you – and you use the various processes to your advantage.

What is PDP?

PDP is a reflective process designed to make you aware of your development whilst a student – so that you can 'sell' yourself better to employers. As a busy student you may not want to engage in PDP – it may feel like yet more stuff that you are being asked to do. But you are at university and you are doing many amazing things and developing in many different ways. It really is to your advantage to take a few moments every month to reflect on all this development and to capture some of it before you forget.

There is so much about university that is also useful on the job market: you are developing personal and interpersonal skills, you are leaning how to organise and manage your time. You are learning your subject and its skills – and you are learning team and group work strategies. You are researching your essays and projects – and perhaps you are also a peer mentor or a student ambassador. The idea of PDP is to become conscious of all the various skills, strategies and practices that all these things are refining in you. In this way, you start to discover the sort of person you really are and the different things that you like and that engage you. This helps you know what sort of jobs to apply for – and gives you evidence to use so that you then get that job.

Whatever else employers want, they will also be seeking someone with key transferable skills. For example, they may write: 'Candidates should have a track record of effective communication skills'. This is your opportunity to let your PDP process do the talking for you. For example, see how your participation in clubs and societies may give you information:

> In my first year at university I joined the Drama Society which developed my ability to speak in public and my self-confidence. In the second year I became a students' union rep for the Drama Soc – I had to keep minutes and good records. I had to maintain the reputation of the Drama Soc. I also began writing about our productions for the student newsletter. I found that working as both SU rep and journalist for the Drama Soc meant that I managed to refine many of the 'soft skills' that my degree modules were seeding: organisation and time management, interpersonal skills and excellent all round communication skills.

Why PDP?

> One of the things I say to my students is, look at all the different sorts of jobs open to people with your degree. What are they like? What sort of person would enjoy which job? What sort of person are you? Therefore – which jobs out there are more suitable for you – the person you actually are? Now – think about developing those aspects of yourself that will fit you for the job that you actually want – and make sure you collect evidence on this as you go through your degree.

Any university's PDP process – no matter how formal or informal it is – is designed to give you the push to capture, reflect upon and learn from your experiences whilst a student – and to capitalise on them when you apply for your jobs. In our opinion this whole book is also about Personal Development Planning – for we invite you to use the book to become the student you want to be and PDP at university invites you to become the graduate – the person – that you want to be.

PDP invites you to formally reflect on all that is happening for you inside and outside the university classroom – so that you can build a portfolio of evidence of your achievements. In the process, you get to know yourself better and this helps you choose a job that will suit you – rather than just thinking that you have to do this or that job just because you are now qualified to. It really matters that you match yourself to the right job.

In Chapter 1 we invite you to take a personal skills review – to note your strengths and your needs – and then to use the rest of the book to develop yourself as a successful, engaged and happy student. We hope you use your review to 'sign up for' different chapters in order to develop aspects of yourself – so that you take control of your studies and of your learning. We also recommended that you put the skills review in your CV or PDP file – so you have a record of your starting point – and that you make notes of how you use this book to develop – for that will give you evidence about your progress. This really is the essence of PDP.

Let us consider your development of academic reading strategies – both before and after reading Chapter 4 on how to survive academic reading:

- Reflect back on how you felt about academic reading before you read that chapter. Were you nervous? Were you already confident?
- How did you normally approach academic reading: what did you do? What did that feel like? What planning and preparation – if any – would you do before you read something? How successful was your reading practice or strategy?
- Did your approach to academic reading change after you had read Chapter 4? What did you do differently after you read the chapter?
- How successful are your new reading strategies?
- How do you feel about your academic reading now?
- How will you continue to develop your reading strategies?

This questioning approach is the process that PDP is based upon: active and continuous reflection – so that you continue to *consciously develop* – as a person and as a professional. As university students you are also joining professions – and many of these require you to engage in continuous professional development (CPD). This is another reason that PDP has entered the university curriculum: PDP is a process that starts you on the route to CPD in your job.

Here is an example of a PDP reflection:

> I organised the student conference at my university. I had to book the rooms, get students to run sessions – and other students to attend. I organised the budget and sorted out the catering. I got marketing students to design the posters and flyers for me ... I had to manage the day itself and make sure that it ran smoothly.
>
> I feel that this experience demonstrates my organisational skills; but more than that, I had to use so many different communication skills as well – from setting up a Facebook site to advertise the conference, to tweeting about the event before, during and after – I had to set up EventBrite so that people could book their places. I also had to get posters and flyers produced – and in the right places at the right time. I had to email, phone and meet people from every level of the university hierarchy – and I had to make sure that all the student presenters felt supported and had the rooms and resources they needed to run their workshops.
>
> I did have a wonderful time – I learned much – and I think that this activity proves that I am suited for your post.

As you can see, this PDP review process is more than just a diary. In the example above, the student is practising a reflection on her activity with a student conference, trying it out to see how she would pitch it at a prospective employer looking for someone who must be a good team worker.

A beginner's guide to PDP

 So I get half way through and I say: 'Why, why, why can't I just be happy going to work and going home? Why did I start this? I can't bear it!' … PDP encouraged me to take greater advantage of resources to improve my skills and capabilities.

In most universities, the PDP process – whether it is embedded in a first year 'skills' module, a second or third year 'employability' module or located within your university's personal and academic tutor system – encourages you to actively develop your *transferable skills*: the ones that you develop at university that will also be useful to employers. Typically you might be expected to reflect on:

- How you have taken control of your general skills development.
- How you improved your organisation and time management capabilities.
- How you developed your ICT skills.
- How you developed your communication skills.

PDP is asking you to reflect on and make conscious your *transferable skills* – so that you can refer to them when you apply for jobs.

What are transferable skills?

Universities often develop their PDP resources around what are known as transferable skills. The term 'skills' can sometimes be contentious in higher education – some prefer the term 'attributes', some use 'practices' and some use the term 'competencies'. Nevertheless, whatever we call them, *noting* the development of these 'skills' will also contribute hugely to your employability. The core transferable, employability skills are taken to include:

- *Self-awareness*: knowing your strengths and skills and having the confidence to put these across.
- *Initiative*: anticipating challenges and opportunities, setting and achieving goals and acting independently.
- *Willingness to learn*: being inquisitive, enthusiastic and open to new ideas.

- *Action planning*: prioritising, making decisions, assessing progress and making changes if necessary.
- *Interpersonal skills*: relating well to others and establishing good working relationships.
- *Communication:* listening to other people and clearly getting your point across orally, in writing and via electronic means, in a manner appropriate to the audience.
- *Team work*: being constructive, performing your role, listening to colleagues and encouraging them.
- *Leadership*: motivating others and inspiring them to take your lead.
- *Client/customer service*: being friendly, caring and diplomatic with clients and customers.
- *Networking*: building effective relationships with business partners.
- *Foreign language*: specific language skills.
- *Problem solving*: thinking things through in a logical way in order to determine key issues, often also including creative thinking.
- *Flexibility*: ability to handle change and adapt to new situations.
- *Commitment/motivation*: energy and enthusiasm to achieve goals.
- *Numeracy*: competence and understanding of numerical data, statistics and graphs.
- *Commercial awareness*: understanding business and how it affects the organisation and sector.
- *IT/computer literacy*: office skills, ability to touch type and use common software packages.

These are the skills, attributes or practices that all students are expected to develop in the process of their studies – and in their life beyond the university. So, check out your course documentation for PDP opportunities – and keep a notebook or a spreadsheet handy where you can jot down reminders, or evidence, of things that might be useful to recall for your CV.

For example, if you have just completed a group work task, you could note things like: your role in the team; what went well, what didn't go so well and why; how problems were solved and disagreements handled; whether team members all contributed equally and if not how was this resolved; whether the work was completed on time.

Now – think about all the things that are important to you – and use these things to help shape *your* PDP. Think: how can I make the most of this? Be prepared to keep notes and reflect regularly. Here are some questions to help you:

- Do you have paid work? If so, what skills are you developing at work? What skills are you developing by balancing work and study? Reflect on how these can be transferred to other aspects of your life.
- Do you play sport? Reflect on the many ways that playing sports can enhance your life, think about the skills and qualities that you are acquiring.
- Are you a member of any clubs and societies? What are you getting from that? Are you running a club or society? What extra experience does that give you?

- What extra contributions are you making in your local community? Are you helping out at your local school or youth club? Do you run an adventure playground? Make notes about what you do in these activities – they will give you lots of positive things to say about yourself.
- Are you prepared to get involved at university? For example, are you an elected course representative, or elected students' union official?
- What hobbies do you have and how do these contribute to the whole you?

Remember – it will *not be enough* just to say, 'I can work well in a team – and I can work on my own as well'. That is a meaningless statement unless you give evidence from your course, your work placement or your volunteering activities that prove what you are saying.

TIPS

- **You will not collect evidence for your PDP or CV folders without having an *active system* for collecting examples of your good work – and your brilliant experiences. Get that habit started!!**
- **Use the transferable skills listed above – and make notes under those headings at least once a month.**
- **Keep blogging about your learning – and use your blogs to remind you of good things that you have done and learned, as evidence of your engagement and development.**

Reflection and reflective cycles: Kolb

 I doubted the point of it at first – but actually it did help me to produce a better CV.

Many articles and texts on PDP also include reference to Kolb (1984) and the reflection cycle. The Kolb cycle suggests that learning is a process, a cycle – that goes through specific phases of: action – reflection – reference to research or theory – improved action … more reflection … and so on. Whilst there are no fixed timescales for each phase, the phases are described as flowing into each other in a cyclical way. There are critics of this model, some suggest that it is too simplistic in the way that it describes the very complex process of reflection and meta-cognition. It is argued that Kolb's cycle is too mechanistic and does not capture the way that we really interact with the world – with ideas – and with our own actions. Nevertheless, Kolb is a useful model to use when attempting your own PDP.

The four phases of the Kolb cycle:

1. *Concrete experience*: what happened? What took place? What was the experience? Don't forget the journalism questions: who, what, why, when, where and how!
2. *Reflection*: your own personal analysis – what skills, attributes, competencies, did you draw on to complete the task – or just to survive it? How did you grow or develop? How might you have performed better? If others were involved in the activity – how do you think they might think back on the experience? Will you refer to theory from your subject to help you understand the experience? (That is – how do the books help you understand and explain what happened?)
3. *Abstract conceptualisation*: what final thoughts do you have about the whole experience? How do you finally understand what happened – and why? What generalisations can be made about the experience? That is, what lessons were learned? What concrete advice might you give to someone else based on your analysis of all that took place? Do you need more information before you draw conclusions?
4. *Active experimentation*: planning for the future, based on experience and reflection. What would you do differently next time and why? What would you do in exactly the same way, and why? Who could you get help from next time to improve something? What resources do you need? What further reading might you do?

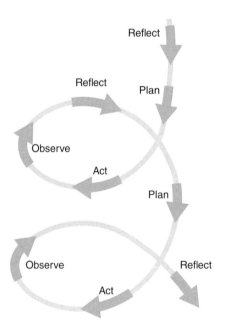

FIGURE 13.1.1   The reflective cycle

All that is a rather complicated way of saying that we can do something – reflect on it – read about it – think about it some more – adapt our behaviour to take account of all of this …

HEAR

Higher Education Achievement Records (HEAR) are also developing currency in university at the moment. HEAR are often small certificates awarded for a student's engagement in some form of extra-curricular (outside the course or classroom) activity. The HEAR is designed to capture a wide range of experience and expertise – allowing us to award recognition for student engagement with and contribution to the whole of the university life cycle – and all of its life.

As we argue in Chapters 3 and 13.2, yes, university is obviously about developing your academic and professional knowledge; but it is also so much more than that. University really is where you can have some space and time to develop yourself in ways that you could not imagine until you actually arrived at the university. Find out about all the opportunities open to you – and get involved. Write for the SU newspaper, joint the United Nations Society, join the Drama Society. Become the Entertainments Officer – and put on bands and dances for your fellow students.

Any and all of these things can be wonderful experiences in themselves – and they can all provide you with materials for your CV and your PDP portfolio … many of them will also attract a HEAR certificate, which you can use as evidence of your ability and effort.

For more information on HEAR you can search out the national website – which also has information for students: www.hear.ac.uk/ – we would recommend that you also investigate whether or not your university has its own HEAR programme – and what you have to do to benefit from it.

Summary

‘ I wish I had known about this at the start of the year. It is something that I will definitely get involved with now that I am more aware about it. ’

PDP really is an opportunity, not a problem. *Reflecting* on your own progress and development makes you more self-aware. This self-awareness can make you see aspects of yourself that you value and like – and that you know will help you do the job that you want to do; it could help you to *discover* the job that you would really like to do. Engaging with PDP takes some time – and this worries students who are already time-poor and stressed. The trick is to see PDP as a process – a little bit of time you put aside every month or every term to develop your self-awareness, your meta-cognition: to deepen your knowledge of yourself and build your profile and self-confidence. Taking control of and responsibility for all your learning and development in this way helps you get the most from your studies and enhances your capacity – and your self-confidence. Whether you view PDP as an investment in yourself or a waste of time is up to you. Engaging with PDP can take time and can also be challenging, but the payoff is that you will find out more about yourself, you will get more out of your studies, and you will be better prepared as a graduate seeking employment.

Activity

Get involved with how your university tackles PDP and HEAR

- How is PDP referred to in your university prospectus, on your university website and in your course documentation?
- Find a job description for the sort of job that you actually want to get – note the knowledge and skills that are being looked for. Make notes – make a decision to develop the skills that the job you want actually requires.
- Look at the detailed information provided about each of the units or modules that you will be taking on your course, and list all the terms that might come under the PDP umbrella, e.g. group project (working in groups), research skills (information handling), etc.
- Jot these down and think about your previous experiences, think about what went well last time you worked in a team, what didn't go so well, what you could do to make yourself a more effective group member, what resources or support you need to do this.
- You may also find that your university provides you with a progress file, or portfolio, where you can record your goal setting, skills audits, action plans, transcripts, etc. This is a very useful way of recording your reflections, action plans and achievements and can be drawn

upon when preparing your CV or planning for an interview. Find out if your university has an e-portfolio, if not, find out whether they can support you in setting one up for yourself, or, alternatively, create your own paper or online record.

- In some universities, the students' union is actively engaged with facilitating PDP activities, e.g. leadership courses, volunteering, representation, etc. These extra-curricular activities are an excellent way of 'adding value' to your time at university. Find out what happens where you are and perhaps get involved.
- Find out if your university has a HEAR initiative or a more formal HEAR programme … get involved!

13.2

How to Move on ... and Get that Job

How to use all your experiences to help you build your CV and get that job or apply for further study.

- Introduction   296
- Improve your prospects   296
- CVs and covering letters   297
- How to write a bad application   298
- What employers want   299
- Going on to further study   299
- Making the most of university   300
- Summary   307
- Activity: what to do right now   308

Introduction

> You call this, 'Moving on' ... but in fact your future career should be planned from very early on. Whatever you do, don't do what I did: wait till the last minute and hope something turns up.

You may already know what you intend to do after you leave university – but not everybody does. Some come to university and hope that a career will become obvious by the end of their degree; others have a particular career in mind and they aim at that in a very systematic and targeted way. Still others have a career in mind, but this changes, and by the end of their degrees they want something very different; they may even decide that they want further study rather than that job.

This chapter discusses preparing for work or further study with an emphasis on using your time at university to develop you as a person – a happy, confident, employable person. Quiet, noisy, shy, brash, extrovert, introvert – there are jobs out there that suit us all. The trick is to know who we are and what we really want – and then to take steps to get that.

We direct you to the Prospects website – and discuss how to develop your CV over your time at university. We conclude with a section offering advice from graduates, careers advisers and many others from around the typical university. Our friends want to say something to you – the new students starting out – about how to enjoy yourself and make the most of university.

Improve your prospects

> I see students who think that after university they ought to get a job that pays lots of money. They strive for this ... they panic about this. On my self-awareness course they may realise that they are not that sort of person – that it is okay not to chase money. It's wonderful to see people appreciate who they are and what they want – and then to go for that.

Whether or not you know what you want to do when you leave university, the Prospects website has been designed to help graduates and prospective graduates discover the jobs or further study opportunities for which they might be suitable – and to help them to apply for those jobs or courses, see: www.prospects.ac.uk/careers.htm.

There is no point in us attempting to replicate all Prospects' useful information, the real trick is for you to use it early on in your degree programme, but we give a quick overview of its contents here:

- CVs and covering letters
- Job application guidance
- Interview tips
- Interview tests and exercises
- Job hunting
- Options
- What do graduates do?
- Using your language skills
- Country profiles
- Careers fairs
- Careers services
- Forum
- Leaving your course.

If you do not know what sort of job you would like to do after university, go to 'Starting out', which has advice for those unsure about what work they might be interested in. Check out their career planning tool: 'What jobs would suit me?' Try also the psychometric testing site and personality questionnaire to get you thinking about who you are and the sort of work that you would enjoy doing and would be a good fit for.

CVs and covering letters

 There are ways an undergrad can stick out from a crowd, including extra-curricular academic and community activities, general volunteering, work experience, involvement in sport teams and development projects, students' union and cultural pursuits (choir/drama and other cultural-type stuff). You could do a meaningful internship over the summer after your second year or get involved in Erasmus programmes.

The information in your CV and your covering letter is a key aspect of getting an interview – and without an interview you do not get that job. Employers will not want you to send your CV when applying for a specific job, but you can copy and paste from your CV to their job application forms.

Warning: an application form is not asking for your autobiography. What they do want to see is that you have understood the job requirements, that you have read the person specification and that you have written something about each of their requirements – proving that you could be the person described in the person specification.

- Keep a CV file. Maintain this file regularly, updating it as you do new things – including at university.
- When you apply for a job copy and paste relevant sections of your CV file into your online application forms – *changing the wording to make it fit the actual job* you are applying for.
- Talk to the careers service to discover the jobs, or further study, that you might apply for.
- Find useful blogs for your subject – this one's for life science students: http://aspiringprofessionalshub.com/2015/07/23/career-option-for-life-science-graduates-uncertain-about-what-to-do/.
- Find websites for the professional bodies for your subject.
- Use the PDP process to know your skills (13.1).
- Check out the University of Aberdeen's Bringing Graduate Attributes to Life (www.abdn.ac.uk/bgatl/), which features video clips that show how people understand graduate attributes. Find out what students (www.abdn.ac.uk/bgatl/students) are learning about the attributes, how academics (www.abdn.ac.uk/bgatl/academics) are helping them to develop them, and how they align with a range of employers' (www.abdn.ac.uk/bgatl/employers) key competencies.

How to write a bad application

It is really easy to write a bad CV, a poor job application and a terrible covering letter – but here are our top tips for getting it all wrong:

- Don't do the research: do not know or find out anything about the company with whom you are applying for a job. Do not write about them. Ignore them. Make it all about you – or about nothing in particular. Keep it general and superficial.
- Make sure that everything you write is riddled with poor spelling, bad punctuation and laughable grammar. Dash off just one version. Do not read through. Do not revise and improve. Do not proof read.
- Write just one CV and one covering letter and send that to every job you apply for – no matter how different the jobs are – no matter that they want different skills and attributes.
- Make sure that everything you produce and send to prospective employers has poor layout and a sloppy and careless appearance. If possible add coffee stains and let the dog chew them.
- Write a general covering letter that is not interesting and not tied to the specific job you are applying for. Make it so boring that you almost fall asleep writing it.

Obviously – we are joking! You *must* address the job requirements and you must know the company that you are applying to work for. Search their website – see what they do and what they are known and respected for. Check out their values and any social responsibility statements they have made, or their commitments to equality or sustainability. Show that you know them in the way that you write your application. You must tailor your application to who they are, otherwise you are naively thinking that *they* are going to adapt to fit *you*. Not going to happen! Every time you apply for a different job – revise your covering letter to fit that job. Do not have one generic thing that you send to everyone – they will spot this – and they will bin it.

If you are not good at spelling, punctuation and grammar – or at laying out information – then get someone to do this part of the process for you. If your application form looks messy and uncared for, *it goes straight in the bin!* Your communication with prospective employers must be tailored, professional and well-presented. You must address their person specifications specifically – giving examples proving that you have done what you say you have. Be intelligent and clever and targeted.

What employers want

A report from the University of Glasgow (Lowden et al., 2011) summarised employers' attitudes to graduate skills – and highlighted what they wanted from universities and from the students themselves.

From the universities, they wanted employability skills that were embedded throughout the whole curriculum – and they wanted a focus on work placements, work-based learning, experiential learning and graduate award programmes that recognised achievement beyond the curriculum.

From students, they wanted the normal transferable skills: team working, communication, leadership, critical thinking and problem solving – but they elaborate upon these. They want proactive employability skills, the ability to engage in multi-layered communication – and innovative team work capable of transforming organisations. Moreover, they wanted graduates to be work ready.

 So there I am waiting for the new recruit to turn up – and his mum phones: 'Sorry he can't come in today, he's taking me to the doctors!' The boss told me to let him go …

Going on to further study

Of course, you may decide that you do not want to move straight into work – you may have a taste for studying and find that you want to do a postgraduate course. More people are aware now that postgraduate study opportunities exist – and that you can use these opportunities in different ways – to extend your learning or to change direction.

There are Masters or other postgraduate courses where you can deepen and develop the knowledge gained in your first degree. If you want to become an academic or a researcher, you could take, for example, an MPhil (Master of Philosophy) and move on to a PhD (Doctor of Philosophy) programme. You could use a postgraduate course to change direction, the Postgraduate Certificate of Education (PGCE), for example, is designed to prepare a graduate of any subject for a career in teaching.

Discuss your interest in further study with a sympathetic tutor on your degree programme – and with the careers service. It may be that you do not know all the possible options available to you – so it is important to find out about all the study opportunities that exist – and to consider who you are and what you really want. Do not leap into the next course – or onto a PGCE – just because you cannot think of anything else, or because you do not immediately get the job you want.

Once you have an idea of what you want to do next – think about whether you want to stay at your current institution, or whether you want to spread your wings and experience a whole different system somewhere else. Ask if your university even does what you want. Speak to your postgraduate unit. Speak to students in the students' union. Explore the options for further study on the Prospects site, and again, prepare for applying for a further course the way you would prepare for an especially tricky assignment.

TIP

For advice on how to prepare for further study in social sciences – or even an academic career – check out these podcasts: www.social-policy.org.uk/uncategorized/employability-soundbites/.

Making the most of university

In this section we have gathered advice and tips to share with you from past students and current university staff. All of them stress the importance of making the most of what is on offer at your university. Have a read – make some notes – take action!

A Dean of Students' open letter to new students

I hope that you are excited but you may be nervous at the same time. Joining the university is like joining the gym. You pay for the facilities, the instructors, the classes, the towels … *But* you have to do all the work yourself. So … welcome to the brain gym!

In the first few weeks you'll probably be worried about getting along with your fellow students, you'll try to compare yourself with others, and you'll have a few wobbles: is this the right course for me? Will I be able to write a long essay? How on earth will I be able to read all these books?

Well, this is all part of becoming a student. In fact, I would be worried if you did not feel that way. You will find your place and your friends very soon. You will also develop your own study skills soon. This will make things less daunting. Here are a few tips for you:

- Learning is personal. If your tutor's style does not match yours, talk to them. Ask if they could re-phrase, present the facts in a different way. Take charge. Tutors will love the attention!
- The most important factor for high achievement is attendance. So, enjoy the evenings but forget the lie-ins …
- Education is painful. It means changing the way you think, challenging your truths, saying it in a different way. It is life changing. You will be unsettled, pushed and pulled. So empower yourself and take on the challenge.
- The more you learn, the more you realise how much you don't know (Einstein), so what seems a step back, could be a massive jump ahead!
- Have fun and share the love of learning …

I hope you'll enjoy making new friends, learning new skills, being independent – and finding your path in life.

What the graduate said

As a mature student, I was already thinking about my future career before I started my course. I wanted to get the most out of university as I thought that it would benefit me when I later had to find a job, so I was determined to experience and participate in things I had never done before and looked out for extra-curricular activities. I joined clubs at the SU, learnt to play volleyball, went to lectures from visiting academics, politicians and celebrities and generally immersed myself in uni life. I did a bit of volunteering, helped out at the drama club behind the scenes and in my final year got the opportunity to participate in academic research (they even paid me for it!).

In my final semester I actively looked for companies recruiting graduates – and I visited the careers service. They translated some of the experiences I had had into actual skills I could put on my CV, plus they gave me tips for where to look for work. I participated in a mock interview, which helped build my confidence. Probably the best thing they gave me, though, was an email address which I could use to contact them when I was struggling.

After leaving uni I sent out my CV and a letter to companies I was interested in working for, applied for graduate positions and joined agencies. I used Facebook, LinkedIn and Twitter to promote what I was doing, which resulted in friends looking out for jobs for me and sending advice/links, etc. After four months of looking, I finally got an offer and I got the job.

My main advice to other people looking for work is to plan ahead, make use of what facilities the uni offers and don't be afraid to ask questions when you need help. If you are determined, you will find that job sooner or later.

Message from the careers service

 I didn't realise I could use the careers service after I graduated. I could have really used their help and support, because at times I felt quite lost.

Sometimes in your student journey, there will be situations that often appear as obstacles, preventing you from reaching your career goals – do not despair. You will find a great deal of help in student services at your university that can support you in developing your confidence, help you to manage your funding, give you assistance if you have a disability and offer professionally trained staff who can help you reach your goals. Your careers service at your university is there specifically to help you achieve your career goal. Seek them out and meet with their experienced staff to help you get ahead in your career.

Did you know:

Businesses want graduates who not only add value but who have the skills to help to transform their organisation in the face of continuous and rapid economic and technological change. All graduates – whatever their degree discipline – need to be equipped with employability skills.

Employability covers a broad range of non-academic or softer skills and abilities which are of value in the workplace. It includes the ability to work in a team; a willingness to demonstrate initiative and original thought; self-discipline in starting and completing tasks to deadline.

(*Source*: CBI – UK's premier business lobbying organisation, providing a voice for employers at a national and international level – www.cbi.org.uk/business-issues/education-and-skills/in-focus/employability/)

It can be daunting to know where to begin to move forward in your career but do talk to staff in your careers service to help you get started with exploring career options and looking at how to develop your skills.

Work experience whilst you are a student will provide you the opportunity to build the skills you need for the future. This can be done through placements or internships and/or through volunteering in the not-for-profit sector. Placements are normally focused on a particular occupational area, can be short or long in duration and are a great way to 'test drive' a job during your course to see if it's the right one for you. Not only do you need the experience to gain employment after graduation but it gives you a great opportunity to see if you are suited to working for a large or small company or in the commercial or non-commercial sector as well as helping you to discover what you like doing and what skills you still need to develop.

Potential employers will want to know about the work experience you have gained whilst at university. Employers are keen to know about your transferable skills gained at university, so any work experience and extra-curricular activities you undertake that develop your skills will be valuable. Getting involved in activities can also be a great way to make friends and have fun.

─ TIPS ─

Top tips throughout your time at university

- Start to explore your career options – if you don't know where to start try: www. prospects.ac.uk or www.targetjobs.co.uk.
- Develop your CV through work experience, internships, placements or volunteering.
- Engage with any employability or enterprise activities offered within your university.
- Attend workshops held by your careers service.
- Join any clubs or societies of interest – find out what is on offer through your students' union.
- See if you can get a careers mentor – many careers services have mentoring programmes which connect students with business professionals. This allows you to extend your network of contacts as well as giving additional insight into your chosen sector.
- Make use of social media – use LinkedIn as a tool for networking and research.

In particular in your penultimate and final year:

- If you are interested in postgraduate study, start to research your options and explore possibilities for funding.
- Start to plan for your job applications. Employers will actively advertise specific schemes for penultimate year students and you can see deadlines advertised

through your university careers service and websites such as www.prospects.ac.uk and www.targetjobs.co.uk.

- If you are interested in graduate programmes, apply early in your final year, many closing dates will be in the autumn term.
- Use your careers service to access graduate opportunities, and use the resources available to find out about other job search sources.
- Use social media as a means of researching opportunities and marketing yourself.
- Go along to careers workshops and events and seek individual help from a careers consultant to make sure your applications are of a high standard.

What the head of department says

Although I am now approaching the end of my career as an academic, going to university and leaving home many years ago still ranks as one of the best experiences of my life because it changed everything ... even if it wasn't always easy. One of the reasons for this is that university is very different from school and college.

People may have told you that you have to be more independent, even that your lecturers may not know who you are or give you as much time as your teachers did, so that you are expected to work things out for yourself. It may look and feel like this sometimes, indeed it may even be true, and, although I don't think it should be, remember three things:

1. If you don't feel you are being heard, find someone who will take up your cause.
2. If you don't understand something, chances are others don't either but are too scared to ask.
3. Even super-humanly confident people worry about understanding lectures, reading fast enough and being understood by others when they speak – school is behind you, so let your education begin!

Remember also, *everyone* at university is a learner and being at university is about engaging with ideas as they are being formed and debated and finding your own identity as a scholar. Sure, it is vital to pass assignments, get a degree and get a good job – that's what we want for you as well – but finding your voice and being able to take pride in your work because it is *your work* is also your entitlement as a graduate – and will do at least as much to make you attractive to employers as high marks.

What the peer-learning programme leader says

As course leader and leader of a Peer Mentoring in Practice (PMiP) module, I strongly recommend that you use every opportunity to gain practical work experience related to your field of study whilst being at university. This can be either as part of your course or alongside your study. Work experience can be gained through placements and internships, paid or unpaid, and also by engaging with the university community. This 'internal engagement' can be on a voluntary basis through participation in societies and clubs, or incorporated into some form of optional module (work placement or peer mentoring) where you gain additional credits for your learning.

A good way of gaining internal work experience is by taking part in a peer-learning scheme. Most universities offer schemes where students support other students with their education. These schemes are sometimes called PASS (Peer-Assisted Support System) or PAL (Peer-Assisted Learning) – or, in the case of the course I lead, the scheme is referred to as peer mentoring. The benefits of taking part in a peer-learning scheme are that it helps you to develop a range of transferable skills; enhance your CV; gain useful contacts for networking; explore possible career options; pursue your personal and development goals; and, last but not least, make a good impression on a future employer.

The students undertaking my PMiP module said that peer mentoring has helped them to:

Develop and share my knowledge with others.

Build relationships with new people.

Become more confident.

Move on with my career planning.

This means, peer-learning can help you to enhance your career prospects whilst also helping you with your own studies. The pool of experience, knowledge and skills benefits all students taking part, both mentors and participants. Peer-learning is for every student, and can be a good, fun opportunity to get your foot into the job market.

However you decide to gain work experience, please make sure you organise the work experience so it suits you, your career plans and your study. Your time is precious, so spend it wisely – and be realistic about what you can take on.

What the student ambassador leaders say

The Student Ambassador Programme is a fantastic way to develop your own skills as well as improve your CV. Ambassadors work on programmes aimed at raising the attainment, aspiration and retention levels of under-represented students in higher education. The roles of the student ambassador can be diverse, including:

- Working on university recruitment events such as open days and higher education fairs.
- Advising students from schools and colleges who are interested in attending university.
- Mentoring students who require support in order to achieve the results they need to get to higher education.

Our ambassadors have found that this type of work particularly strengthens their communication and soft skills as well as builds confidence and enables them to work better in groups.

Most ambassador positions in higher education institutions are now paid roles and a very convenient way to earn some extra money whilst studying. The work is very flexible as your institution realises that your studies are the most important thing – the reason why you are there. It is also a great way to give something back to your university – and, by working on various outreach activities, you will also be promoting social justice and mobility within your community. Here's what our ambassadors have to say:

 I feel honoured to be an ambassador. It makes me feel confident and proud of myself. I get the opportunity to lead, inspire, support and influence young and old people from all backgrounds. I take my job as an ambassador very seriously and it has helped me become such a different person emotionally and intellectually. In fact, I am actually in love with my role as it gives me so much power, confidence, happiness, strength, and freedom, both in my personal and professional life.

What the lecturer says

Don't just look for jobs that are obviously linked to your subject, there may be jobs for you under different names so get creative … For my computing students that might be to look at Information Systems, Media and IT, New Media, Databases, Creative Industries, Telecommunications, Infrastructure, Marketing, Advertising, Management, Publishing, Manufacturing, Web Developer, Web Designer, Graphic Designer, Content Developer, Graphic Creator/Artist … and even Communications Developer.

If there are that many ways of describing ICT jobs – imagine how *your* jobs could be described! Ask your tutor or careers service or your librarian what sorts of jobs you might be able to apply for – and research sectors, job profiles and job vacancies using: www.prospects.ac.uk.

A student's journey

I joined university in 2003 as a mature, female student from a white working-class background. I managed to obtain a place on the BA Education Studies programme through the then New Labour government's widening participation programme, which aimed to increase diversity in the student body and provide a more socially just higher education landscape.

After leaving school at 15 and spending 11 years as an administrator and then a secretary, I had had enough of 9–5 working and low status employment. My intention was to return to higher education and become a primary school teacher.

But something happened somewhere in the first year of my course as knowledge opened up to me. A whole new world appeared possible, a world I had never even thought of before my first day at university! I decided I wanted to pursue academic work.

I gained a distinction in my BA studies and swiftly moved on to pursue an MA. I gained another distinction. I then decided to apply for a PhD scholarship … And after much support, sponsorship and hard work from the staff and myself, I was awarded that scholarship.

Three years later I had completed my PhD and found myself in an academic post. Who knew?! Not me that's for sure! My journey to the academy highlights the transformative potential of university for non-traditional students. Without the family and cultural capital necessary to understand the inner workings of higher education, it was the support, commitment, passion and dedication of all the staff I encountered that made my journey possible. I feel incredibly privileged to do my job.

Summary

The whole of ESS4 is designed to develop you as someone who can succeed on a course and at any task that you set yourself – and this includes finding and getting that great job. We have focused on some of the big things that stand out for us: finding out exactly who you are, what you enjoy and what you are good at – and using that to discover what it is that you want to do. We suggest that you use, shape and refine all the experiences in your life – both inside and outside the university – for your job applications. We have captured top tips from past students, a head of department and a dean of students, peer mentor and student ambassador leaders, a careers adviser and a subject lecturer – the rest is up to you. Use and enjoy your time at university – find and get that great job. Good luck and good wishes …

Activity

What to do right now

- Go to the careers service – see what jobs are available to someone on your degree programme.
- Look up a job advert in your possible career – see what sorts of skills and experience you will need to get such a job. Discuss with the careers service how you can get that experience whilst at university.
- Write your CV and take it to the careers service for feedback.
- Give the same time to writing your CV that you would give to writing an assignment for which you wanted to get an A – it's that important.
- Practise job interviews with other students: predict questions from the job description – then rehearse how you would handle yourself in a real job interview
- Visit the Prospects careers website early in your course and set yourself the goal of working through the different sections and benefiting from them.

Bibliography and Further Reading

Abegglen, S., Burns, T. and Sinfield, S. (2015) 'Voices from the margins: Narratives of learning development in a digital age', *Journal of Education Innovation, Partnership and Change*, 1(1). Available at: https://193.60.48.124/index.php/studentchangeagents/article/view/148 (accessed 1 July 2015).

Ahearn, A. (2006) 'Engineering writing: Replacing "writing classes" with a "writing imperative"', in L. Ganobcsik-Williams (ed.), *Teaching Academic Writing in UK Higher Education*. Basingstoke: Palgrave Macmillan.

Akerlind, G.S. and Trevitt, C. (1999) 'Enhancing self-directed learning through educational technology: When students resist the change', *Innovations in Education and Teaching International*, 36(2): 96–105.

Anie, A. (2001) *Widening Participation – Graduate Employability Project*. University of North London (now London Metropolitan University).

Archer, L. (2002) 'Access elite', *Times Higher Education Supplement*, 18 January.

Archer, L. (2003) 'Social class and higher education', in L. Archer, H. Hutchings and A. Ross (eds), *Higher Education and Social Class: Issues of Inclusion and Exclusion*. London and New York: RoutledgeFalmer.

Archer, L. and Leathwood, C. (2003) 'Identities, inequalities and higher education', in L. Archer, H. Hutchings and A. Ross (eds), *Higher Education and Social Class: Issues of Inclusion and Exclusion*. London and New York: RoutledgeFalmer.

Bakhtin, M. (1981) *The Dialogic Imagination: Four Essays*. Austin: University of Texas Press.

Barrow, M. (2006) 'Assessment and student transformation: Linking character and intellect', *Studies in Higher Education*, 31(3): 357–72.

Barthes, R. (1957/1972) *Mythologies*, trans. A. Lavers. London: Paladin.

Barton, D. and Hamilton, M. (1998) *Local Literacies: A Study of Reading and Writing in One Community*. London; Routledge.

Beck, U., Giddens, A. and Lash, S. (1996) *Reflexive Modernization*. Cambridge: Polity Press.

Beetham, H. and Sharpe, R. (2007) *Rethinking Pedagogy for a Digital Age: Designing and Delivering E-Learning*. London: Routledge.

Belbin, R.M. (1981) *Management Teams: Why They Succeed or Fail*. London: Heinemann.

Bennett, N., Dunne, E and Carré, B. (2000) *Skills Development in Higher Education and Employment*. Buckingham: Open University Press/Society for Research into Higher Education.

Bennett, R. (2002) 'Lecturers' attitudes to new teaching methods', *International Journal of Management Education*, 2(1): 42–58.

Blalock, A. (1999) 'Evaluation research and the performance management movement: From estrangement to useful integration?', *Evaluation*, 5(2): 117–49.

Bligh, D. A. (1998) *What's the Use of Lectures?* (5th edn). Exeter: Intellect.

Boud, D. (2001) 'Introduction: Making the move to peer learning', in D. Boud, R. Cohen, and J. Sampson (eds), *Peer Learning in Higher Education: Learning from and with Each Other*. London: Kogan Page.

Boud, D., Cohen, R. and Sampson, J. (eds) (2001) *Peer Learning in Higher Education: Learning From and With Each Other*. London: Kogan Page.

Bourdieu, P. (1977) *Reproduction in Education, Society and Culture*. London: Sage.

Bourdieu, P. and Passeron, J.-C. (1979) *Reproduction in Education, Society and Culture*. London: Sage.

Bowstead, H. (2011) 'Coming to writing', *Journal of Learning Development in Higher Education*, 3. Available at: www.aldinhe.ac.uk/ojs/index.php?journal=jldhe&page=article&op=view&path%5B%5D=128&path%5B%5D=88 (accessed 1 July 2015).

Bradley, C. and Holley, D. (2011) 'Empirical research into student mobile phones and their use for learning', *International Journal of Mobile and Blended Learning*, 3(4): 38–53.

Brockes, E. (2003) 'Taking the Mick', *Guardian*, 15 January. Available at: www.guardian.co.uk/politics/2003/jan/15/education.highereducation (accessed 20 September 2009).

Brown, G., Bull, J. and Pendlebury, M. (1997) *Assessing Student Learning in Higher Education*. Oxon and New York: Routledge.

Burke, P.J. (2005) 'Access and widening participation', *British Journal of Sociology of Education*, 26(4): 555–62.

Burns, T. and Sinfield, S. (2004) *Teaching, Learning and Study Skills: A Guide for Tutors*. London: Sage.

Burns, T., Sinfield, S. and Holley, D. (2006) 'The silent stakeholder: An exploration of the student as stakeholder in the UK government e-learning strategy 2005', paper presented to the International Corporate Social Responsibility Conference, Idrine, Turkey, May.

Buzan, B. and Buzan, T. (1999) *The Mind Map Book*. London: BBC Publications.

Buzan, T. (1989) *Use Your Head*. London: BBC Publications.

Carroll, J. (2002) *A Handbook for Deterring Plagiarism in Higher Education*. Oxford: Oxford Centre for Staff and Learning Development.

Cheng, W. and Warren, M. (2007) 'Online collaborative learning and assessment', in S. Frankland (eds), *Enhancing Teaching and Learning through Assessment: Deriving an Appropriate Model*. Dordrecht: Springer.

Cohen, S.B. (1997) *The Maladapted Mind*. London: Psychology Press

Conole, G., Smith, J. and White, S. (2006) 'A critique of the impact of policy and funding', in G. Conole and M. Oliver (eds), *Contemporary Perspectives on E-learning Research*. London: RoutledgeFalmer.

Cottrell, S. (2001) *Teaching Study Skills and Supporting Learning*. Basingstoke: Palgrave Macmillan.

Crème, P. (2003) 'Why can't we allow students to be more creative?', *Teaching in Higher Education*, 8(2): 273–77.

Curry, M.J. (2006) 'Skills, access and "basic writing": A community college case study from the United States', in L. Ganobcsik-Williams (ed.), *Teaching Academic Writing in UK Higher Education*. Basingstoke: Palgrave Macmillan.

Davies, J. (2011) *Don't Waste Student Work* [video]. Available at: http://tedxtalks.ted.com/video/TEDxOttawa-Jim-Davies-Dont-Wast (accessed 1 July 2015).

Deleuze, G. and Guattari, F. (1987/2005) *A Thousand Plateaus: Capitalism and Schizophrenia*. Minneapolis and London: University of Minnesota Press.

Department for Education and Skills (now Business, Innovation and Skills) (2005, revised 2008) *Harnessing Technology: Transforming Learning and Children's Services*. London: HMSO.

Devine, T.G. (1987) *Teaching Study Skills*. Newton, MA: Allyn and Bacon.

Dewey, J. (1997). *Democracy and Education: An Introduction to the Philosophy of Education*. New York: The Free Press.

Feather, H. (2000) *Intersubjectivity and Contemporary Social Theory*. Farnham, UK: Ashgate.

Fergusson, R. (1994) 'Managerialism in education', in C. Clarke, A. Cochrane and E. McLaughlin (eds), *Managing Social Policy*. London: Sage.

Finnigan, T., Burns, T. and Sinfield, S. (2009) 'Tell us about it', workshop presented at ALDinHE Symposium, Bournemouth.

Foucault, M. (1980) *Power/Knowledge*. Brighton: Harvester.

Foucault, M. (1988) *History of Sexuality. Vol. 3: The Care of the Self*. Harmondsworth: Penguin.

The Free Dictionary (2015) 'Lecturer' [dictionary]. Available at: www.thefreedictionary.com/lecturer (accessed 1 July 2015).

Freire, P. (1977) *The Pedagogy of the Oppressed*. Harmondsworth: Penguin.

Freire, P. (1996) *Pedagogy of Hope* (3rd edn). London: Penguin.

Gamache, P. (2002) 'University students as creators of personal knowledge: An alternative epistemological view', *Teaching in Higher Education*, 7(3): 277–94.

Gibbs, G. and Makeshaw, T. (1992) *53 Interesting Things to Do in Your Lectures*. Bristol: Technical and Educational Services.

Giddens, A. (1996) *Consequences of Modernity*. Cambridge: Polity Press.

Gravett, S. and Henning, E. (1998) 'Teaching as dialogic mediation: A learning centred view of higher education', *South African Journal of Higher Education*, 12(2): 60–8.

Haggis, T. and Pouget, M. (2002) 'Trying to be motivated: Perspectives on learning from younger students accessing higher education', *Teaching in Higher Education*, 7(3): 323–36.

Healey, M., Flint, A. and Harrington, K. (2014) *Engagement through Partnership: Students as Partners in Learning and Teaching in Higher Education*. York: The Higher Education Academy.

Higher Education Academy (2014) *Framework for Partnership in Learning and Teaching in Higher Education*. York: The Higher Education Academy.

Hodge, M. and Saunders, C. (2003) 'Fact: term jobs damage grades', *Times Higher Education Supplement*, 7 February.

Holmes, L. (2009) 'Graduate employability: the graduate identity approach', www.graduate-employability.org.uk (accessed 15 August 2010).

Hutton, W. (1995) *The State We're In*. London: Cape.

Ingle, J. (2013) 'Writing: An exclusive practice?', paper delivered at the conference Discourse, Power and Resistance 2013: Discourses of Inclusion and Exclusion, Greenwich: 9–11 April 2013.

Jackson, S. and Burke, P.J. (2007) *Reconceptualising Lifelong Learning: Feminist Interventions*. Oxon and New York: Routledge.

Jamieson, C. and Morgan, E. (2008) *Managing Dyslexia at University: A Resource for Students, Academic and Support Staff*. Oxon and New York: Routledge.

Jeffers, S. (1997) *Feel the Fear and Do It Anyway*. London: Century.

Kapp, R. and Bangeni, B. (2005) 'I was just never exposed to this argument thing: Using a genre approach to teach academic writing to ESL students in the humanities', in C. Moran and A. Herrington (eds), *Genre Across the Curriculum*. Logan, UT: Utah University Press.

Keenan, C. (2014) *Mapping Student-led Peer Learning in the UK*. York: The Higher Education Academy.

Kirkpatrick, I. and Lucio, M. (1995) *The Politics of Quality in the Public Sector*. London: Routledge.

Knapper, C.K. and Cropley, A.J. (2000) *Lifelong Learning in Higher Education* (3rd edn). London: Kogan Page.

Kolb, D.A. (1984) *Experiential Learning: Experience as the Source of Learning and Development*. Upper Saddle River, NJ: Prentice-Hall.

Krueger, R.A. (1994) *Focus Groups*. London: Sage.

Land, R. (2010) 'Threshold concepts: undergraduate teaching, postgraduate training and professional development: a short introduction and bibliography'. Available at: www.ee.ucl.ac.uk/~mflanaga/thresholds.html (accessed 14 October 2015).

Lea, M. and Stierer, B. (eds) (1999) *Student Writing in Higher Education: New Contexts*. Buckingham: Open University Press/Society for Research into Higher Education.

Lea, M. and Street, B. (1998) 'Student writing in higher education: An academic literacies approach view', *Studies in Higher Education*, 23(2): 157–72.

Leathwood, C. and O'Connell, P. (2003) 'It's a struggle: The constructions of the "new student" in higher education', *Journal of Education Policy*, 18(6): 597–615.

Leathwood, C. and Read, B. (2009) *Gender and the Changing Face of Higher Education: A Feminised Future?* Maidenhead: Open University Press.

Lewis, S.E. and Lewis, J.E. (2005) 'Departing from lectures: An evaluation of a peer-led guided inquiry alternative', *Journal of Chemical Education*, 82(1): 135–9.

Lillis, T. (2001) *Student Writing, Access, Regulation, Desire*. London: Routledge.

Lillis, T. (2003) 'Student writing as "academic literacies": Drawing on Bakhtin to move from *critique* to *design*', *Language and Education*, 17(3): 192–207.

Lowden, K., Hall, S., Elliot, E. and Lewin, J. (2011) *Employers' Perceptions of the Employability Skills of New Graduates*. University of Glasgow, SCRE Centre. Available at: www.edge.co.uk/media/63412/employability_skills_as_pdf_-_final_online_version.pdf (accessed 9 October 2015).

Lyotard, J. (1984) *The Postmodern Condition: A Report on Knowledge*, trans. G. Bennington and B. Masumi. Minneapolis, MN: University of Minnesota Press.

Macherey, P. (1990) 'The text says what it does not say', in D. Walder (ed.), *Literature in the Modern World: Critical Essays and Documents*. Oxford: Oxford University Press.

May, T. (2003) *Social Research: Issues, Methods and Processes*. Buckingham: Open University Press.

McInerney, D.M. and Brown, G.T.L. (eds) (2009) *Student Perspectives on Assessment: What Students Can Tell Us about Assessment for Learning*. Greenwich, CT: Information Age Publishing.

Medhurst, A. (2000) 'If anywhere: Class identifications and cultural studies academics', in S. Munt (ed.), *Cultural Studies and the Working Class*. London: Cassell.

Medhurst, N. (2010) 'Collaborative online design: A pedagogical approach to understanding student multiliterate creative practice'. Available at: www.londonmet.ac.uk/fms/MRSite/acad/foc/research/seminars/09–10/nigel-abstract.html (accessed 31 August 2010).

Mitchell, S. and Evison, A. (2006) 'Exploiting the potential of writing for educational change at Queen Mary, University of London', in L. Ganobcsik-Williams (ed.), *Teaching Academic Writing in UK Higher Education*. Basingstoke: Palgrave Macmillan.

Moon, J. (2005) 'Coming from behind: An investigation of learning issues in the process of widening participation in higher education', abstract of the final report published November 2008 at http://escalate.ac.uk/1109 (accessed 31 August 2010).

Morrice, L. (2009) 'The global in the local: Issues of difference (mis)recognition and inequity in higher education', paper presented at the ESRC seminar series: Imagining the University of the Future.

Mullin, J.A. (2006) 'Learning from – not duplicating – US composition theory and practice', in L. Ganobcsik-Williams (ed.), *Teaching Academic Writing in UK Higher Education*. Basingstoke: Palgrave Macmillan.

Munt, S. (ed.) (2000) *Cultural Studies and the Working Class*. London: Cassell.

Murray, R. (2006) 'If not rhetoric and composition, then what? Teaching teachers to teach writing', in L. Ganobcsik-Williams (ed.) *Teaching Academic Writing in UK Higher Education*. Basingstoke: Palgrave Macmillan.

Nancy, J.L. (2000) *Being Singular Plural*. Stanford, CA: Stanford University Press.

Newman, J. and Clarke, J. (1994) 'Going about our business? The managerialism of public services', in C. Clarke, A. Cochrane and E. McLaughlin (eds), *Managing Social Policy*. London: Sage.

Noble, C. (2015) *Learning Log – Week 27* [blog]. Available online: https://noblechloe.word press.com/first-year-learning-logs/first-year/learning-logs-21–to-30/learning-log-week-27/ (accessed 1 July 2015).

Noble, D. (2002) *Digital Diploma Mills: The Automation of Higher Education*. New York: Monthly Review Press.

Northedge, A. (2003a) 'Rethinking teaching in the context of diversity', *Teaching in Higher Education*, 8(1): 17–32.

Northedge, A. (2003b) 'Enabling participation in academic discourse', *Teaching in Higher Education*, 8(2): 169–180.

Norton, L.S. (2009) *Action Research in Teaching and Learning: A Practical Guide to Conducting Pedagogical Research in Universities*. Abingdon: Routledge.

Paczuska, A. (2002) 'The applications process', in A. Hayton and A. Paczuska (eds), *Access, Participation and Higher Education*. London: Kogan Page.

Palmer, R. and Pope, C. (1984) *Brain Train: Studying for Success*. Bristol: Arrowsmith.

Pollitt, C., Birchall, J. and Putman, K. (1998) *Decentralising Public Service Management*. London: Macmillan Press.

Prensky, M. (2001) 'Digital natives, digital immigrants', *On the Horizon*, 9(5): 1–6.

QAA (2002) *Subject Review for Business*, London Metropolitan University.

Quinn, J. (2003) *Powerful Subjects: Are Women Really Taking Over the University?* Stoke-on-Trent: Trentham Books.

Quinn, J. (2004) 'Understanding working-class "drop-out" from higher education through a socio-cultural lens: Cultural narratives and local contexts', *International Studies in Sociology of Education*, 14(1): 57–74.

Ridley, P. (2010) 'Drawing to learn: Making ideas visible', workshop for staff and students – see GetAhead 2010. Available at: www.catsconsulting.com/getahead2010/# (accessed 31 August 2010).

Rogers, C. (1994) *Freedom to Learn*. Upper Saddle River, NJ: Merrill.

Rose, C. and Goll, L. (1992) *Accelerate Your Learning*. Aylesbury, UK: Accelerated Learning Systems Ltd.

Satterthwaite, J., Atkinson, A. and Martin, W. (eds) (2004) *The Disciplining of Education: New Languages of Power and Resistance*. Stoke-on-Trent: Trentham Books.

Schwandt, T. (1997) *Dictionary of Qualitative Enquiry*. London: Sage.

Seale, C. (1999) *The Quality of Qualitative Research*. London: Sage.

Silverman, D. (ed.) (1997) *Qualitative Research: Theory, Method and Practice*. London: Sage.

Silverman, D. (ed.) (2004) *Qualitative Research: Theory, Method and Practice* (2nd edn). London: Sage.

Sinfield, S., Burns, T. and Holley, D. (2004) 'Outsiders looking in or insiders looking out? Widening participation in a post 1992 university', in J. Satterthwaite, A. Atkinson and W. Martin (eds), *The Disciplining of Education: New Languages of Power and Resistance*. Stoke-on-Trent: Trentham Books.

Skillen, J. (2006) 'Teaching academic writing from the "centre" in Australian universities', in L. Ganobcsik-Williams (ed.), *Teaching Academic Writing in UK Higher Education*. Basingstoke: Palgrave Macmillan.

Stierer, B. and Antoniou, M. (2004) 'Are there distinctive methodologies for pedagogic research in higher education?', *Teaching in Higher Education*, 9(3): 275–85.

Tett, L. (2000) '"I'm working class and proud of it": Gendered experiences of non-traditional participants in higher education', *Gender and Education*, 1(2): 183–94.

Themetrogirl (2015) 'The get ahead conference' [blog]. Available at: https://themetrogirl. wordpress.com/2015/03/12/the-get-ahead-conference-2015/ (accessed 1 July 2015).

Thomas, E. (2001) *Widening Participation in Post-compulsory Education*. London: Continuum.

Thomas, L. (2002) 'Student retention in higher education: The role of institutional habitus', *Journal of Educational Policy*, 17(4): 423–32.

Tinto, V. (1998) 'Colleges as communities: Taking research on student persistence seriously', *Review of Higher Education*, 21(2): 167–77.

Walberg, H.J. (1998) 'Foreword', in K. Topping and S. Ehly (eds), *Peer-assisted Learning*. Mahwah, NJ: Laurence Erlbaum Associates.

Webb, W.T. (1920/2013) *How to Write an Essay: With Sample Essays and Subjects for Essays*. London: George Routledge & Sons Limited/New York: E.P. Dutton & Co.

Wenger, E. (2009) 'Social learning capability: Four essays on innovation and learning in social systems', *Social Innovation*, Sociedade e Trabalho Booklets, 12 – separate supplement. Lisbon: MTSS/GEP & EQUAL.

Wenger, E. (2010) 'Communities of practice and social learning systems: The career of a concept', in C. Blackmore (ed.), *Social Learning Systems and Communities of Practice*. London: Springer and The Open University.

Willetts, D. (2010) Speech to the CBI. Available at: http://news.bbc.co.uk/1/hi/uk_politics/ 6662219.stm (accessed 30 September 2010).

Wingate, U. (2006) 'Doing away with study skills', *Teaching in Higher Education*, 11(4): 457–69.

Winnicott, D.W. (1971) *Playing and Reality*. London: Tavistock.

Wyatt, A. and Cash, C. (2012) 'i-write: Animating essay writing', paper presented at ALDinHE Conference, Leeds University.

Index

abstract 209–12
academia, fears of 7, 38, 257
academic communities 130, 186
academic forms
 of communication 13
 essay writing 168
 see also presentations and reports
academic groups 116–26
academic offence 58, 186
academic practices 80–1, 155
academic tutors 43
action plan 288
 term plan 33
 transferable skills 287
 weekly plan 34
 writing skills 221
active and interactive learning 6, 11, 18, 25, 36
activities of learning (Devine) 19
Adair, J 122–4
analytical and critical reading 52–60
see also QOOQRRR
annotated bibliography, defined 170
appendices (of a report) 209, 211, 214, 253
assessment 145–280
 dissertation 168–9, 251
 essay 168, 191
 exams 169, 263
 formative and summative 176–7
 group work 117
 literature review 169
 presentations 169, 225
 report 168, 207
 seminars and workshops 169, 241
 virtual 141
assignments 167
 assignment journey 170–5, 176
 creativity 11–2
auditory learning 20, 269

Belbin, RH 120–2
Bibliography 196–7
 annotated 170
 preventing plagiarism 58, 184
 of a report 211, 214, 253
block, writing 154, 160–2
blog (web log) 6, 111
board games 270–1
body language, presentations 227
Book (Reading) List 149
bookmarking 138
 tools 138
 Delicious 139
 Endnote 138
 Mendeley 138
 REFworks 138
 Zotero 138
books 6–7, 43
 course/module handbooks 148, 150
 Google books 138
 using this book 6
brainstorming 82–4, 156
 collage 87
 pattern notes 83
 question 83
 ten-minute brainstorms 83
Buzan, B and Buzan, T 71–2, 81, 266, 268

calendar, events and deadlines 32–4
careers 44
 adviser 302–4
 Prospects 296–7
checklist 14–5
 assessment success 202
 essay writing 205
 exam preparation 278–9
 expenditure 46–7
 library 62

checklist *cont.*
  presentations 239–40
  study tips 14–5
cognitive psychology 37
commitment (to study) 30
communication, effective 42, 123
  academic forms 168–70
  and a job skill 231
  oral 169, 231
  presentations 169, 231
  in SOCCER 11, 13
  tools (social media) 137–40
  transferable skills (PDP) 287–9
computing 127
  digital 130
  ICT (information and communications technology) 128, 287
concept maps 70–1
conclusion
  of an essay 194–5, 197
  of a report 211, 213
confidence
  positive thinking 36, 46
  self 231
  seminars 246
  see also checklists
contents page (reports) 210, 212, 253
contract (learning) 29–30
counselling services 45
counter loans (library) 61–2
course overview 150
course tutors 43, 287
course/module handbooks 148
covering letters 297–8
creativity 12, 79–92
  brainstorming 82–4, 156
  draw-to-learn 84–92
  pattern notes 72–5
  question matrix (QM) 101–4
  SOCCER 12
critical thinking 93–104
curriculum vitae (CV) 297–8
  covering letters 297–8
  employability 281–94, 299, 302
  Personal Development Planning (PDP) 283–93
  Higher Education Achievement Records (HEAR) 291

data and resources, websites 259
deadlines, pressure 15, 26, 33
deep learning 85, 196
Delicious (social bookmarking) 138
Devine, TG, on learning 19
diary, reflective learning 106
digital artefact 170

dissertation, defined 168
drafts 172–3, 194
  reflection 113
  pattern notes 72–4
dyslexia 44

Endnote and REFworks 138
e-learning 134–5
  MOOC (Massive Open Online Course) 131–3
electronic library resources 57
emotional aspects 113
employers (what they want) 299
employability 281–293, 302
  see also transferable skills
epistemology 26
essay writing 192–205
  assessment forms 19, 210–1, 256–7, 263
  body 193–7
  checklist 205
  conclusion 195–6
  essay explained/defined 192
  introduction 195
  paragraph questions 194–5
  plan, prepare and draft 197
  structure of essay 194
  see also assignments
ethics and legal constraints 256
events and deadlines, calendars/plans 31–34
exam preparation 263–79
  checklist 278–9
  fear 264, 275
  memory 266–7
  past papers 272, 275
  revision cycle 75–6
  three-minute presentation 238
exam success, SQP4 270
  survey 271
  question 272
  predict 272
  plan 273
  prepare 273
  prepare 401
examination day 274
  apportioning time 275
  handling the exam 277
  night before 276
  positive thinking 276
  relaxation 276
  after the exam 277
exercise(s)
  hopes and fears 358
  group building 116
  positive thinking 120
  prompted writing 163–4
  time sponge 28
  writer's block 160–2

fears 37
    of academia 38
    re-framing 38
feedback 175–8
findings (of a report) 211, 213, 221
first year at university 116
first day experiences 13, 307
formative and summative assessment 176–7
forming a group 116
free writing 158–60
Fun
    make reading fun 59
    revision games 269–70
further study 299–300

Gibbs, Graham 81
glossary, of a report 211, 214, 253
goal setting 110, 113
Google
    Google+ 132
    Google books 138
    Google documents 129
    Google Scholar 137
grammar 158
group processes (Adair's) 122–3
group roles (Belbin) 121–2
group work *see* study groups

handbooks, course/module 148, 150
Harvard System, referencing 196, 214
hopes and fears (statements and responses) 7, 9

independent learning 25
    see also study
informal learning 219
ICT (Information and Communications Technology)
    128, 287
information handling 292
information sources 61
instructions, three-minute test 238
internet 135
    see also Web
Internet Detective 140–1
introduction
    of a dissertation 253
    of an essay 194–5, 197
    of a presentation 228–9
    of a report 210, 213, 220

Jeffers, Susan 37, 40
    Feel the Fear and Do It Anyway 39
job
    application 298
    careers service 302
    covering letter 297–8

job *cont.*
    curriculum vitae (CV) 297–8
    search 304
journalism questions (5Ws and H) 95–8
journals 61

kinaesthetic learning 20
Kolb Cycle 289–91

laboratory report 209
learning 17–34
    definition 19
    development and support 237
    Devine on activities 19
    monotonous 69
    outcomes 148, 150
    primary school 267
learning contract 65–8, 250
learning journeys 29–30
learning style 20
lectures 24
library 61–3, 135
    electronic resources 135
    subject librarians 135
literature review 168

memory 266
    Buzan 266
    Revision cycle 75
    revision games 269–70
    short and long-term memory 266–7
Mindmaps 71–2, 221–2
    Buzan 71–2
    pattern notes 72–4
mnemonic triggers 267–8
monotonous learning 69
Moodle 136
motivation 26, 197, 288
mourning 123

negative thoughts 23
    see also positive thinking
networking 288, 303
norming 123
notemaking 65–77
    concept maps 70–1
    Cornell notes 69–70
    ideal notes 68
    linear notes 68
    matrix notes 101–3
    mindmaps 71–2
    notemaking – why, what, how 66
    pattern notes 72–4
    revision cycle 75–6
numeracy, Personal Development
        Planning (PDP) 288

oral communication 169, 231, 288
    fears 38
    skills and job prospects 231, 288
organising skills 8, 19
    Devine's list 19
    Seminars 242
Overview 11–2, 55, 75, 271, 296
    in QOOQRRR *(cooker)* 55
    in SOCCER 11–2

4Ps plan/prepare/practise/present (presentations) 232–6
paper(s)
    past examination papers 150, 271
    seminars 243
    see also reports
pattern notes 72–5
    beginner's guide 73
peer-learning 304
    mentor 34
    support 44
performing 123
Personal Development Planning (PDP) 283–93
    beginner's guide 287
    definition 284–5
    HEAR 291
    Kolb cycle 289–91
    terms and phrases 287–8
    transferable skills 287–8
personal skills review 7–9
personalised learning environment 23–4
plagiarism 58
positive thinking 46, 102
    believe in yourself 36
    emotions rule 13
    'fifth P' 239
    presentations 235
    SWOT analysis 237
postgraduate 262, 299–300
preparation for research 171
presentations 225–40
    4Ps plan/prepare/practise/present 232–6
    beginner's guide 229
    body 229–30
    checklist 239
    conclusion 230
    creativity 238
    defined 226
    essentials 238
    formal convention 229
    interactive 228
    introduction 229
    positive body language 227
    question and answer session 230
    rehearsal 234

presentations *cont.*
    structure (fig.) 228
    SWOT analysis 237
    tips and tricks 235
Professional Development Process (PDP) 283–93
prompted writing 163–4
proof reading 174, 198
publishers, referencing 182–3
pyramid discussion 118

QOOQRRR *(cooker)* approach to reading 54–6
    Active research and reading 57
qualitative research 258
quantitative research 258
question matrix (QM) 102
questionnaires 211, 213, 218
quizzes 259, 270

reading 52–62
    active strategy (QOOQRRR approach) 54–6
    analytical and critical reading 52–60
    attitude 53–4
    creating outlines 80
    free write 54
    index cards 56
    make reading fun 59
    pattern notes 72–4
    plagiarism 58
    reading dossier 59
    resources, online 60
    strategies 57
    targeted research 171
    visual summary 59
    see also study
reading list 149
Reading Record, defined 170
recommendations
    report 211, 213
    dissertation 253, 260
referencing 182–4
    annotated bibliography 170
    index cards 56, 186
    Harvard System 196, 214
    should I reference? 182
    websites 184
reflective account 120, 124
reflective cycle 289–90
reflective practice/learning 106, 215
reflective question 310
relaxation 22, 27, 276
reports 207–24
    beginner's guide 216–7
    defined 208
    getting started 219
    key questions 215

reports *cont.*
  method 217–8
  preparing 219–20
  presentation and style 214
  report v essay 216
  sections of a report 210–4
  structure 210–1
  student reports 221–3
  types 209
research folder 171
research project 223, 252–62
  beginner's guide 254–5
  ethical and legal constraints 256–7
  methodology and interpreting data 257–8
  qualitative/quantitative research 258
  question 255–6
  resources, websites 259
  stages 253
  structure 252
  student research 256
  thinking about time 254
  also see dissertations
responsibility 39–40
revision
  active 268
  cycle 75–6, 107, 268
  exam technique SQP4 270–4
  games 269–70
  memory 266
  timetable 29
key words, use of 68, 108, 137
  common instruction words 199–201
  illustrate 87
  revision cycle 75–6
  revision games 269–70
Rogers, Carl 80

self-belief 40
self-confidence 46, 91, 156, 231
seminars 241–49
  advantages and disadvantages 246–7
  confidence and enthusiasm 246
  defined 242–3
  get visual 247
  planning 244–5
  practise 244
  workshops 247
  write to learn 248
skills audit 292
skills review 7–9
SOCCER (six steps to success) 9–14
  study techniques and practices 11
  overview 12
  creativity 12
  communicate effectively 13

SOCCER (six steps to success) *cont.*
  emotions 13
  review 14
social media 131, 137–40, 222, 303
sources
  Harvard System 196
  information handling 292
  and plagiarism 58
  and referencing 182–4
  quotes 184–5
SQP4 (survey/question/predict/plan) 270–4
storming 122
stress control 236
student attitudes to reading 53–4
student support services 44
Students' Union (SU) 44
study 17–34
  beginner's guide 26
  how/when/where of study 21–5
  independent learning 25
  techniques and practices in SOCCER 11
  see also checklists; reading
study groups 116–7
  advantages and disadvantages 119
  beginner's guide 124
  business-like approach 120
  definition 117
  stages to success 121–4
  SWOT 120
  Ten stage approach 125–6
Study partner 272
study space 23
success
  free write 54
  presentations 232–6
  Ten steps to 170–5
  writer 178
SWOT analysis (strengths, weaknesses, opportunities, threats) 229, 331–2, 354–6
  group work 120
  feedback, essays 204
  positive thinking 102
  presentations 237
  seminars 246
syllabus 150

teaching and learning 25, 109, 130
team work 239
Ten stages to better assignments (writing skills) 202–4
term and weekly plans 33–4
test
  dyslexia 264
  multi-sensory approach 20
  three minute 238
  two minute 268

think smart 276
time
    allowances in exam preparation 274
    effective use on exam day 275
    events and deadlines 33
    for studying 22
    Personal Development Planning (PDP) 292
    while at university 303
time management 254
timetables 23, 30–4
title page 209–11, 253
transferable skills 287–8
tutorial 25
tutor, academic and personal 43

university
    finances 46–7
    first year 116, 158, 182, 307
    networking 303
university library *see* library
useful people and places 43–4

Virtual Learning Environments (VLEs) 25
    Blackboard 136
    Moodle 136
    Web CT 136
visual learning 91
    Brighton 91, 218
volunteering 45
Von Rostorff effect 68

Web CT 136
Websites 140
web tools, examples of 138
Wikipedia 140
work placement or volunteering 45
workshops 169
World Wide Web 136
worrying 36–9
    see also fears
writing blocks 160–3
writing skills 153–65
    blog to learn 157
    discomfort 163
    free writing 158
    getting it right 162
    group 157
    ideas 162
    practise 156
    prompted writing 163
    proofreading 174, 198
    rich writing 165
    speed writing 156
    strategies 156
    tool 158
    see also essay writing

YouTube 139

Zotero 138